CRUSADES – MEDIEVAL WORLDS IN CONFLICT

Crusades – Medieval Worlds in Conflict

Edited by
THOMAS F. MADDEN, JAMES L. NAUS, VINCENT RYAN
Saint Louis University, USA

Routledge
Taylor & Francis Group

LONDON AND NEW YORK

First published 2010 by Ashgate Publishing

2 Park Square, Milton Park, Abingdon, Oxfordshire OX14 4RN
711 Third Avenue, New York, NY 10017

Routledge is an imprint of the Taylor & Francis Group, an informa business

First issued in paperback 2018

British Library Cataloguing in Publication Data
International Symposium on Crusade Studies (2006)
    Crusades : medieval worlds in conflict.
    1. Crusades – Congresses. 2. Civilization, Medieval – Congresses.
    I. Title II. Madden, Thomas F. III. Naus, James L.
    IV. Ryan, Vincent.
    909'.07–dc22

Library of Congress Cataloging-in-Publication Data
Crusades : medieval worlds in conflict / [edited by] Thomas F. Madden,
James L. Naus, Vincent Ryan.
        p. cm. Includes index.
    Selected papers originally presented at the first International Symposium on
Crusade Studies in Saint. Louis, Mo., Feb. 2006.
    ISBN 978-1-4094-0061-5 (hardcover : alk. paper)
    1. Crusades—Congresses. I. Madden, Thomas F. II. Naus, James L.
III. Ryan, Vincent. IV. International Symposium on Crusade Studies
(1st : 2006 : Saint. Louis, Mo.)
    D157.C785 2010
    909.07—dc22

                                                                        2010021524

ISBN 978-1-4094-0061-5 (hbk)
ISBN 978-1-138-38393-7 (pbk)

Contents

List of Plates

Contributors

Sam Zeno Conedera, SJ, recently completed his PhD in History at UCLA. His areas of interest include Iberia, crusading spirituality, and the military orders. He is currently pursuing a degree in philosophy at Fordham University as part of his Jesuit formation.

Walker Reid Cosgrove is a doctoral candidate at Saint Louis University working under the direction of Thomas F. Madden. He is currently writing a dissertation on the episcopate in southern France at the turn of the thirteenth century, and the impact the Albigensian Crusade had on the church in the region.

Thomas Devaney, currently a PhD candidate at Brown University, previously studied at the University of Chicago with Walter Kaegi, to whom this essay is greatly indebted. His research interests are focused on the interactions between different religious groups in the medieval Mediterranean. He is writing a dissertation on frontier culture and public spectacle in both Iberia and the Latin East under the direction of Amy Remensnyder.

M. Cecilia Gaposchkin received her PhD from UC Berkeley in 2001. She teaches at Dartmouth College, and works on late medieval French cultural history. She has published on the intersection between politics, kingship, and representation, and is currently interested in art and culture under the Capetian kings, as well as the influence of crusading and crusade ideology on culture and kingship in the West. Her first book, *The Making of Saint Louis: Kingship, Sanctity, and Crusade in the Later Middle Ages*, was published by Cornell University Press in 2008.

Carole Hillenbrand is Professor Emerita of Islamic History at the University of Edinburgh, United Kingdom. Her two most recent books are *The Crusades: Islamic Perspectives* (Edinburgh, 1999), and *Turkish Myth and Muslim Symbol: The Battle of Manzikert* (Edinburgh, 2007).

Robert Hillenbrand was educated at the universities of Cambridge and Oxford. He has taught for most of his career at the University of Edinburgh, with Visiting Professorships at the universities of Princeton, UCLA, Bamberg,

Dartmouth College and Groningen. He has written eight books, edited or co-edited 10 books, and published over 150 articles or contributions to books.

Michael Lower is Associate Professor of History at the University of Minnesota. He received his PhD from Cambridge University in 1999 and is the author of *The Barons' Crusade: A Call to Arms and Its Consequences* (Pennsylvania, 2005). He was a residential fellow at the Institute for Research in the Humanities at the University of Wisconsin-Madison in 2007 and is a Mellon Foundation New Directions Fellow for 2010–2011. He is currently working on a comparative history of Christian mercenaries in North Africa and Muslim mercenaries in Spain in the medieval and early modern periods, tentatively titled *Fighting for the Enemy*.

Thomas F. Madden is Professor of History and Director of the Center for Medieval and Renaissance Studies at Saint Louis University. His publications include *The Fourth Crusade: The Conquest of Constantinople* (with Donald E. Queller) (University of Pennsylvania Press, 1997), *Enrico Dandolo and the Rise of Venice* (Johns Hopkins University Press, 2003), and *The New Concise History of the Crusades* (Rowman and Littlefield, 2005).

James L Naus is a doctoral candidate at Saint Louis University working under the direction of Thomas F. Madden. He is currently writing a dissertation on the Capetian monarchy's use of crusade memory during the twelfth and thirteenth centuries.

David Alan Parnell is a doctoral candidate at Saint Louis University and a historian of Late Antiquity and the Byzantine Empire. His dissertation is entitled "Justinian's Men: The Ethnic and Regional Origins of Byzantine Officers and Officials, ca. 518–610." He is also interested in the relationship between the crusades, the crusader states, and the Byzantine Empire.

C. Matthew Phillips is Assistant Professor of History at Concordia University-Nebraska and resides in Lincoln, Nebraska. He completed his PhD in medieval history at Saint Louis University in 2006. He is currently working on writing a book on the relationship between monastic preaching on devotion to the cross and crusade propaganda during the twelfth and thirteenth centuries.

Jennifer A. Price completed a M.Phil at Cambridge University under the supervision of Jonathan Riley-Smith and a PhD at the University of Washington in 2005. She is completing a monograph with the working title,

"*Cruce Signatus*: Crusaders and their vows, 1095–1291." Her current research focuses on the communication and transformation of the crusading idea, the visual representation of the crusader in medieval art, and the ongoing cultural dialogue between Christian and Muslim communities. Dr. Price currently serves as an adjunct professor of History at Seattle University.

Vincent T. Ryan to received his Ph.D. from Saint Louis University and is one of the co-founders of the Crusades Studies Forum. He is the author of "Richard I and the Early Evolution of the Fourth Crusade" in *The Fourth Crusade: Event, Aftermath, and Perceptions* (Ashgate, 2009). His dissertation is a study of the relationship between crusading and Marian piety during the Middle Ages.

Caroline Smith studied History at the University of Cambridge, from which she received her PhD in 2004. She is the author of *Crusading in the Age of Joinville* (Aldershot: Ashgate, 2006) and translator of Geoffrey of Villehardouin's "The Conquest of Constantinople" and John of Joinville's "The Life of Saint Louis," published together as *Chronicles of the Crusades* (London: Penguin Classics, 2008).

Brett Edward Whalen is Assistant Professor of medieval history at the University of North Carolina, Chapel Hill. He works on Christian intellectual and cultural history during the High Middle Ages. His recent book, *Dominion of God: Christendom and Apocalypse in the Middle Ages* (Harvard, 2009), explores how the Roman papacy, its supporters, and its critics invoked prophecy and apocalyptic thought to theorize the proper ordering of the world during the age of European expansion from the eleventh to the fourteenth century.

Abbreviations

BC   *Bulario de la Orden Militar de Calatrava* (Barcelona, 1981)

CCCM   *Corpus Christianorum, continuatio Medievalis*

MGH   *Monumenta Germaniae Historica, Scriptores,* ed. G.H. Pertz et al., 32 vols. (Hannover, 1826–1934)

PL   *Patrologia cursus completes. Series Latina,* ed. J.P. Migne, 217 vols. (Paris, 1844–64)

RHC Oc.   *Recueil des historiens des croisades: Historiens occidentaux,* 5 vols. (Paris, 1844–95)

RHC Or.   *Recueil des historiens des croisades: Historiens orientaux,* 5 vols. (Paris, 1872–1906)

RHGF   *Recueil des historiens des Gaules de la France,* ed. M. Bouquet et al., 24 vols. (Paris, 1737–1904)

Introduction

At one time the crusades were regarded as a sidelight of the Middle Ages – peripheral campaigns fought thousands of miles from Europe for a variety of religious, economic, and political reasons. Historians have come to know better. The crusades stood not at the periphery of the medieval world, but at its core. They were the product of events separated by thousands of miles and across complex frontiers of culture and religion. They owed their existence as much to Muslim expansionism and Byzantine instability as they did to the articulation of ecclesiastical reform to a Western feudal nobility. It is within the context of the crusading movement that each of the major medieval cultures – Latin West, Byzantine, and Muslim – came into contact. That contact, of course, resulted in conflict, cooperation, collaboration, and individual assimilation, accommodation, or rejection of the newly encountered other. Crusade studies is not simply the study of campaigns and battles (although those are by no means excluded), but the examination of a context in which the medieval Mediterranean and its disparate cultures both acted and interacted.

The purpose of this volume is to bring together recent research into the ways in which those medieval worlds were affected by the crusading movement. All of the studies here were presented initially at The First International Symposium on Crusade Studies held on the campus of Saint Louis University between 15 and 18 February 2006. The title of the symposium, like that of this volume, was *Crusades: Medieval Worlds in Conflict*. Its goal was to bring together scholars at all career levels and from a wide variety of disciplines to present research and respond to the work of others. In that respect, and many more, it was a highly successful event.

The Symposium was originally conceived by a group of graduate students at Saint Louis University – primarily Vincent T. Ryan and James L. Naus – who were working on the history of the crusades under the direction of Thomas F. Madden. With some modifications, Madden took their idea to the university administration, which very generously supported it. The Symposium itself took place in two distinct phases. The goal of Phase I was to present new research from distinguished scholars in a venue approachable to fellow scholars, interested specialists in other fields, and the general public. On the evenings of 15, 16, and 17 February two lectures were delivered in the magnificent Pere Marquette Gallery with questions and discussion after each. Free and open to the public, all of these lectures attracted standing-room-only crowds. Phase I lecturers were Jonathan Riley-Smith (Cambridge University), John France (University of Wales, Swansea), Robert Hillenbrand (University of Edinburgh), Jaroslav Folda (University of North Carolina, Chapel Hill), and Carole Hillenbrand (University of Edinburgh).

Phase II of the symposium took place on 18 February. This provided an opportunity for participants to present specialized research in a traditional conference environment. More than 40 papers were delivered in both plenary and concurrent sessions. Taking advantage of the venue, a special plenary session was devoted to the crusader king, Saint Louis IX. Although originally intended for a scholarly audience, many people from the Saint Louis region attended the plenary session making it yet another overflow event. Among the attendees were clergy from the nearby Cathedral Basilica of Saint Louis who had days earlier allowed participants to view relics of both Louis IX and the True Cross. After papers were presented by M. Cecilia Gaposchkin (Dartmouth College), Michael Lower (University of Minnesota), and Caroline Smith (Saint Louis University) a comment was delivered by William Chester Jordan (Princeton University). Jordan remarked on the exceptional quality of the papers and reflected on the passing of the torch of Louis IX studies to a new generation of scholars.

After the papers were delivered, the banquets and receptions enjoyed, and the participants had departed, the Symposium nevertheless continued to bear fruit. Aside from this volume, it also brought into being the Crusades Studies Forum, a new, permanent venue for the presentation of research, the discussion of recent scholarship, and the exploration of new directions in topics relating to the crusades. The Crusades Studies Forum now meets approximately 15 times per year at Saint Louis University. Half of those meetings provide an opportunity for participants to discuss and debate new publications in crusade studies. The rest of the meetings host visiting crusade scholars who deliver lectures and discuss their own work with participants. For a full list of past presenters and current schedules, see the Crusades Studies Forum website at http://crusades.slu.edu.

This volume includes a select group of the papers delivered at the symposium in 2006. They were chosen not only because of their quality and importance, but also because they illuminate several of the diverse medieval worlds in which the crusades took place. All three of the studies from the session on Louis IX are here included. Although Jordan's comment is not included directly, its insights and suggestions are woven into the studies as they stand in their current form.

The first section explores worlds of conflicting sanctity within the framework of the crusades. Across the battlefields two religious cultures constructed narratives of the sacred while simultaneously describing the other as polluted and therefore worthy of destruction. In the Islamic world old conceptions of *jihad* against Christians were retooled to meet the challenges of the crusades. Carole Hillenbrand demonstrates in her essay the ways in which jihad poetry, an established genre of propaganda during the centuries of warfare against Byzantium, was modified to focus on the Latins in the East, especially during the years leading up to 1187. While earlier jihad poetry made much of the importance of Constantinople, the new poets were able to replace the Byzantine capital with Jerusalem itself. Thus, the message of the poet went from conquest to restoration, from expansion to redemption. Jihad poetry during this period described a sacred Jerusalem now polluted by idolators and pork-eaters. It cried out for rescue.

On the other side of sanctity was the Christian understanding of crusade, particularly after the loss of Jerusalem and the True Cross in 1187. C. Matthew Phillips uncovers the monastic roots of crusading spirituality that emphasized self-denial and the communal life as the bearing of one's own cross. Like jihad poets, monastic sermon writers took existing concepts – in this case the equation of monastic rigor with the imitation of the crucified Christ – and adapted them to new circumstances. Not only the monk, but the crusader was crucified by his trials and sacrifices to restore Jerusalem. The loss of the True Cross, which remained a source of profound concern for Europeans, brought into sharp relief this metaphorical image. These sermons made clear that the crusader was called to take up the cross of self-denial in order to redeem the cross on which Christ himself had been (and continued to be) crucified. And these crusaders need not only be bound for Jerusalem. Crusaders in Iberia were affected by the same concepts of sanctity which interwove monasticism and crusade. Sam Conedera illuminates one such manifestation of this with his examination of the *hermandades*, religious military confraternities in Spain that played an important part in the *reconquista*.

The second group of essays focuses on the crusades and contested worlds of ideas. Robert Hillenbrand begins by demonstrating how the crusades and the presence of Latin Christians in the East may have set off cultural ripples that affected expression within Islamic art in Syria and Jazira. Although contacts between the Byzantine and Muslim worlds were plentiful, Islamic art had long ago left behind Byzantine and classical styles. However, in Syria and Jazira in the twelfth and thirteenth centuries, many of those styles returned. Hillenbrand posits that the presence of the crusader states isolated the area from both Cairo and Baghdad, leading to an independence that naturally manifested itself in artistic expression. By examining the practice of including author portraits in Islamic books Hillenbrand finds a classicizing influence which simultaneously depicted and elevated the author. After the fall of the Latin East, however, this trend began to subside and finally collapse utterly, leaving only epigraphy, with no author portrait at all. The influence of Mamluk Egypt from the south and the Mongols from the East, unhindered by the foreign buffer of the Latin East, displaced the classicizing independence of the area.

Jennifer Price tackles the difficult question of the Spanish *reconquista*. Scholars have long wrestled with attempts to define and relate this concept to the crusading movement. Rather than deal in generalities, however, Price trains her analysis on the ways that warfare against Muslims in Spain was re-understood in the wake of the First Crusade. She finds that the two activities continued to be regarded as different – that the crusade remained an armed pilgrimage to Jerusalem. However, particularly in the court of Alfonso I of Aragón-Navarre, crusade components came to be used to support local warfare against Muslims.

Perhaps the thorniest problem at the intersection of the crusades and ideas is one of definition. Crusade scholars have sometimes found it difficult to agree on what was and was not a crusade. In part, this mirrors a similar uncertainty in the medieval world as the concept of crusade developed and changed over time. Although the majority opinion now appears to have accepted Riley-Smith's expanded definition, there remain important challenges. These include Christopher Tyerman's assertion that the crusades were born only during the pontificate of Innocent III and Michael Markowski's claim that even Innocent did not consider all of the crusades of his pontificate to be, in fact, crusades. Walker Reid Cosgrove responds to Markowski's use of language as evidence, arguing that the use of the word *crucesignatus* cannot reliably be used as a window into the medieval understanding of crusade. Instead, Cosgrove finds that it was one word among many that Innocent and other popes employed to describe the crusades of their time.

Since the crusades (if we assume that their origins can, indeed, be traced to the Council of Clermont in 1095) were conceived in part as a rescue for the Byzantine Empire, some attention should certainly be paid to the intersection of crusades with Byzantium. Brett Edward Whalen begins his study in the immediate aftermath of the First Crusade. He argues that scholars have been too quick to project later crusader/Byzantine animosity onto the events of 1107 when they describe Bohemond's attack on Alexius I as a sanctioned crusade. Whalen demonstrates that an unbiased reading of the sources does not bear this interpretation. Rather, the attack on Durazzo should be seen as an episode in the continued belligerence between the Normans and Byzantines, not as the opening salvo in a war that would continue until 1204.

Likewise, the Venetian Crusade of 1122 was not a war against Byzantium, but that certainly did not stop the Venetians from using it to punish John II Comnenus for his revocation of their commercial privileges in the empire. Thomas Devaney provides a comprehensive examination of this crusade within the context of Byzantine/Venetian relations. He argues that John's actions constituted one part of a larger policy to consolidate and reclaim powers and assets lost in previous years. John erred by assuming that the Venetians would accept his decision, something unlikely given their increased wealth and power. The crusade, therefore, provided a means for them to make that case, although in so doing they laid the seeds of the Byzantine seizure of Venetians and their assets 50 years hence.

John II's policy toward Venice may have been problematic, but it did not attract near the attention that he gave to his plans in the East. David Parnell examines John's policy toward crusader Antioch. He finds that, unlike his Venetian strategy, John II initially continued the policy of his father, Alexius I, toward Antioch. However, when he saw the need to expand, John quickly pressed his claim to the city. Parnell believes that John's plan was to conquer Aleppo and other parts of Syria or Mesopotamia in order to create buffer states to be handed over to the Latin rulers of Antioch, thus freeing up the city for direct imperial control. In this way, John could place the barbarians again beyond the empire's border while providing for the long-term security of the eastern frontier. His sudden death, however, ended that plan while it was still in execution.

The last set of essays is the product of the symposium's special session on the crusade and Louis IX. Caroline Smith provides a truly fascinating study of the fear with which crusaders, in this case those on the first crusade of Louis IX, approached travel by sea. More than the battlefield, the capricious sea put crusaders in direct contact with the divine, for it was only by God's will and the intercession of his saints that they could hope to survive. The sea served as a test of courage and devotion. It was both a journey and a destination, for it was itself a penance. Louis mightily struggled with this test, dramatically stretched out before the consecrated host in prayer while his vessel seemed lost. Smith reminds us not only of the hardships of the crusade, but the anxious feelings of helplessness that accompanied the seaborne journey of the crusaders.

Michael Lower next focuses our attention on the Second Crusade of Louis in 1270. Scholars have long puzzled over the reasoning behind the destination of this crusade. Why did Louis choose to sail to Tunis? Lower convincingly argues that the king did so with two goals in mind. First, he hoped to use the wealth of Tunis to help fund his crusade. It was this sort of strategy of using confiscated non-Christian wealth that had served him well in the past. The Jews in France had previously had their usurious funds confiscated by the king to fund his crusade. Second, Louis seems to have believed that the emir of Tunis was willing to convert to Christianity. This intelligence, Lower believes, came not from Tunisian envoys, but from Dominicans who Louis knew and who were connected to the Dominican mission in Tunis. Lower's explanation is compelling, for it not only brings new evidence to bear on the problem, but it places the decision within the constellation of previous decisions made by the crusader king.

Finally, this volume ends where it begins, by tying together the crusade career of Louis IX with competing concepts of sanctity. M. Cecilia Gaposchkin investigates this theme within the various approaches to the sanctity of Louis himself. Louis was canonized quickly after his death, but neither as a crusader nor as a martyr. Indeed, as Gaposchkin points out, Louis was not alone in this since no crusader was ever canonized as a crusader. The crusade therefore was a vehicle, an activity, and a penance. It was not in and of itself evidence of sanctity. Instead, Louis was canonized for his exemplary life. Impossible to ignore his crusading career, this served only as evidence of Louis' willingness to suffer with humility for Christ. Ironically, Louis' captivity, the mark of his first crusade's failure, was a powerful argument for his sanctity for it put in clear light his patient and steadfast humility.

Together these essays reveal more of the seemingly endless facets of medieval life that touched and were touched by the crusading movement. With each new investigation into the crusades we learn more about the conflicting medieval worlds that they themselves mirrored.

PART I
The Crusades and Conflicting Worlds of Sanctity

Chapter 1

Jihad Poetry in the Age of the Crusades

Carole Hillenbrand
University of Edinburgh

Introductory Comments

Medieval Arabic poetry, spanning the period from around 500 to 1800, has rarely found favour with Westerners. It has been criticized for its lack of "spontaneity," the absence in it of the personal note, its emphasis on form over content, and its excessive indulgence in verbal pyrotechnics – antithesis, synonyms, puns, and other devices – not to mention its self-consciously inkhorn vocabulary. Indeed, the extraordinarily rich vocabulary of classical Arabic – with literally hundreds of words denoting, for example, the camel, the camel's trappings and the beauties of the desert – does not lend itself easily to translation into other languages. The frustrated and impotent translator ends up with a prose version, which is workmanlike, but flat and lifeless, in comparison with the resonance and force of the original.

In the period before Islam, poetry recited orally within the tribe was the vehicle for recording the genealogies of the ancient Arabs and for lauding their heroic exploits. After the advent of Islam, and the creation of a vast world empire, caliphs and governors encouraged court poets to compose panegyrics to vaunt their regimes and their personal prestige. Nobody thought that the writing of verse was easy; poetry was recalcitrant material, to be tamed only by painful and prolonged effort. The words had to be fashioned by constant arrangement and rearrangement. Rarely are medieval Arab poets found boasting of their ability to compose verse quickly. Poems had to be meticulously crafted. Nevertheless, inspiration and natural talent were indispensable; no amount of effort could succeed without an innate disposition towards poetry.[1]

---

[1]   There are many introductory works on classical Arabic poetry; two works which are still very useful are A.Hamori, *On the art of medieval Arabic literature* (Princeton, 1974) and H.A.R. Gibb, *Arabic literature* (Oxford, 1974).

The Concept of *Jihad* and Its Manifestation in Poetry before the Coming of the Crusades

Jihad is enjoined on the believer several times in the Qur'an and indeed has sometimes been called the sixth pillar of Islam. From the earliest period, the notion of *jihad* (struggle) as a spiritual concept for individual Muslims was paramount. Two kinds of *jihad* were identified, however: the greater *jihad* and the lesser *jihad*. The greater *jihad* is the struggle which man has to wage against his lower self and is, indeed, more meritorious than the lesser *jihad*, the military struggle conducted against infidels, either to defend or to expand the world of Islam.[2]

The conflict of the Crusades did not create the first *jihad* poetry in Arabic. The pre-Islamic poetic tradition with its weapons of glorification of the tribe and satire of the enemy could be used to extol the new faith and castigate polytheists and infidels. The 'Abbasid poet Abu Tammam (*floruit c.*805–45) laid a number of the foundations for later *jihad* poetry in his praise of the annual campaigns against the Byzantines led by the caliph al-Muta'sim in the ninth century, and in particular the Muslim victory at the battle of Amorium in 836: the poem is a literary *tour de force*, with every line ending in the letter "b":

> O day of the battle of 'Ammuriyya, hopes have returned from you overflowing with honey-sweet milk.
> You have left the fortunes of the sons of Islam in the ascendant,
> And the polytheists and the abode of polytheism in decline.[3]

Thus we see a single Muslim military triumph being elevated to the status of a grandiose struggle between Islam and polytheism.

The favourite classical Arabic poet of all time is the Syrian al-Mutanabbi (d. 965), a professional panegyrist who travelled with his poetic wares in search of patronage.[4] The religious flavour of his name – al-Mutanabbi – meaning "he who aspires to be a prophet" – indicates some politico-religious activities in his youth which caused him to end up in prison for a while. Later, he spent nine years in the service of an Arab prince, the remarkable Hamdanid ruler of Aleppo, Sayf al-Dawla, who fought more than 40 battles against the Byzantines. Bedridden from 962 onwards, Sayf al-Dawla would be carried into battle on a litter and

2   Cf. D. Cook, *Understanding Jihad* (Berkeley, 2005); C. Hillenbrand, *The Crusades: Islamic perspectives* (Edinburgh, 1999), pp. 89–92.
3   *Arabic poetry*, ed. and trans. A.J. Arberry (Cambridge, 1965), p. 52.
4   Cf. R. Blachère, *Un poète arabe du IVe siècle de l'Hégire (Xe siècle de J.-C): About-Tayyib ul Motanabbi* (Paris, 1935).

when he died, he was buried in his mausoleum, in the manner of a martyr, with a brick covered in dust from one of his campaigns placed under his cheek. He was a real model for later *jihad* warriors to follow. The period he spent with Sayf al-Dawla brought al-Mutanabbi the most satisfaction and it was then that he produced his finest poetry, excelling in the description of fierce combat, often put into the mouth of the warrior himself:

> Now I face war and I will go to the end.
> I will leave horses startled by the burning battle.
> They are so pierced with blows, so panic-stricken by shouting,
> That they seem to be afflicted by a kind of madness ...
> More delicious than the generous wine,
> More gentle than the clinking of goblets
> Are for me the handling of sabres and lances
> And the impact, at my command, of one army against another.
> To expose myself to death, in combat, is my life.
> For me living is spreading death ...
> I have exhausted the utmost measure of patience. I will
> Now hurl myself into the perils of war ...
> Tomorrow is the rendezvous between slender blades.[5]

The capture by Sayf al-Dawla of the Byzantine border fortress of al-Hadath in 954 gives al-Mutanabbi the opportunity to conjure up a most memorable poetic *tour de force*, replete with rhetorical devices and powerful images:

> According to the degree of the people of resolve come resolutions,
> And according to the degree of noble men come noble actions.
> Small deeds are great in the eyes of the small
> And great deeds are small in the eyes of the great.[6]

Here we see the rigidly symmetrical antitheses so beloved of classical Arab poets. But we see and hear more than this – the hypnotic rhythmic succession of a torrent of words which sound similar – paronomasia – and which fit together in ways that defy easy definition. The *jihad* evoked in the poetry of al-Mutanabbi is not limited to his master's campaigns; it is viewed on a much wider canvas:

---

[5] *Ibid.* 76, *apud* E. Dermenghem, *Les plus beaux textes arabes* (Paris, 1951), p. 105 (my English translation).

[6] *ʿala qadr-i ahl al-ʿazm-i taʾti al-ʿazaʾimu / wa-taʾti ʿala qadr-i al-kiram al-makarimu wa-taʿzumu fi ʿayn i al-saghir sigharuhum/wa-tasghuru fi ʿayn-i al-ʿazim al-ʿazaʾimu*, Arberry, *op.cit.*, p. 84.

> You were not a king routing an equal,
> But monotheism routing polytheism,
> We put our hope in you and your refuge, Islam.
> Why should merciful God not guard it, when through you
> He cleaves the unbeliever asunder?

Al-Nami, a much lesser-known poet than al-Mutanabbi, who held public poetry competitions with his great rival, also gives fulsome praise to his patron Sayf al-Dawla, and he hints at the link between *jihad* and martyrdom, should his master fall on the field of battle in the path of *jihad*:[7]

> Illustrious prince! Your lances gain you glory in this world and in Paradise thereafter.
> Every year which passes finds you with your sword in the necks of enemies
> And your steed harnessed with bit and saddle.
> Time rolls on, and still your deeds are all for glory.

But such *jihad* campaigns as those of Sayf al-Dawla on the Byzantine border, and those of others on the Central Asian steppes against the pagan Turks or in Muslim Spain against the Christians of the north, should not blind us to the prevailing context of the Muslim world before the coming of the Crusades. The predominant ethos, after the initial Arab conquests of the seventh century, was *not* one of *jihad*; it was rather one of fairly fixed frontiers and of generally pragmatic tolerance of Christians and Jews. An intensifying of the Muslim *jihad* spirit was to return as a result of the coming of the Crusaders.

An Overview and Analysis of *Jihad* Poetry Written During the Muslim/Crusader Conflict

The body of poetry about *jihad* that has survived from the twelfth and thirteenth centuries is quite substantial. It is therefore somewhat surprising that such poetry has not been discussed, either under the category of religious or political poetry, in any of the standard works of scholarship on classical Arabic literature. Take the example of Saladin's famous friend and biographer, 'Imad al-Din al-Isfahani (d. 1201), whose historical works, written in a formidably difficult ornate prose, are frequently mentioned in surveys of Arabic literature, usually as models

---

7   Ibn Khallikan, *Wafayat al-a'yan*, trans. W.M. de Slane as *Ibn Khallikan's Biographical Dictionary* (Paris, 1843), I, p. 111.

to be avoided.[8] But his poetry is almost totally ignored, despite its value as a background to Saladin's career. And this neglect extends to the whole corpus of *jihad* poetry, which is scattered through Muslim chronicles, biographical dictionaries and medieval anthologies.

It is well known that when the forces of the First Crusade hit the Muslim world in 1098, the spirit of *jihad* was far from being in the forefront of Muslim minds and that it was a good half-century before the inhabitants in Syria and Palestine were able to forget their political and religious squabbles sufficiently to reunite under strong leadership and the banner of revitalized *jihad*. The prospect of Jerusalem lost to the Crusaders would provide an intense spur to the Muslims in their struggle. In a period almost totally devoid of contemporary Muslim chronicles, the poetry which has survived from the early twelfth century provides valuable testimony to the Muslim experience of grief and anguish at the loss of Jerusalem and to the gradual reawakening of the *jihad* spirit. These poems, composed by poets such as al-Abiwardi and Ibn al-Khayyat,[9] reflect the anguish and shame of loss.[10] The Franks are portrayed as religious infidels and despoilers of all that the Muslims hold sacred, both in the public domain and in their homes, since the sanctity of their mosques and their women is endangered. Sadly for the Muslims, the warnings contained in these poems remained unheeded for several decades, but their themes would be adopted and elaborated by poets later in the twelfth century and thereafter.

The great Muslim leader who began to turn the tide significantly in the fight against the Franks, Nur al-Din (d. 1174), is often portrayed as the very prototype of the *jihad* warrior. Ideally, personal and public *jihad* combine in the person of the ruler and this is certainly the way in which Nur al-Din is presented in the Muslim sources. During his period in power, *jihad* books, *jihad* sermons, and works praising the Holy City – the *Merits of Jerusalem* genre – proliferate. But perhaps the most rousing literary vehicle for *jihad* was the poetry written for and about Nur al-Din. This poetry stresses the spiritual dimensions of his *jihad* much more than the usual public ones. Saladin's future biographer, 'Imad al-Din al-Isfahani, joined the service of Nur al-Din and he wrote poetry in praise of

---

[8]   One of the early biographers of Saladin, Lane-Poole, for example, is very critical of the rhetorical flourishes of 'Imad al-Din; cited in H.A.R. Gibb, "The Arabic sources for the life of Saladin," in H.A.R. Gibb, *Studies in Islamic history*, ed. Y. Ibish (Beirut, 1972), p. 54. This view is shared inter alios by Gabrieli who complains of the "wearisome obscurities" of 'Imad al-Din; cf. F. Gabrieli, *Arab historians of the Crusades* (London, 1969), p. 114.

[9]   For references to the poems, cf. E. Sivan, *L'Islam et la Croisade* (Paris, 1968), pp. 18, 24, 32, and 36.

[10]   For a detailed discussion of these poems, cf. Hillenbrand, *Islamic perspectives*, pp. 70–1.

his master's pursuit of *jihad,* putting the following lines into the mouth of Nur al-Din:

> I have no wish except jihad
> Repose in anything other than it is exertion for me.
> Seeking achieves nothing except by striving.
> Life without the striving of jihad is an (idle) pastime.[11]

The successor of Nur al-Din, Saladin, is also the great *mujahid* in the Islamic sources. As in the time of Nur al-Din, the poets in Saladin's entourage also stress his prosecution of *jihad,* combined with his role as the ideal Sunni ruler. The well-known travelogue (*Rihla*) of the Spanish Muslim Ibn Jubayr, who wrote *inter alia* about the Holy Land when he passed through it in 1184 in the time of Saladin, has often been translated and used by historians. Nobody, however, seems to have paid due attention to a poem of his addressed to Saladin. This poem is to be found at the very beginning of the standard Arabic edition of the *Rihla* and is included amongst a series of extracts from later medieval Arab writers who used the work of Ibn Jubayr.[12] One such borrower was a later travel writer from Valencia, Muhammad al- 'Abdari, who made the pilgrimage to Mecca in 1289.[13] In view of references in the poem to Saladin having purified Jerusalem from the infidel, the poem must have been written after 1187.[14]

It is a long poem, containing fifty-three lines. It can be divided loosely into four sections: praise of Saladin who has conquered Syria, a description of the illegal way in which pilgrims to Mecca have been treated by Saladin's customs officials in Alexandria, an appeal to him to rectify this matter, and finally a eulogy of Saladin.[15] Here are a few key lines from it:

> How long have you been hovering among them (that is the Franks),
> A lion hovering in the thicket?

---

[11]   Abu Shama, *Kitab al-rawdatayn*, ed. M.H.M. Ahmad, I (Cairo, 1954), p. 625.

[12]   Ibn Jubayr, *Rihla*, ed. W. Wright (Leiden, 1907), pp. 28–31.

[13]   Al-'Abdari, *Al-rihla al-maghribiyya*, ed. M. El-Fasi (Rabat,1968); cf. *Encyclopedia of Islam*, second edition (*EI2*), s.v. Misrata (T. Lewicki).

[14]   Ibn Jubayr made two further journeys east, one between 1189 and 1191, and then a second one in 1217. He died that same year in Alexandria; cf. *EI2*, s.v. Ibn Djubayr (C. Pellat).

[15]   In view of the fact that Broadhurst, the English translator of Ibn Jubayr's work, mentions that Ibn Jubayr's "high literary reputation" among the Arabs was "partly due to his poetical works," it is a pity that he does not translate any of the verses about Saladin; cf. Ibn Jubayr, *The travels of Ibn Jubayr*, trans. R.J.C. Broadhurst (London, 1952), p. 20.

You have broken their cross by force
And what a fine breaker you are!
Their kingdom has retreated in Syria
And has turned its back as if it has never been.
You have avenged the religion of corrections on your enemies.
God has chosen you as avenger.

It will be noted here that Ibn Jubayr, though a visitor to the Levant, speaks of Saladin as a lion, and as God's instrument on earth, and he uses the familiar image of the "breaker of crosses" found in other anti-Christian *jihad* poetry.

Amongst the successors of Saladin, namely his family dynasty of the Ayyubids, the tradition of *jihad* poetry continued unabated, although some of its claims rang rather hollow in this age of relative *détente* with the Franks. However, it is important to mention here a poem composed by the professional poet, Ibn 'Unayn, to celebrate the victory of Saladin's descendant, the sultan al-Kamil, over the Franks at Damietta in 1221:[16]

On the morning we met before Damietta a mighty host of Byzantines, not to be numbered either for certain or (even) by guesswork.
They agreed as to opinion and resolution and religion, even if they differed in language.
They called upon the companions of the cross, and troops (of them) advanced as though the waves were ships for them.

This poem begins as it means to go on; it is infused with gloating irony, a poetic *topos* which had been developed by the 'Abbasid poet, Abu Tammam, to deal with Muslim triumph over another Christian enemy, the Byzantines. Indeed, in the poem, the Crusaders are called "a mighty host of Byzantines"; this is historically inaccurate, but it echoes a continuous past of adversarial conflict between Christendom and Islam. Yet, clearly, with the specific reference to Damietta, it is the hosts of the Fifth Crusade that are being routed.

In the rhythmic symmetry of the third line, the poetic device of *tibaq* (the placing of two words of opposite meanings in the same line) – "they agreed ... and they disagreed" ... – is employed to suggest the shared ideological purpose of the European crusading Christian army, despite the multiplicity of their differing linguistic backgrounds. Europe as a whole is pitted against the forces of Islam. In the fourth line we hear one of the most common titles for the Crusaders in medieval Muslim writings – they are called *ansar al-salib* (the supporters,

---

[16] Arberry, *Arabic poetry*, pp. 122–5.

helpers, protectors of the Cross). There is also here probably a deliberate echo of the Arabic term for Christian, *nasrani*, which comes from the same Arabic root as *ansar*. It must be admitted that the symbol of the Cross became a focus of Muslim animosity in the Crusading period. It was a symbol of the conquests and occupation of a foreign invader, the Franks. Breaking crosses in battle was a symbolic act in which Christianity was defeated and Islam was triumphant.

In the fourth line there is an allusion to the fabled maritime skills of the Franks, skills not shared by their Muslim opponents in this period. According to the poet, the troops of the Franks pour forth as though the waves of their battle lines are like ships cresting the waves of the sea. Yet, despite the awe-inspiring billows of the advancing torrent of the Crusader armies – a deliberate attempt by the poet to inflate the magnitude of the Christian enemy – Muslim victory is assured.

The climax of the poem turns to the victor himself, the Muslim sultan, al-Kamil:

> We are led by a noble scion of the House of Ayyub,
> whose resolution disdains to be settled in any place of contentment.
> Noble in praise, devoid of shame, valorous, handsome of countenance,
> perfect in beauty and beneficence.

These lines praise the sultan al-Kamil directly and more allusively. In the first line he is called a noble scion of the family of Ayyub, Saladin's father, and is thus given an impeccable pedigree for leading the war against the Franks. In the next line he is the exemplar of physical and moral qualities, "perfect in beauty and beneficence" (*kamil al-husni wa'l- husna*) – a deliberate pun on the sultan's name of al-Kamil, meaning "the perfect one").

The next line reads as follows:

> By your life, the signal deeds of 'Isa are not hidden,
> They shine out radiant as the sun upon the farthest and the nearest.

The poet's choice of one of al-Kamil's long list of names, 'Isa, is probably deliberate too: a taunt at the Christian enemy, since 'Isa is, of course, the Arabic version of the name Jesus.

The poet continues as follows:

> He marched towards Damietta with every highborn champion,
> Viewing the descent into battle as the most salubrious of descents,
> And he removed from there the miscreants of Byzantium, and the

Hearts of certain men were gladdened that afterwards made compact with sorrow;
And he cleansed her of their impurity with his sword – a hero
Regarding the acquisition of praise as the noblest of prizes.

The first hemistich of the last line is particularly significant – the Arabic is very forceful indeed:

And he cleansed her of their impurity with his sword

The word used for "filth" (*rijs*) is that denoting ritual impurity. Indeed, images of pollution and purification abound in the Muslim *jihad* literature of the Crusading period. And the poetry reflected real events: for example, Saladin purified the Dome of the Rock in Jerusalem with rosewater in 1187 when he recaptured the Holy City for Islam.

Ibn 'Unayn then reaches the rousing climax of his celebratory ode, with a triumphal threat and a solemn warning: the present victory belongs to the Muslims, but the *jihad* is still ongoing:

His swords have immortalised the memorable deeds of glory,
Whose report will never pass away, though time itself shall perish.
Our swords and their necks have known their places of encounter there;

The last words of the ode sound very grim indeed:

And if they return to the attack, we too shall return!

General Reflections

We should remember that a wide range of *jihad* literature flooded into being at the time of Nur al-Din and Saladin and it remained an important instrument in the propaganda war against the Franks – letters exulting in victory, sermons rousing the faithful, books extolling the merits of *jihad* and of *jihad* in particular to regain Jerusalem. So poetry was only one of a number of overlapping literary genres that flourished, but clearly it was the one that was most intimately linked to the ruler and his court, a genre for his public prestige and personal gratification. Monumental inscriptions and even coins contained further allusions to *jihad*.

Who wrote the *jihad* poetry? The obvious pool of writers comprised the peripatetic poets, who still went from one small court to another, often travelling vast distances in search of fame, fortune and, above all, the patronage of a ruler, provincial governor or military commander. The life of the professional poet was not without its hazards. Ibn 'Unayn (d. 1233), the author of the poem about Damietta already discussed, satirized Saladin so sharply that he was sent off into exile. He came back after Saladin's death and ingratiated himself with one of Saladin's successors at Damascus, even becoming his chief minister.[17]

Poetry did not, however, remain the preserve of the professional poet. An interesting development in the twelfth and thirteenth centuries was the greater involvement by the bureaucratic elite in the writing of such poetry in the wake of the strong revival of Sunni Islam, especially under Turkish rule. It was, after all, only a short step from written high-flown rhyming prose (*sajj*), much in favour with the scribal elite of Syria and Egypt at the time of the Crusades, to composing panegyric poetry about the exploits of their military overlords in the *jihad*. So the scribes, advisers, and ministers who travelled around in the entourage of the Turkish or Kurdish rulers – including Nur al-Din, Saladin and Baybars – enthusiastically picked up the pen and composed a substantial corpus of verse. Baybars' biographer, Ibn 'Abd al-Zahir, wrote vast amounts of poetry about his master – occasional poetry written to celebrate his master's victories, an elegy to be read over his tomb, and many other pieces.[18] Another government official, Ibn Mammati, who happened to be involved in the collecting of taxes, wrote a versified history of Saladin and many poems besides.[19] An intriguing example of a government official with a predilection for poetry is the famous chief minister of the Seljuq sultanate in Iraq and Iran, and a veritable polymath, al-Tughra'i (d. 1121), who is described by his biographer as surpassing "all his contemporaries in the art of composing in prose and verse." His most celebrated ode, written in 1111, contains sixty lines, all ending with the letter "l."[20] 'Imad al-Din al-Isfahani, Saladin's biographer and, as already mentioned, the author of high-flown rhyming prose, collected with enormous energy a 20-volumed anthology of twelfth-century poetry (*Kharidat al-qasr*), written by over a thousand poets. But by general consensus he was himself only a mediocre poet.

Why and when were the *jihad* poems written? Frequently, such poems were written after a conquest, whether great or small: the capture of a minor citadel could produce poetry just as much as a major victory, such as the fall of Edessa to Zengi in 1144,[21] or the battle of Hattin in 1187. A number of poems were indeed composed praising Zengi's *jihad*. An ode was also written congratulating

17   Arberry, *Arabic poetry*, p. 174.
18   Ibn 'Abd al-Zahir, *Al-rawd al-zahir*, ed. A. A. Al-Khuwaytir (Riyadh, 1976).
19   Ibn Khallikan, *Wafayat*, de Slane, I, p. 192.
20   *Ibid.*, p. 462.
21   Imad al-Din, *Kharidat al-qasr: qism shu'ara' al-Sham*, pt. 1 (Damascus, 1955), p. 110.

Zengi's son, Nur al-Din, on imprisoning the Crusader leader, Joscelin.[22] The death of a ruler was especially, of course, the ideal moment to extol in poetic form his exploits in the *jihad*.

It is legitimate to ask to what extent such flowery Arabic *jihad* poetry was understood by the Turkish and Kurdish rulers of Syria, Egypt, and Palestine, to whom it was addressed. After all, this was a court literature which rejoiced in rhetorical devices and carefully selected abstruse vocabulary which many Arabs themselves could not understand, let alone Turks and Kurds, who had often only recently entered the Arabic-speaking world and who spoke their own languages in their homes. Contemporary prose writing was also ornate in character and favoured form over content. Whether or not the non-Arab military leaders understand this literature remains uncertain, but it is clear that it was indeed read out in their presence as part of the ceremonies of the court. Perhaps an interpreter was used to explain the subtleties of the work as the public recitation proceeded. It is impossible to judge what the audience outside court circles might have been (and the word "audience" is used advisedly here, for it was certainly poetry which was meant to be declaimed in public). There is no doubt that the Muslim elite – preachers, judges, and teachers in the *madrasa*s (religious colleges) – would have approved of the religious ethos of the poetry and would have appreciated the high level of its Arabic. But it is doubtful how much troops, from a multiplicity of ethnic backgrounds, standing for inspection on the parade ground, or about to enter the fray or to celebrate a victory, would have comprehended of such stylized Arabic material. Yet its public declamation would have enabled them to catch its solemn tone and to have been roused by it, in much the same way as non-Arabic speakers often did not understand the text of the Qur'an but were nevertheless moved by it, sometimes to tears. Poetry, the quintessential Arabic literary genre, can be said to work at a deep subliminal level on the emotions of its hearers.

The major themes, images, and *topoi* of this *jihad* poetry were largely inherited from a military past spent fighting Byzantium. The concept, though not the exact image, of conquest as resembling the deflowering of a virgin, an image beloved of the ninth-century poet, Abu Tammam, who spoke of "swords swaying unsheathed" winning "many a branch quivering on a sandhill,"[23] is easily transferred by the poets of the early 1100s who described "young girls" as "almost wasting away with fear"[24] at the prospect of the Franks' approach.

---

22 'Imad al-Din, *Kharidat al-qasr*, p. 157.
23 Hamori, pp. 127 and 129.
24 Ibn al-Khayyat, *Diwan*, editor unidentified (Damascus, 1958), p. 185.

20

Abu Tammam celebrates the Muslim victory over Byzantium at Amorium in the following lines, proclaiming:

> The days of victory have left pale of face as their name the sons of the Yellow Ones
> (the Byzantines) and have brightened the faces of the Arabs.[25]

Yellow, the colour of flight and cowardice, had long been associated in the medieval Muslim sources with Byzantines and this epithet was easily transferred to the Crusaders, who were known as the Yellow Tribe (*Banu'l-Asfar*).[26]

As in the past, the *jihad* poets of the twelfth and thirteenth centuries give a religious framework to the military activities of Muslim leaders. Muslim victories are divinely ordained. The poet Ibn al-Qaysarani, praising Zengi's conquest of Edessa, suggests that he was helped in his endeavours by divine assistance:

> Hosts of angels have provided you with regiments, surrounded by more regiments.
> For him who has heavenly angels for an army
> What country is there where his horses would not tread?[27]

It is common too for Muslim poets to liken great victories, such as Hattin, to those fought in the exemplary life of the Prophet Muhammad.

Among the new emphases to emerge in the poetry of this period are the twin religious themes of Christian pollution and Muslim purification, which are omnipresent in the *jihad* poetry of the time. The identification of the Franks with the pig, an animal included in the Qur'an under the same divine anathema as the monkey, is a key image. The Ayyubid poet Ibn al-Nabih praises Saladin's brother, al-'Adil, declaring:

> You have purified Jerusalem of their (the Franks') filth
> After it had been a refuge for pigs.[28]

Despite the use of this familiar stereotypical imagery for the Christians, it is probable that it acquired new relevance and edge in the twelfth century when, for the first time in history, the Muslim monuments in Jerusalem, the Dome of the Rock and the Aqsa Mosque, were occupied and in Muslim eyes, "polluted" by the presence of the Franks, an occupation symbolized by the giant cross placed atop the Golden Dome and visible for miles around.

---

[25]   Arberry, *Arabic poetry*, p. 62.
[26]   Cf. the discussion in Hillenbrand, *Islamic perspectives*, pp. 240, and 255.
[27]   'Imad al-Din, *Kharidat al-qasr*, p. 110.
[28]   Ibn al-Nabih, *Diwan*, editor unidentified (Beirut, 1881), p.121.

New use of old imagery could be also be made in the case of Jerusalem itself. In the early centuries of Islam the Muslims were used to focusing on the conquest of the nearest seat of Christendom, Byzantium. High and low literature still cherished dreams of conquering Constantinople for Islam. Poets flattered their patrons who achieved minor victories on the Byzantine frontier: the capture of a single Byzantine fortress could permit expectations to be raised all over again.

In the twelfth century, the longed-for conquest of one great Christian capital is soon replaced by an intense desire to recapture another city, the very epicentre of Christianity – Jerusalem. And poets have a stock of well-tried *topoi* and rhetorical devices ready on the tips of their pens. Yet there were new aspects on which the poets could concentrate. The shift of emphasis from Constantinople to Jerusalem brought important changes with it; after all, Constantinople remained proudly unconquered and it contained no major Muslim holy sites. So the poetic focus on a humiliated Muslim Jerusalem is, of course, a theme unknown to earlier *jihad* poetry.

It must be admitted that this *jihad* poetry, much of it produced by the scribal class in Syria and Egypt, is not to be found nowadays in anthologies of the finest Arabic verse. Such poetry is clearly less focused on the elitist literary aims of the court poet of earlier generations; it is far more hortatory and didactic in nature and can be seen as an adjunct to the *jihad* sermons, the books of *jihad* and those belonging to the *Merits of Jerusalem* genre. The *jihad* poetry is functional and largely derivative in form and imagery. But it is not doggerel, either. It was recited at key historical moments; and afterwards, the medieval Muslim chroniclers place it deliberately and strategically in their works, at moments of high tension or significance in their narratives. So there too, on the pages of history books written for contemporaries and also for posterity, the *jihad* poetry serves as a solemn, if somewhat bombastic, reminder of the wider backcloth – a titanic struggle between Islam and Christianity – against which these events are being played out. The poetry is competent enough for its immediate purpose and occasionally, in the pen of real professional poets, such as Ibn al-Khayyat, lamenting the fall of Jerusalem, or Ibn ʿUnayn, exulting in victory at Damietta, it is poetry which reaches much greater heights.

How useful is this *jihad* poetry as historical evidence of the Muslim military and religious environment in Syria in the twelfth and thirteenth centuries? Much of the poetry follows a long-established tradition, with a repertoire of set images and themes. These images and themes are also found in kindred religious literary genres, such as *jihad* sermons, which display the same rhetoric but which are based more explicitly on the Qurʾan and the sayings of the Prophet. The same holds good for the wording of monumental inscriptions and official letters written by Muslim scribes on behalf of rulers. All this material reflects a milieu geared for *jihad,* even if Muslim rulers did not always prosecute it. In such a stylized literary genre as panegyric poetry, it is rare to find specific nuggets of "fact." There are, of course, references in the poems to names of citadels, cities, and individual warriors or rulers. But it is hard to construct a narrative from such references. It captures an atmosphere rather than relaying facts.

However, the very profusion of such *jihad* poetry is a clear indication of the nature of the religious milieu within which the Turkish "Counter-Crusade" leaders operated. The theme of Jerusalem, for example, becomes more pressing and urgent in the poetry of Saladin's adviser, 'Imad al-Din al-Isfahani: his insistence on the recapture of the Holy City reaches a powerful crescendo in his extant verse from the period 1180–87 and may have had an impact on Saladin's final decision to focus ever more intently on fighting the Franks.

Conclusions

This discussion has shown how the pre-Islamic ode with its pagan tribal character could be transformed into a core component in Arabic Muslim religious literature. Indeed, it proved to be elastic enough to adapt itself to the realities of running a vast Muslim empire. Moreover, this conventional form of medieval Arab panegyric poetry came to be deployed as a political and religious tool in the monumental struggle between Western Christendom and the Muslim world at the time of the Crusades. To state the obvious, *jihad* poetry is poetry in the service of religion. Its function mattered more at the time than its intrinsic quality.

Jihad poetry was not the creation of Muslim poets as a response to their unprecedented contact with *Western* Christendom at the time of the Crusades. What we see in twelfth and thirteenth century *jihad* poetry is in fact the easy and seamless transfer of earlier invective against Christian Byzantium to a new Christian target, the Crusaders. The Muslim poets of the twelfth and thirteenth centuries built on the traditions of the great al-Mutanabbi who wrote in ringingly grandiose terms about the small-scale *jihad* warfare of his patron, Sayf al-Dawla, against Byzantium. The Muslim poets who extolled the virtues of Nur al-Din, Saladin and their successors in the *jihad* do not belong in the pantheon of the greatest names of medieval Arabic poetry. But their verses resonate with the spirit of a period which would change the relationship between Christendom and the Muslim world and would harden the ideological battle lines between them. The *jihad* poetry gives us insights into the stereotypical way in which the Muslims viewed the Christian "other." But the proliferation of such poetry at key historical moments, and especially in the build up to Hattin and the recapture of Jerusalem, is significant. Nor is this all. The selfsame tropes and stereotypical language resurface throughout the Ottoman period in prose and poetry alike, from an anonymous Ottoman account of the Turkish victory over the Hungarians at Nicopolis in 1396 to the inflated and vainglorious ode written by al-Budayr to celebrate the victory of Jazzar Pasha over Napoleon near Acre in 1799.[29] These formulae, then, survived in almost unaltered form for almost a millennium – and their day is not yet over.

[29]   C. Hillenbrand, *Turkish myth and Muslim symbol: the Battle of Manzikert* (Edinburgh, 2007), pp. 169–70, and 182–4.

Chapter 2

Crucified with Christ: The Imitation of the Crucified Christ and Crusading Spirituality

C. Matthew Phillips
Concordia University-Nebraska

In his *Exordium magnum cisterciense*, a collection of stories for spiritual instruction, Konrad von Eberbach recounted a famous tale concerning Bernard of Clairvaux's devotion to the cross. A certain monk saw Bernard lying prostrate before an altar with a crucifix placed on the floor in front of him. As the abbot of Clairvaux adored and kissed the crucifix with great devotion the corpus separated itself from the cross and embraced him. This legend reflects a graphic depiction of a central teaching of twelfth-century monastic and canonical preachers, namely, devotion to the cross and the imitation of the crucified Christ.[1]

Building on Holy Scripture and patristic tradition, twelfth-century monastic and canonical preachers encouraged their audience to subdue carnal desires through the physical pain associated with abstinence, fasting, vigils, and flagellation. However, they also exhorted monks to transform themselves spiritually through crucifying carnal vices while simultaneously inculcating the divine virtues associated with the cross of Christ. Indeed, they defined the religious life as a metaphorical crucifixion of body and soul with Christ. Increasingly, twelfth-century preachers and devotional writers associated this

---

[1] Konrad von Eberbach, *Exordium magnum cisterciense* 2.7, ed. Bruno Griesser, CCCM 138 (Turnhout, 1994), pp. 78–79. On the importance of this story and the Cistercians' devotion to the crucified Christ see Sheryl Frances Chen, "Bernard's Prayer Before the Crucifix that Embraced Him: Cistercians and the Devotion to the Wounds of Christ," *Cistercian Studies Quarterly* 29 (1994), 23–54. On the twelfth century in general see Giles Constable, *The Reformation of the Twelfth Century* (Cambridge, 1996), pp. 278–82; idem, "The Ideal of the Imitation of Christ," in *Three Studies in Medieval Religious and Social Thought* (Cambridge, 1995), pp. 194–217.

inner crucifixion with meditation on relics of the True Cross, crucifixes, and Christ's passion.[2]

Beginning with Urban II's proclamation of the First Crusade, preachers had promoted an interior conversion through bearing the crusader's cross. In so doing, they appropriated the devotional and theological concepts formerly used to describe the monastic life. Their spiritual rhetoric aimed at potential crusaders included a focus on the believer's co-crucifixion with Christ via meditation on the Lord's passion and infusion of the virtues; especially love for God and one's neighbor, associated with his cross.[3] In this paper, through a close analysis of monastic and crusade sermons, I will demonstrate how crusade propagandists formed an integral part of crusading ideology through this adoption of the devotional concept of the imitation of the crucified Christ.

Chroniclers of the First Crusade and the preachers of the Second Crusade, many of whom were monks themselves, certainly depicted the crusaders as bearing the cross for individual salvation. However, the Frankish army's loss of the relic of the True Cross to Saladin in 1187 inspired crusade preachers to focus more specifically on the cross. While the Holy Sepulcher remained an important part of their propaganda, crusade preachers associated with the moral reformers at the schools of Paris and their monastic and ecclesiastical colleagues made Gregory VIII's call for the Third Crusade into an exhortation for personal

---

[2]   On the significance of the relationship between physical pain and spiritual conversion see Karl F. Morrison, *Understanding Conversion* (Charlottesville, 1992), pp. 66–91. See also Caroline Walker Bynum, *Jesus as Mother: Studies in the Spirituality of the High Middle Ages* (Berkeley, 1982), pp. 82–109, on how exterior behavior and interior conversion complemented one another in twelfth-century religious thought. Three studies on medieval artistic depictions of virtues and vices that refer to sermons are Adolf Katzenellenbogen, *Allegories of the Virtues and Vices in Medieval Art* (London, 1939; reprint, Toronto: University of Toronto, 1989); Jennifer O'Reilly, *Studies in the Iconography of the Virtues and Vices in the Middle Ages* (New York, 1988); Gertrud Schiller, *Iconography of Christian Art*, vol. 2, *The Passion of Jesus Christ*, trans. Janet Seligman (Greenwich, 1972), pp. 137–40. On the development of the visual element in meditation on the crucified Christ see Constable, "Imitation of Christ," pp. 210–11; and most recently, Sara Lipton, " 'The Sweet Lean of His Head': Writing About Looking at the Crucifix in the High Middle Ages," *Speculum* 80 (2005), 1172–1208.

[3]   See Jonathan Riley-Smith, *The First Crusade and the Idea of Crusading* (Philadelphia, 1986), p. 2, where he stated that three significant crusade chronicles agreed with the eleventh-century reformers' goal of infusing "secular life with monastic values." On the significance of the love of one's neighbor for crusade propaganda see idem, "Crusading as an Act of Love," *History* 65 (1980), 177–192.

and social reform through devotion to the cross and imitation of the crucified Christ.[4]

Before turning to crusade propaganda, we will examine the texts of some key twelfth-century preachers and devotional writers. The famous monastic and crusade preacher, Bernard of Clairvaux discussed the struggle between the two crosses that occurs within every monk. He told his brothers that the virtues of Christ's cross, that is, the fear of the Lord, eternal hope, divine love, and perseverance overcame the vices of the devil's false cross, which were self-exaltation, despair, fleshly lust, and obstinacy.[5]

Additionally, Bernard also taught that Christ's cross should crucify the faithful monk carnally and spiritually. While monks crucified the flesh on the cross of abstinence, they bore the cross of love, on which Christ hung daily in the heart. If they feared falling into desperation, Bernard advised his monks to imagine Christ crucified for them. Hanging on the cross of Christ's love, Bernard

---

[4]   On importance of the True Cross see Alan V. Murray, "Mighty Against the Enemies of Christ: The Relic of the True Cross in the armies of the Kingdom of Jerusalem," in *The Crusades and Their Sources*, eds. John France and William G. Zajac (Brookfield, 1998), pp. 217–238. On Gregory's call for the Third Crusade and the loss of the True Cross see Jean Richard, "1187, Point de départ pour une nouvelle forme la croisade," in *The Horns of Hattin*, ed. B.Z. Kedar (London, 1992), pp. 254–55; Penny J. Cole, "Christian Perceptions of the Battle of Hattin (583/1187)," *Al-Masaq* 6 (1993), 19–21; idem, " 'O God, the Heathen Have Come Into Your Inheritance' (PS. 78.1): The Theme of Religious Pollution in Crusade Documents, 1095–1188," in *Crusaders and Muslims in Twelfth-Century Syria*, ed. Maya Shatzmiller (Leiden, 1993), pp. 104–11; and Christopher Tyerman, *The Invention of the Crusades* (Toronto, 1998), pp. 26–29. On the Parisian reformers' cooperation with religious orders in combining crusade preaching with moral reform see Penny J. Cole, *The Preaching of the Crusades to the Holy Land, 1095–1270* (Cambridge, Mass., 1991), pp. 112–17; Jessalynn Bird, "Heresy, Crusade and Reform in the Circle of Peter the Chanter, c.1187– c.1240." (D.Phil. University of Oxford, 2001), pp. 1–296; idem, "Reform or Crusade? Anti-usury and Crusade Preaching during the pontificate of Innocent III," in *Pope Innocent III and His World*, ed. John C. Moore (Aldershot, 1999), pp. 165–85; idem, "Innocent III, Peter the Chanter's Circle, and the Crusade Indulgence: Theory, Implementation, and Aftermath," in *Innocenzo III: Urbs et Orbis, Atti del Congresso Internazionale Roma, 9–15 settembre 1998*, ed. Andrea Sommerlechner (Rome, 2003), pp. 501–24. Cf. Colin Morris, *The Sepulchre of Christ and the Medieval West* (Oxford, 2005), pp. 269–70; and Jonathan Riley-Smith, "The Politics of Holy War: France and the Holy Land," in *The Book of Kings: Art, War, and the Morgan Library's Medieval Picture Bible*, eds. William Noel and Daniel Weiss (London, 2002), p. 79.

[5]   Bernard of Clairvaux, *Sententiae* 3.74, eds. Jean Leclercq, C.H. Talbot, and H.M. Rochais, *Sancti Bernardi Opera* 6/2 (Rome, 1957–1977), p. 114; *The Parables and the Sentences*, Trans. Michael Casey and Francis R. Swietek (Kalamazoo, 2000), pp. 255–57. On the significance of Bernard's *Sententiae* as sources for his monastic preaching see Jean Leclercq, *Monks and Love in Twelfth-Century France* (Oxford, 1979), pp. 86–87.

exhorted them to chastise their bodily members, so that neither their feet nor hands would commit evil actions.[6]

Mid twelfth-century Cistercian abbots, Guerric of Igny and Aelred of Rievaulx, exhorted their monks to embrace the spiritual cross of Christ in their sermons for Palm Sunday and Easter. They believed that the faithful could transform themselves in their affections and actions through the liturgical remembrance of the crucified Christ. Thereby they would crucify sinful vices, while simultaneously strengthening their virtues. Those who were nailed to the cross and died with Christ became spiritually wise, righteous, holy, and free from sin.[7]

They exhorted their fellow monks to be fastened to the cross by the deeply-driven nails of the fear of the Lord. Thereby, their bodily members now could only serve righteousness and not iniquity. Although sin remained in the body, those in Christ continually crucified their vices. Christ's method of redemption, the cross, had become the pattern for living righteously through torturing the flesh. They urged their monastic brothers to persevere with Christ by hanging voluntarily on the cross of penance until death. Aelred of Rievaulx dramatically described the cross as the monastic *ordo* or way of life.[8]

While the Cistercians certainly understood the monastic life as a metaphorical crucifixion with Christ, the traditionalist black monks described their religious devotion with similar spiritual rhetoric. In his treatise on the cloistered life Peter of Celle stated that the devout religious must crucify the flesh and its vices in the same manner that the naked Christ was nailed to the cross.[9] He compared the monastic life to the scene of Christ's crucifixion and burial. As Christ's feet were

---

[6]   Bernard of Clairvaux, *Sententiae* 3.74, p. 115; Swietek, *Sentences*, pp. 257–58. Cf. Martha G. Newman, *Boundaries of Charity: Cistercian Culture and Ecclesiastical Reform, 1098–1180* (Stanford, 1996), p. 9, where she argues that the Cistercians "associated caritas with their efforts to control their own physical nature and their desire to help their fellow monks to do the same." Bernard's description of the crucifixion on the Christ's cross of love (*caritas*) affirms Newman's view.

[7]   Guerric of Igny, *In ramis palmarum. Sermo* 2.1, eds. John Morson and Hilary Costello, *Sources chrétiennes* 202 (Paris, 1973), pp. 172–74; *Liturgical Sermons*, trans. Monks of Mount Saint Bernard Abbey, vol. 2 (Kalamazoo, 1971), pp. 59–60; Aelred of Rievaulx, *In hebdomada sancta. Sermo* 36.2, 10–14, ed. Gaetano Raciti, CCCM 2A (Turnhout, 2001), pp. 294–97.

[8]   Guerric of Igny, *In ramis palmarum. Sermo* 2.5–6, pp. 180–87; Monks, *Liturgical Sermons*, pp. 63–65; Aelred of Rievaulx, *In ramis palmarum. Sermo* 10.31, p. 88; *The Liturgical Sermons*, trans. Theodore Berkeley and M. Basil Pennington (Kalamazoo, 2001), p. 180.

[9]   Peter of Celle, *De disciplina claustrali* 6, ed. Gerard de Martel, *Sources chrétiennes* 240 (Paris, 1977), pp. 160–63; *Peter of Celle: Selected Works*, trans. Hugh Feiss (Kalamazoo, 1987), pp. 81–82.

nailed to cross, the monk must not leave the cloister. Obediently, the monk must stretch forth his hands for almsgiving and bodily mortification. The cloistered one's eyes should look to God in prayer, to Mary with petitions, and to John in reading the gospel. As Christ bowed his head and gave his spirit to God, the monk should look down in public, but lift up his head in prayer. The monk's back may be whipped for sins, in thanksgiving, or as compensation for Christ's passion. Whenever a monk confessed sins to a superior, the blood and water of compunction symbolically flowed forth from his side.[10]

Another twelfth-century Benedictine, Ekbert of Schönau, contemplated the crucified Christ from whose wounds blood flowed copiously. The devout monk prayed for the Lord to place on his shoulders the sweet, most heavenly cross.[11] Ekbert petitioned the suffering Lord to fasten his limbs to this cross and conform his life to Christ's passion. In order to avoid carnal works and act rightly, he begged for the nails of self-control and righteousness to pierce his left and right hands. Alternatively, he asked that the nails of prudence and fortitude would fasten his right and left feet to the cross. Then, Ekbert pleaded for the crown of thorns to be placed metaphorically on his head through contrition, compassion for his neighbor, and zeal for living rightly in tribulation. Next, he compared the sponge and bitter wine given to Jesus on the cross to the monk's rejection of the world and its lusts. Similar to the blood and water that flowed from Christ's pierced side, the sharp lance of God's word would pierce the monk's heart from which divine love for one's brothers would emanate.[12]

The Cistercian monk who later preached and participated in the Third Crusade as the archbishop of Canterbury, Baldwin, emphasized the transformative effects of meditation on Christ's cross and passion. In a sermon in praise of the cross he exhorted his audience:

> Gaze carefully at Jesus of Nazareth, and
> him crucified zealous for us, desiring us
> from the depths of his heart, stretching
> out His arms on the cross as if to embrace
> us, prepared to receive everyone who comes
> to Him.

---

[10]   Peter of Celle, *De disciplina claustrali* 7, pp. 170–73; Feiss, *Peter of Celle*, pp. 84–85.

[11]   Ekbert of Schönau, *Stimulus amoris*, PL 158:756A, 758C–759A. (Falsely attributed to Anselm of Canterbury here and in PL 184:953D-966A to Bernard of Clairvaux.) On Ekbert's authorship of this text, and its influence on later medieval devotion to the Christ's passion see Thomas H. Bestul, *Texts of the Passion* (Philadelphia, 1996), pp. 40–41, 188, 205, ns. 56–63. Cf. Constable "Imitation of Christ," p. 210.

[12]   Ekbert, *Stimulus amoris*, PL 158:759A-760A.

Describing the Lord's passion in detail, Baldwin explained that Christ desired to transfigure those who deserved crucifixion themselves and to raise them up conformed to God's image through his own death and resurrection.[13] Metaphorically, the cross became the instrument which brought about this transformation. He described the cross as the foundation of monastic discipline, the mortification of the flesh, and the mark of Christ on the body. Imprinted on each Christian's forehead and heart, Christ's cross, as the origin of virtues and the destruction of vices, renewed the old self.[14] According to Baldwin, the cross truly became the pattern for living when its memory continually inspired those who followed Jesus.[15]

Preachers associated with the twelfth-century schools of Paris described the religious life with similar terminology. Examples include the anonymous homiletic miscellany from the canonry of St. Victor in Paris, and the sermons of the twelfth-century masters, Peter Lombard and Peter Comestor.[16] For example, in a Good Friday sermon, Peter Lombard taught that Christians should hang on the cross in spirit and thereby fasten their bodily members with the spiritual nails of God's commands.[17]

However, it was the Parisian master with significant connections to the Cistercian Order, Alan of Lille, who purposely appropriated this theology of the cross in his *Sermo de cruce Domini*. Originally preached on the eve of the Third Crusade, Alan explained that those who bore the imprint of the cross on the front of their bodies also carried it in their minds through faith.[18] Similar to other preachers of the Third Crusade, such as Henry, Cardinal-Bishop of

---

[13]   Baldwin, *Sermo de sancta cruce* 8.1–2, ed. David N. Bell, CCCM 99 (Turnholt, 1991), p. 127; Jane Patricia Freeland and David N. Bell, "The Sermons on Obedience and the Cross," *Cistercian Studies Quarterly* 29 (1994), p. 276. The quote (Sermo 8.1 in CCCM 99, 127) reads, "Intuemini diligenter Iesum Nazarenum, et hunc crucifixum, pro nobis zelantem, cupientem nos in visceribus suis, in cruce brachia tendentem quasi ad amplexus, paratum suscipere omnem hominem venientem ad se."

[14]   Baldwin, *Sermo de sancta cruce* 8.8, pp. 128–29; Bell and Freeland, "Sermons on Obedience and the Cross," p. 278.

[15]   Idem, *Sermo de sancta cruce* 8.28–31, 35–36, pp. 134–36; Bell and Freeland, "Sermons on Obedience and the Cross," pp. 284–88.

[16]   Attributed to Hugh of St Victor, *Miscellanea* 31, PL 177:653; Peter Comestor, *In purificatione Beatae Virginis. Ad claustrales. Sermo* 9, PL 198:1748B.

[17]   Peter Lombard, *De laudibus sanctae crucis*, PL 171: 691 (Falsely attributed to Hildebert of Le Mans.)

[18]   Alan of Lille, *Sermo de cruce Domini*, ed. Marie-Thérèse d'Alverny, *Alain de Lille, Textes inédits* (Paris, 1965), pp. 279–80. I have discussed this sermon in Matthew Phillips, "The Thief's Cross: Crusade and Penance in Alan of Lille's Sermo de cruce domini," *Crusades* 5 (2006), 143–156.

Albano, Alan related this emphasis on the mystical sign of the cross to the loss of the relic of True Cross to Saladin in 1187.[19] In response to this loss of the symbol of the Lord's passion, he exhorted crusaders to reject a mere external mark of the cross, but rather patiently bear Christ's cross inwardly. According to Alan, the crusader's cross signified God's burdensome yoke that Christ's love made attractively light. Notably, in Alan's manual for preachers he identified this charity as the spiritual cross for God and one's neighbor and the root of all virtues that inspires Christians to willingly embrace physical adversities and reject worldly honor and fleshly lusts.[20]

Although Alan encouraged love-inspired crusaders to take up the penitential cross, he proclaimed the imitation of the crucified Christ as the crusader's ultimate goal. Drawing upon the image of the crucifix, he presented Christ's passion as a triumph over the Christian's true enemies: the world, the flesh, sin, and the devil. Alan stated that Christ had affixed these enemies to the cross with his own body, therefore, counteracting the vices represented by various body parts. For instance Christ had turned back the devil's head, pride, through his own humility. He crucified the devil's hand, inordinate desire, by condemning worldly things. Christ also pierced the devil's side, debauchery, and fastened his feet, cunning. Alan then described how the crucified Christ overcame the vices that he associated with the world and the flesh. Through a graphic depiction of the Jesus' Passion, he revealed to his audience what Christ had willingly undergone to overcome their sinful enemies and vices. Thereby he presented a model for the crusaders to imitate.[21]

Similar theological and devotional themes appeared in songs and poems written to promote the crusading venture. A French song, probably written around 1189, delineated between faithful crusaders who suffered the pain of the cross daily for their love of Christ and those who deserted their Lord. Most significantly, the song described the unfeigned love which the crucified Christ demonstrated for humanity when he carried the holy cross and received nails into his hands and feet. Roger of Howden recorded the song of Berter of Orleans, a cleric who inspired others to take up the cross for the Third Crusade. Lamenting the loss of the True Cross, he warned sinners against the rejection of the crucified Christ's embrace, but called upon them to take up the cross of him who gave up body and soul for them. In his work on poetry and rhetoric

---

[19] On Henry's crusade preaching see Cole, *Preaching of the Crusades*, pp. 65–71.

[20] Alan of Lille, *Sermo de cruce Domini*, p. 281. See Matt. 11.30. Alan of Lille, *Summa de arte praedictoria* 20, 21, PL 210:151B-152D, 153C-55D; *The Art of Preaching*, trans. Gillian R. Evans (Kalamazoo, 1981), pp. 86–94.

[21] Alan of Lille, *Sermo de cruce Domini*, p. 282. See Phillips, "The Theif's Cross," pp. 153–54.

the thirteenth-century Parisian master, John of Garland, portrayed the crusade as a spiritual battle of the virtues of the cross against the vices of the world, the flesh, and the devil.[22]

The anonymous model sermon for crusading, entitled *Brevis ordinacio de predicacione sancte crucis*, demonstrates early thirteenth-century crusade preachers' focus on the crusader's inner conversion through a metaphorical crucifixion of body and soul with Christ. In the first section of this text the preacher exhorted crusaders quickly to embrace Christ's cross, thereby fulfilling the commandment to love God and one's neighbor with all one's heart.[23]

The anonymous preacher explicitly set forth the crucified Christ as an example for the potential crusader. He explained how various elements of the crucifixion exemplified the bearing of the penitential cross. Christ offered peace to sinners on the cross as he expanded his arms to embrace them. The single nail that fixed Christ's feet to the cross symbolized the love of God that should pierce the crusader's heart and from which all other virtues should spring. The two nails in Christ's hands signified good works that those in the active and contemplative lives performed.[24]

According to the anonymous preacher, the crucified Lord became the crusader's ultimate object of imitation because all of Christ's actions were lessons for living. Therefore, he exhorted crusaders to keep their hearts, hands, and feet from forbidden acts. Instead, following Christ, they should keep their bodily members from all illicit things. Since the nail-pierced Lord did not want sinners to be lost forever, he has given them the opportunity to cleanse themselves in flesh and spirit through taking up this crusader's cross and thereby gaining heaven through physical tribulation and inner conversion.[25]

---

[22]   *Vos qui ameis de vraie amour*, eds. Joseph Bédier and Pierre Aubry, *Les chansons de croisade* (Paris, 1909), pp. 20–22; Louise Riley-Smith and Jonathan Riley-Smith, trans. *The Crusades: Ideal and Reality, 1095–1274* (London, 1981), pp. 89–90. Roger of Howden, *Chronica magistri Rogeri de Hovedene*, vol. 2, ed. William Stubbs (London, 1869), pp. 330–32; John of Garland, *Parisiana Poetria*, ed. and trans. Traugott Lawler (New Haven, 1974), pp. 69–71. See also Elizabeth Siberry, *Criticism of Crusading, 1095–1274* (Oxford, 1985), p. 98.

[23]   *Brevis ordinacio de predicacione sancte crucis*, ed. Reinhold Röhricht, *Quinti belli sacri scriptores minores* (Geneva, 1879), p. 4. The author quotes Matt. 22.37–40. Cf. Riley-Smith, "Crusading as an Act of Love," 180.

[24]   *Brevis ordinacio*, pp. 11–12. See James Powell, *Anatomy of a Crusade, 1213–1221* (Philadelphia, 1986), pp. 52–53; Cole, *Preaching the Crusades*, p. 121; Bird, "Heresy, Crusade and Reform," p. 157. These authors identify the image of the crucified Christ as a source for crusade preachers.

[25]   *Brevis ordinacio*, pp. 13–14. See Cole, *Preaching of the Crusades*, pp. 122–23; Powell, *Anatomy of a Crusade*, p. 53.

In a manner similar to Alan of Lille, the *Brevis ordinacia* depicted the crusader's cross as the means to conquering the devil, the flesh, and world with the inspiration of the Holy Spirit. Since the Lord thirsted for the salvation of sinners on the cross, the sinner should offer himself to Christ through receiving the sign of the holy cross on the shoulder and commending himself to the Lord in the heart. Similarly, the crucified Christ's consumption of wine mixed with bitter gall symbolized the fleshy, worldly delicacies that would bring only bitter sadness in the end. The text called upon the crusader to reject these things, follow Christ, and run to the cross. It was on the cross that the baptism of blood and water flowed from Christ's side for their salvation. Finally, the preacher exhorted the crusaders to "arise and direct the eyes of the heart to the Crucified suspended for you on the cross."[26]

These examples demonstrate how crusade preachers, especially following the loss of the True Cross in 1187, appropriated the theology of the cross exemplified in the sermons of twelfth-century monastic and canonical preachers. The crusade became a metaphorical crucifixion of body and soul in imitation of the crucified Christ which was analogous to the religious life exemplified in Bernard of Clairvaux as he embraced the crucified Lord. Thereby, crusading spirituality imbibed the same theological and devotional concepts that shaped the religious renewal movements of the twelfth and thirteenth centuries. For this reason, the crusading venture became a means by which lay Christians participated more fully in this expanding devotion to the crucified Christ.

---

[26] *Brevis ordinacio*, pp. 18–20. "surgas et erigas oculos cordis ad crucifixum pro te suspensum in cruce."

Chapter 3

Brothers in Arms: *Hermandades* among the Military Orders in Medieval Iberia

Sam Zeno Conedera, SJ
Fordham University

"But let it be known that we make this pact so that there might be a bond of greater love between us."[1] The above quote is taken from a thirteenth-century agreement, known as a *hermandad*, between military orders in Iberia. The word *hermandad* literally means "brotherhood" in Spanish; equivalents in Latin include *fraternitas, confraternitas and pactum*. Antonio Álvarez de Morales, while noting the conceptual ambiguity of the word, defines it as "a type of association that has spiritual objectives."[2] My analysis of these *hermandades* indicates that up to the early fourteenth century, the military orders in Iberia together pursued the Reconquest and built up networks of religious fraternity, while maintaining a certain distance from political and dynastic conflicts within and between the Christian kingdoms. The *hermandades* were not merely expressions of high ideals, but evidence of the common interests and strategies that the orders pursued in military campaigns, religious life and relations with outside powers. The decreasing frequency and observance of the *hermandades* from the early fourteenth century can be attributed to the slowing of the Reconquest, royal interference, and the "nationalization" of the orders, which sapped their original energy, independence, and cohesion. Scholars have previously studied the *hermandades* and commented on cooperation between the military orders, but no one has analyzed in detail the formation of these brotherhoods or considered their social and cultural significance.

---

[1] Madrid, Archivo Histórico Nacional, Sign 1046 B, *Tumbo menor de Castilla*, Liber III, no 101, pp. 337–9. *Hoc autem factum esse dignoscitur ut inter nos maioris dilectionis vinculum habeatur.*

[2] Antonio Álvarez de Morales, *Las hermandades, expresión del movimiento comunitario en España* (Valladolid, 1974), p. 9. "La palabra hermandad no expresa un concepto preciso y determinado cuando la encontramos empleada en las fuentes medievales...En los siglos altomedievales, en que este fenómeno se da únicamente en el ámbito religioso, designa un tipo de asociaciones que tienen objetivos espirituales."

Hermandades

There are a total of twelve *hermandades* from the late twelfth to the early fourteenth centuries for the military orders in Iberia, some of which have been studied by Derek Lomax and Joseph O'Callaghan, among others.[3] While most of these agreements directly concern only the orders of Santiago and Calatrava, others involve the international orders as well, and all give evidence of extensive mutual cooperation. O'Callaghan sees these pacts as not only strategic attempts to prevent and resolve conflicts, but also as part of "a continuing desire to achieve a true spiritual fraternity which could be translated into cooperative action on the field of battle."[4]

One agreement in particular offers insight into the development of these documents over time. The original agreement, signed by the Masters of Santiago and Calatrava, dates from 1221, but its terms were expanded in 1243.[5] It is written in fairly elegant Castilian and includes a lengthy preamble expressing the masters' desire to establish "unity of brotherhood" on account of the "spiritual friendship" between them.[6]

The agreement first stipulates that the orders will help each other when one of them makes war upon the Moors, and that neither order can sign a treaty with the enemy without mutual consultation.[7] If, in spite of an existing royal treaty, the Moors should attack one of the orders, the other must come to its defense.[8] The orders agree to honor each others' peace agreements with Moors or with municipalities. Santiago and Calatrava agree to march together in battle or on raids, unless the king should order them otherwise. If the master of one order is present in battle and the other is not, the brothers of both orders agree to obey the one, or in the absence of any master, they will both obey any commander present.[9] If one order suffers some offense at the hands of a third party, such as

---

[3]   Derek Lomax, *La Orden de Santiago (1170–1275)* (Madrid, 1965); Joseph O'Callaghan, "*Hermandades* between the Military Orders of Calatrava and Santiago during the Castilian Reconquest," *Speculum* 44 (1969), 609–618.

[4]   O'Callaghan, "Hermandades between the Military Orders," 609.

[5]   *Bulario de la Orden Militar de Calatrava* (Barcelona, 1981), pp. 683–686.

[6]   *BC*, p. 683. "Unedad de hermandad" and "espirital amiganza."

[7]   Ibid. "E si por ventura los Freyles de Calatrava ovieren guerra con Moros sin consejo de los Freyles de Uclés, non puedan firmar treuga, nin los Freyles de Uclés sin consejo de los Freyles de Calatrava."

[8]   Ibid. "los Freyles de Calatrava non dexen por treuga del Rey de ayudar a los Freyles de Uclés, nin los Freyles de Uclés por la paz del Rey non dexen de ayudar a los Freyles de Calatrava."

[9]   Ibid., p. 684. "O quier que el Maestre qualquier destas Ordenes, con los Freyles de ambas estas Ordenes, acaescier no estando i el Maestre de la otra Orden, todos los Freyles, tan

the loss of property, the other order must come to its aid against the offenders. There are two variations in this section of a phrase that will be repeated numerous times throughout the agreement: "that they may be seen to be brothers of one order."[10]

The next provision deals with visits. When the master of one order visits the other, the host brethren will obey him as if he were their own master, and likewise with commanders.[11] The orders promise equal division of spoils taken from the Moors, regardless of how many members of each order participated in the battle.[12] When passing through the territory of the other order, each is to follow the other's commander as a leader and guide. In the case of unspecified scandals arising between the orders, *cosa que Dios no mande*, the masters are each to choose three brothers from the other order, forming a committee to settle the matter. This power of appointment passes to the grand commander if the masters are unavailable. A year-long, biweekly fast is imposed on any commander who handles this responsibility in a negligent manner. Stricter punishments are meted out to those brothers who violate any of the above provisions. A brother who is disobedient to a commander is to be stripped of his habit and thrown out of his order.[13] Violations of hospitality earn the offender a barefoot pilgrimage to the other order's headquarters for a biweekly, six month fast, after which time he is allowed to return to his own convent. With respect to more explicitly spiritual concerns, the agreement declares that both orders will offer three Masses a year for each others' deceased members, and that general chapter meetings will offer a *missa general* for the same intention.[14]

Twenty-three years later, additional sets of provisions were added, so that the *hermandad* would be "stronger for all time." The number of Masses to be said for deceased brethren is increased from three to six. In the case of brothers who are expelled from their own order for disobedience, the members of the other order are to plead on their behalf and try to amend whatever offense they have

---

bien los otros, como los suyos, todos le obedescan... a un Comendador obedescan."

[10]   Ibid, p. 683. "que todos sean vistos por todas cosas seer Freyles de una Orden."

[11]   Ibid, p. 684. "quando el Maestre de la una Orden fuere en la Casa de la otra Orden, assi les obedescan como a su Maestre. E otrosi obedescan, e sirvan al Comendador, como al su Comendador propio."

[12]   Ibid. "maguer que la una parte de los Freyles sea menor que la otra, toda la quenta sea partida por medio."

[13]   Ibid. "E el Freyle, que non fuere obediente a estos Comendadores, a todas cosas que ellos mandaren, sin habito sea echado de la Orden."

[14]   Ibid. "E cada uno de los Freyles por aquellos diga tres Missas: e otro dia del Cabildo, missa general sea celebrada."

caused.[15] The agreement also envisions a scenario in which the masters of each order plead personally on behalf of an expelled brother, though the language is too murky to understand precisely what is meant. At the very least, deliberate mutual action to bring back brothers to their own communities is intended.[16] In keeping with this theme, both orders are to exchange their own prisoners of war for any brother held captive by the Moors.[17] If a brother becomes sick while at the house of the other order, he should be cared for with much honor and love; if he dies, his body should be buried in the nearest cemetery of either order.[18]

The orders also commit themselves to further military and political cooperation. Besides fighting side by side in battle, they agree to protect each others' standards and to obey each others' masters and commanders in the field.[19] All brethren are to offer their horses to any superior from either order if he loses his horse while fighting.[20] A system of exchanging mounts while traveling is also established, so that brothers can obtain a fresh horse at the other order's houses.[21] The orders pledge to help each other in everything, before the king's court or anywhere else, and especially concerning the defense of property. In the

---

[15]   Ibid, p. 685. "E quando este Freyle fuere echado de la Orden, la otra parte sea tenuda de rogar por el, emendando el Freyle lo que oviere de emendar, o de entregarm que sea rescebido por aquel ruego."

[16]   Ibid. "E quando acaescier que por ventura algun Freyle destas Ordenes salier de alguna dellas, quier que salga él, quier que faga cosas porque lo hayan de echar de la Orden, que quando vinier a la puerta dalguna destas Ordenes, e el Maestre de la otra Orden acaesciendo i si por él rogare, e si el Freyle soviere fuera, que sea cabido a la puerta por su ruego. E si soviere rescebido a la puerta, quel sea dado el habito, e que por su ruego haya misercirodia, todavia el Maestre que este ruego fizier; haviendo antes consejo, que mja se faga con el otro Maestre."

[17]   Ibid. "quando acaesciere que algun Freyle destas Ordenes ambas cativare, e en alguna destas Ordenes oviere Moro cativo, por que lo tengan, que sea este Moro dado por este Freyle sin contradicho ninguno, por tal Moro cativo, qual cada uno de las Ordenes seria tenida de dar por su Freyle."

[18]   Ibid, p. 686. "E si algunos destos Freyles destas Ordenes enfermar en la otra Orden, que fagan mucha ondra, e mucho amor, E si finar, que lo lieven a la sepultura destas Ordenes, qual mas acerca fuer."

[19]   Ibid. "que la una Orden tambien aguarde la seña de la otra Orden, como la suya misma, e la otra Orden esto mismo sea tenida de fazer. E si fuer uno de los Maestres, e non mas, que todos aguarden adaquel Maestre, e a él obedezcan, o al uno de los Comendadores, si í Maestre non fuere, o í non fuere mas de un Comendador, e cada un Freyle sea tenido en cada una de las Ordenes."

[20]   Ibid. "que si por ventura en batalla mataren Caballo al Maestre, o al Comendor Mayor, que el Freyle de la otra Orden sea tenudo de le dar luego el Caballo."

[21]   Ibid. "E todo Freyle, que por las Casas destas Ordenes passar, si bestias cansadas troxier, que gelas camien fasta la primera Casa de su Orden, e aquellas bestias cansadas, que sean bien guardadas fasta que las otras envie aquel Freyle."

case of either order having a procurator in the Roman Curia or royal court, they are to work for the benefit of both orders.[22]

Economic concerns are also addressed. The orders agree not to steal livestock from each other, and also to provide documentation of their flocks when passing through each other's lands, and to defend each other's animals as if they were their own.[23] They also agree to assist each other in the collection of the tolls at Zorita and Alfariella, held by Calatrava and Santiago respectively. No ferries on the Tagus River are to be maintained, because they reduce the revenues from other toll stations.[24] The orders agree not to collect tolls or other taxes from each other and to share pasture lands.[25] The punishment of a six-month fast for violators is repeated from the previous agreement, and two brothers are to attend the general chapter meetings of the other order with bills of complaints, so that any disputes might be resolved.[26] The final provision makes the agreement binding throughout Castile, Leon, Portugal, and Aragon. The text is ordered to be read aloud at every chapter meeting, so that no one can claim ignorance of its terms.[27] To those who keep the *hermandad*, the orders wish the blessing of Jesus Christ and his Mother Mary.[28]

This amendment of 1243 represents the high-water mark of the *hermandades* between Santiago and Calatrava, as well as the high-water mark of their participation in the Reconquest.[29] The range of collaborative efforts and overtures

---

[22]   Ibid., p. 685. "E quando alguna destas Ordenes, o ambas tovieren Procuradores en la Corte de Roma, o en las Cortes de los Reyes, estos Procuradores sean tenidos de procurar en todos los negocios destas Ordenes, tanbien a la una Orden, como a la otra lealmientre."

[23]   Ibid. "E de los nuestros ganados ponemos assi, que non prendamos unos a otros, nin otrosi de los ganados de nuestros aportellados; pero quando los ganados entraren en termino de alguna destas Ordenes... sean todos tenidos de traer cartas selladas de los Baylios de sus Señores... E en sus ganados, que otrosi se ayuden a defenderlos cada una Orden como los suyos mismos."

[24]   Ibid. "E ningun destas Ordenes non sea tenida de traer barcos en Tajo, porque las rendas de los otros Puertos se minguen en mucho, ni en poco."

[25]   Ibid., p. 686. "E en ningunos nuestros Logares non tomemos portadgos ningunos entre Nos, nin saquemos defessas forras de Cballos, e de Yegua, e de Boys, e de Conejos, en todos los otros Logares cortemos, e pazcamos en sembla."

[26]   Ibid. "que dos Freyles de cada una destas Ordenes vayan todavia a los Cabildos Generales destas Ordenes con sus escritos de las querellas, que ovieren unos de otros."

[27]   Ibid. "E todavia usen estas Ordenes esta composicion desta hermandad en sus Cabildos, e leerla como la sepan bien todos, porque non digan despues los otros, que non lo sopieron."

[28]   Ibid. "E aquellos que nuestra Carta de nuestra hermandad aguarden, e la cumplieren, hayan la bendicion de Jesu Christo, e de su Madre Sancta Maria."

[29]   Carlos de Ayala Martínez, "Tópicos y realidades en torno a las Órdenes Militares," in *Tópicos y realidades de la Edad Media*, ed. Eloy Benito Ruano (Madrid, 2004), vol. 2, p. 131.

of mutual assistance is extensive, touching nearly every aspect of each order's life and mission. More importantly, the documents give evidence of learning from experience and of building upon previous agreements. That the pact of 1221 was amended rather than replaced shows a desire to maintain the continuity of past agreements stretching back to the 1180s and to expand them further.

Although most of the *hermandades* involve only Santiago and Calatrava, the tone and many of the specific provisions involving other orders are similar. These agreements take concrete steps to resolve existing quarrels and prevent the outbreak of future ones by creating procedures for dealing with them. Frequent contact between the orders must have been necessary to maintain these relations, especially given the emphasis on hospitality. Alan Forey sees "little sign that the *reconquista* was harmed by animosities" between the orders, in contrast to the Holy Land. This suggests that cooperative efforts in pursuit of the Reconquest were ultimately quite successful.[30]

But perhaps other goals not specifically military and political should be given more attention. The penances and Masses indicate the desire to create real bonds of religious fraternity that, strictly speaking, were ancillary to the success of the Reconquest. Indeed the classic justification of the "new knighthood," according to St. Bernard, is that it "ceaselessly wages a two-fold war both against flesh and blood and against a spiritual army of evil in the heavens."[31] The orders may have had both battlefields in mind when they made these agreements. There is reason to believe that closer study of the *hermandades* and other sources could reveal a great deal about social and cultural dynamics in the orders, especially their shared spirituality. The barefoot pilgrimages described above are perhaps another manifestation of general enthusiasm for pilgrimages across medieval Europe, including Santiago de Compostela.[32] Cooperation in battle and sharing of horses and arms might be seen as an extension and reinterpretation in a new context of classic monastic ideals of hospitality and obedience, as well as an effort to stand together. The movement away from the cloister into the world brought the orders many dangers and snares, not only from their Moorish foes, but also from their putative protectors.

---

[30]   Alan Forey, "The Military Orders and the Spanish Reconquest in the twelfth and thirteenth centuries" *Traditio* 40 (1984), 228.

[31]   Bernard of Clairvaux, *In praise of the new knighthood*, trans. Conrad Greenia (Kalamazoo: Cistercian Publications, 1977), p. 129.

[32]   The Hospital and Santiago had the strongest presence on the pilgrimage route and cared for the spiritual and bodily needs of travelers. See José Vicente Matellanes Merchán and Enrique Rodriguez-Picavea, "Las Ordenes militares en las etapas castellanas del Camino de Santiago," in Horacio Santiago-Otero, *El Camino de Santiago, la hospitalidad monástica y las peregrinaciones*, (Salamanca, 1992), pp. 343–363.

Early Relations with Monarchs

A persistent factor bearing on the orders' military action and collaboration was their relationship with Iberian monarchs. In many respects, the masters acted as great lords of the realm, judging suits, serving as ambassadors and guaranteeing peace agreements between kings, as Lomax notes.[33] Unlike many other lords, however, the masters tried to remain aloof from internal dynastic struggles and strife between kingdoms, resisting royal attempts to harness the orders' military might to use against their co-religionists.[34] These efforts were not always successful, as there are examples of the orders serving for one Christian monarch against another even in the late twelfth and early thirteenth centuries.[35] Yet in most instances these were defensive actions against an invading army; the orders were more reluctant to engage in wars of aggression against Christians.

Carlos de Ayala Martínez draws a basic distinction between the international military orders and their Iberian counterparts, noting, "In the case of Iberia, crusading is not the military orders' *raison d'être*, but the means of justifying their service to the king."[36] It is true that royal leadership of the Reconquest was predominant in all the Christian kingdoms, and that the orders acted within the boundaries established by royal prerogative, especially in Leon-Castile. According to Alan Forey, the orders were reluctant to break kings' truces, and generally accepted their leadership.[37] Often the monarchs did try to extend their control over the orders. Alfonso VIII and Fernando III, for example, supported the attempted transfer of jurisdiction over Calatrava from the Abbot of Morimond to San Pedro de Gumiel, presumably to make the order more pliable to royal interests.[38]

The distinction between the international and Iberian orders can be taken too far, however, if one forgets that all the military orders in the peninsula pursued essentially the same mission; the Iberian provinces of the Hospital and the Temple were also quite dependent upon royal favor and leadership of the

---

[33]   Lomax, *La Orden*, p. 32.

[34]   Forey, "Spanish Reconquest," 216.

[35]   José Luis Martín, *Orígenes de la Orden Militar de Santiago (1170–1195)* (Barcelona, 1974), pp. 64–65.

[36]   Carlos de Ayala Martínez, *Las órdenes militares hispánicas en la Edad Media (siglos XII-XV)* (Madrid, 2003), p. 700. "La cruzada no es en este caso la razón de ser de la existencia de las órdenes militares sino el medio que justifica su actuación al servicio de los reyes."

[37]   Forey, "Spanish Reconquest," 220.

[38]   Ayala Martínez, *Las órdenes militares*, 704; for the relationship between Calatrava and San Pedro de Gumiel, see Derek Lomax, "Algunos estatuos primitivos de la Orden de Calatrava," *Hispania* 21 (1961), 483–494.

Reconquest. Nor could monarchs simply do as they pleased with the Iberian orders. Modern historiography identifies only one probable instance of direct royal interference in the election of masters before the reign of Alfonso X. The election of Gomez Manrique as Master of Calatrava had provoked schism within the order, and Fernando III appointed another candidate, which was probably intended to restore legitimate governance.[39] In summarizing the relationship during the first century of the orders' existence, Ayala Martínez says, "The alliance with the monarchy is close, but one cannot yet speak of a clear royal directive with the purpose of integrating the military orders into royal policies that were still poorly defined."[40] He also admits that the limited number of suitable monographs on the subject make a comprehensive synthesis difficult.

Nationalization

The historical development of the military orders is often viewed in terms of "nationalization," or the process by which each order's territorial holdings, interests, and politics became associated with one particular kingdom. The timeline for this process is critical to determining the duration of the cooperative period. In Castile, nationalization is evident during the reign of Alfonso X, who in various ways attempted to exert greater control over the orders. This "royal policy" included appointing his own candidate as master on two occasions and usurping the orders' goods.[41] The policy nevertheless must be considered among Alfonso X's many failed ambitions. He was unable to translate his efforts into lasting control over the orders, and all except the Order of Alcántara joined the Castilian nobles in breaking with the king in 1282.[42]

Alfonso XI was the first to establish real royal hegemony over the orders. He appointed his son Fadrique as Master of Santiago and openly asserted that the orders existed for the king's service.[43] Two new developments served to solidify royal domination. First, masters began to receive important offices in the royal household, while laymen who held these same offices were often given masterships as prizes for their service and loyalty. Second, Alfonso XI punished

---

[39]   Francisco de Andres y Rada, *Crónica de las Tres Ordenes de Santiago, Calatrava, y Alcántara* (Barcelona, 1980), *Crónica de Calatrava*, fols. 40v-41r.

[40]   Ayala Martínez, *Las órdenes militares*, p. 705. "La alianza entre monarquía es estrecha pero no cabe hablar todavía de unas claras directrices de la realeza con el fin de integrar en sus todavía balbucientes esquemas a las órdenes militares."

[41]   Ayala Martínez, *Las órdenes militares*, pp. 710–714.

[42]   Ibid., p. 491–492.

[43]   Lomax, *La Orden*, p. 216; Ayala Martínez, *Las órdenes militares*, p. 715.

numerous brothers for treason, even Gonzalo Martinez, Master of Alcántara, who had been the king's creature until his execution in 1339.[44] This changed state of affairs is already reflected in the *hermandad* of 1313, which specifically emphasizes the importance of loyalty to Alfonso.[45] By this time, military orders and crusading had entered a new age. The great Reconquest in Iberia had ended and the military orders had suffered criticism and dramatic setbacks, most notably the Council of Lyons in 1274 and the dissolution of the Templars.[46] Rather than being dissolved, however, the Iberian orders ceased to fulfill a crusading role per se and came under the control of the various peninsular monarchs. The Portuguese branch of Santiago separated from the larger order, and each began to act more and more as factions in the political struggles of the fourteenth and fifteenth centuries.[47] Religious discipline was progressively relaxed in theory and in practice, and military activity, where it existed, was more concerned with internal conflicts. Thus the official royal takeover of Santiago, Calatrava, and Alcántara under Charles V was simply the final stage in a long process.[48] It should be clear, however, that until the fourteenth century, the military orders in Iberia were primarily oriented towards pursuit of the Reconquest, and that they were able and willing to cooperate with one another to achieve that objective.

Conclusion

Interest in the *hermandades* and cooperation is not new; historians of such stature as Joseph O'Callaghan, Derek Lomax, Alan Forey, and Carlos de Ayala Martinez have investigated them. They express little surprise at the relatively high level of cooperation and the relatively low level of conflict manifest in these relations. And yet, when considered against the backdrop of strife between the Temple and the Hospital in the Holy Land, or discord between religious orders in general throughout the Middle Ages, the Iberian situation *is* surprising. The most obvious explanations, such as the precariousness of the frontier with Islam or strong royal leadership, are important, but do not suffice to explain why the military orders responded cooperatively to these exigencies while others,

---

[44]   Ayala Martínez, *Las órdenes militares*, pp. 498–499.

[45]   *BC*, pp. 498–500.

[46]   See Elizabeth Siberry, *Criticism of Crusading, 1095–1274* (Oxford, 1985); Alan Forey, *The Military Orders: From the Twelfth to the Early Fourteenth Centuries* (Toronto, 1992), pp. 204–241.

[47]   Lomax, *La Orden*, p. 50.

[48]   For Leo X's bull conferring the orders' administration to Charles, see *BC*, pp. 503–506.

including the monarchs themselves, continued to quarrel in crisis situations. This paper has not made the necessary distinctions between kingdoms, specific orders, zones of operation and stages in the Reconquest, and the larger social and cultural questions are only hinted at. That work remains to be done. I do believe, though, that some deeper answers lie in the *hermandades*: understood not only as the documents themselves, but the common sense of brotherhood, built upon the spiritual and material networks that existed between the orders' members, which generally carried the day throughout the late twelfth and thirteenth centuries, even in the face of great challenges and setbacks.

PART II
The Crusades and Contested Worlds of Ideas

Chapter 4

The Classical Author Portrait Islamicized

Robert Hillenbrand
University of Edinburgh

The sudden influx of ideas from the Byzantine and Graeco-Roman world into the Middle East during the twelfth and thirteenth centuries, and their equally sudden disappearance, is still a largely unexplained phenomenon. Most general accounts of Islamic art dodge the issue, while the few scholars who have analysed how this classical influence expressed itself do not agree as to why this trend occurred in the first place.[1] Yet that question of motive is of prime importance. Simply put, the brief flirtation with classical forms which manifests itself in the area of Syria and the Jazira between *c.*1100 and *c.*1250 is an aberration in the rational chronological progression of Islamic art. It comes at the wrong time. An openness to classical and Byzantine ideas was only to be expected in the first century of Islamic art, when the new culture was gradually finding its feet in the thoroughly Hellenized environment of the Levant. Many classical features readily found their way into Islamic art at this time and became acclimatised there.[2] In the process of digestion they underwent radical change. Moreover, the incorporation of features drawn from ancient Near Eastern art introduced ways of seeing that were not easily compatible with Mediterranean traditions. Thus within a relatively short time, Islamic art had broken free from the tutelage of the classical tradition and had developed its own distinctive artistic idiom.[3] For centuries there was to be no looking back. And that is why the Byzantine or classical feel of so much Syrian and Jaziran art in the twelfth and thirteenth

---

[1]   See J.M. Rogers, "A Renaissance of Classical Antiquity in North Syria (11th – 12th centuries)," *Annales Archéologiques Syriennes* 21 (1971) (*Proceedings of the 9th International Congress of Classical Archaeology*), 347–61; and, more generally, O. Grabar, "Survivances classiques dans l'art de l'Islam," ibid., 371–80 and R. Hillenbrand, "The classical heritage in Islamic art: the case of medieval architecture," *The Scottish Journal of Religious Studies* VII (1986), 123–40.

[2]   O. Grabar, "Islamic Art and Byzantium," *Dumbarton Oaks Papers* 18 (1964), 69–88.

[3]   R. Hillenbrand, "Islamic Art at the Crossroads: East versus West at Mshatta," in *Essays in Islamic Art and Architecture in Honor of Katharina Otto-Dorn*, ed. A. Daneshvari (Malibu, 1981), pp. 63–86.

centuries is such an anomaly. It would not have been strange in the Umayyad period. But surfacing as it does a full four centuries after classicizing art had fallen out of favour in this area, it does demand an explanation. True, the period 750 to 1100 was a curiously fallow one in the art of the Levant; but 'Abbasid art and its offshoots were at least readily available as an option here as elsewhere in the central Islamic lands.

So why did this classical revival begin, and why did it end? Was it perhaps related to the irruption of the Crusaders into the Levant? Or to a greater degree of cross-cultural contact between Byzantium and Islam in this same period,[4] fostered both by Muslim military encroachment in Anatolia in the century between Manzikert and Myrocephalon and by the initial Byzantine support of the Crusaders?[5] Could these sudden changes in the familiar rhythms of political life have forced Muslims to confront foreign cultures and to reconsider what they had to offer? Violently jolted by a totally unexpected invasion out of the even tenor of provincial life – for the major centres of the region lay at its eastern and western peripheries, at Cairo and Baghdad – the Muslims of the Levant suddenly found themselves at the sharp edge of political events. As they saw it, they had been catapulted to the centre of things. Naturally this realisation did not come overnight, and – as so often happens with political events or trends – there was a time lapse before their impact made itself felt in the visual arts. And the repercussions of this new political order extended beyond the Levant. In particular, the Jazira, ruled by Turcoman dynasties and atabegs of the Zangid house, came to be politically oriented towards Syria and its concerns rather than towards Baghdad.[6] This, together with the presence of a very large Christian minority, may help to explain why Byzantine and classical influences (notably in manuscript painting) are stronger in northern than in central Iraq.[7]

---

[4]   P.Soucek, "Byzantium and the Islamic East," in H.C. Evans and W.D. Wixom (eds.), *The Glory of Byzantium: Art and Culture of the Middle Byzantine Era A.D. 843–1261* (New York, 1997), pp. 402–33.

[5]   C.V. Bornstein and P.P. Soucek (ed. C. Olds), *The Meeting of Two Worlds: The Crusades and the Mediterranean Context* (Ann Arbor, 1981).

[6]   The figural coinage of the Turcoman dynasties is a pointer in this direction. See H.M. Brown, "Some Reflections on the Figured Coinage of the Artuqids and Zangids," in D.K. Kouymjian (ed.), *Near Eastern Numismatics, Iconography, Epigraphy and History. Studies in Honor of George C. Miles* (Beirut, 1974), pp. 353–8; W.F. Spengler and W.G. Sayles, *Turkoman Figural Bronze Coins and Their Iconography. Vol. I – The Artuqids* (Lodi, Wisc., 1992); and W.F. Spengler and W.G. Sayles, *Turkoman Figural Bronze Coins and Their Iconography. Vol. II – The Zengids* (Lodi, 1996).

[7]   H. Buchthal, "The Painting of the Syrian Jacobites and its Relation to Byzantine and Islamic Art," *Syria* XX (1939), 136–50.

At this critical juncture, then, the Muslims of Syria and the Jazira were thrown onto their own resources, since for various reasons neither the Fatimid caliph in Cairo nor the 'Abbasid caliph in Baghdad lent effective aid to their beleaguered co-religionists. Self-help became the order of the day. The new self-reliance and sense of local pride bred by these events would naturally have fostered a comparably new independence in the visual arts, and perhaps even the desire to assert that independence by developing ideas that were distinctively different from those which dominated Cairo and Baghdad.

Specifically local resources in Syria and the Jazira included huge quantities of standing classical and Byzantine buildings, supplemented by manuscripts, coins, and other objects belonging to those same cultures. It was the unexpected willingness to exploit these long-neglected sources which sparked off the classical revival. The long-established Oriental Christians of the area now acquired an importance they had not enjoyed for centuries. Their allegiance was avidly courted, for had they thrown in their lot with the Crusaders the effect could have been catastrophic. Thus two complementary factors, local pride and urgent political expediency, could help to explain the sudden reversal to long-outdated classicising modes.

These remarks, tentative though they are, may help to create a context for the entire trend of classicising art in this period, irrespective of its particular manifestations in architecture or metalwork, coins or manuscripts. And such a general context is especially necessary to establish because this phenomenon has usually been treated piecemeal, that is in one particular sphere such as architecture[8] or coins.[9] Yet its cultural interest extends across the board precisely because it found such manifold expression. To confine it artificially to the context of a single medium is to risk belittling and misunderstanding its significance. It is not surprising that the contemporary art of Western Europe should have struck no chord with the Muslims; the Franks were, after all, their principal enemies.[10] Similarly, it is not surprising that this revival should peter out in the later thirteenth century, in which the principal political events of this area were the ejection of the Crusader presence, the growing power of the Mamluks in

---

[8]   The principal study of the topic is T. Allen, *A Classical Revival in Islamic Architecture* (Wiesbaden, 1986).

[9]   N. Lowick, "The Religious, The Royal and The Popular in The Figural Coinage of the Jazira," in *The Art of Syria and the Jazira 1100–1250*, ed. J. Raby *(Oxford Studies in Islamic Art*, I) (Oxford, 1985), pp. 159–74.

[10]   The plethora of stories told with sly malice against the Franks by Usama b. Munqidh reveals a profound lack of respect for their culture on his part. See P.K. Hitti, *An Arab-Syrian Gentleman at the time of the Crusades, Memoirs of Usamah Ibn-Munqidh*, 3rd edition (Princeton, 1987), passim.

the Levant and the imposition of the new Mongol political order in Iraq. The departure of the Crusaders broadly speaking coincided with a Mamluk takeover in Syria, which meant the severe reduction of Syrian independence and, in the visual arts, drew Syria into the orbit of Egypt. At the same time the Jazira fell under Mongol control. Deprived of their local independence, Syria and the Jazira merged once more into larger political entities, and this process replicated itself in the visual arts.

So much, then, for the historical background to this paper. It is now time to look more closely at one particular manifestation of the classicizing trend outlined above, namely one specific detail from the world of manuscripts. This is the portrait of the author placed at the beginning of a manuscript. It is a topic that can serve almost like a laboratory experiment to show the interaction of two cultures. And in this particular instance Islamic culture responded in almost exactly the same way in the 12th-13th centuries as it had done in the seventh and eighth centuries. First comes a brief period of close, almost literal, copying. Next there develops a more lateral interpretation of the source. Lastly, dependence on the original source is swept away in a brand new solution to the problem. Earlier examples of this same process, with these identical three stages, can be seen in the development of Umayyad coinage[11] or of Samarra stuccowork.[12]

The way that this pattern of response surfaces in the twelfth and thirteenth centuries in secular book illustration is, incidentally, persuasive evidence that such illustration, though known in earlier centuries, was still a relatively new feature in Islamic art at this time. Another pointer in the same direction is the uneven development of frontispiece design in the course of the thirteenth century. It betrays all the signs of a tradition finding its feet – experimenting, rejecting, combining old ideas in a new way.

By the late twelfth century the author portrait had a millennial tradition behind it. Its origins have been traced in exhaustive fashion by Friend in a celebrated *Art Studies* paper, whose main aim was to follow up the varying fortunes of the theme, this time in the guise of the evangelist portrait found in Gospel books, both in medieval Western[13] and in Byzantine art.[14] The dearth of pre-Iconoclastic Byzantine illustrated manuscripts, and the comparable

---

[11]   M.L. Bates, "History, Geography and Numismatics in the First Century of Islamic Coinage," *Revue Suisse de Numismatique* 65 (1986), 231–62.

[12]   E. Herzfeld, *Der Wandschmuck der Bauten von Samarra und seine Ornamentik* (Berlin, 1923).

[13]   A.M. Friend, Jr., "The Portraits of the Evangelists in Greek and Latin Manuscripts, II," *Art Studies* 7 (1929), 3–29.

[14]   Idem, "The Portraits of the Evangelists in Greek and Latin Manuscripts," *Art Studies* 5 (1927), 115–47.

scarcity of their contemporary Western European equivalents, makes it difficult to do more than outline the crucial early stages of this iconography. It has also guaranteed that the very few surviving examples have had a disproportionate weight of speculation loaded onto them. With that warning ringing in our ears, let us look at the first major surviving example of the genre. This is to be found in the Vienna Dioscorides, datable to *c.*512 and in all likelihood produced at Constantinople. The gratifyingly close iconographic links between its author portrait[15] and that of the Arabic translation of the same text, dated 1229 and attributed to Syria or northern Iraq,[16] are offset by a veritable chasm between the two manuscripts in matters of style and technique – as is only to be expected. But there is no need to traverse this familiar ground today. Instead, let us focus on the fact that the Vienna Dioscorides contains a separate opening, preceding the author portrait by one page, which depicts the patron of the book, the Byzantine princess Julia Anicia (pl. 1).[17] This means that Islam could have inherited from the classical tradition not only the author portrait but also the idea of depicting the person who paid for the manuscript. Note that the two images were kept apart and that power took precedence over intellect.

The Vienna Dioscorides of *c.*512 establishes that the close connection between author portraits and images of the patron was already known in pre-Islamic times, though whether it was common is another matter. Moreover, the formula of allocating separate pages to these subjects was not the only solution known to Byzantine painters. Sometimes the author of a book was depicted on the same page and in the same picture space as the patron of that specific copy of the text – a device which could result in gross anachronisms, as for example when St John Chrysostom (died 407) is depicted alongside the Emperor Nicephorus Botaneiates (died *c.*1085) (pl. 2).[18] It might be argued that such a layout paved the way for the eventual suppression of the author portrait and its replacement by an image of the patron. Double portraits of the monarch,[19] or of the monarch and his consort,[20] as well as single portraits of the ruler flanked by their sons, angels or bishops,[21] were increasingly popular in later Byzantine book painting at the expense of images of the authors of the works concerned. In that respect Byzantine practice was remarkably close to that of the Islamic world.

---

[15]   K. Weitzmann, *Late Antique and Early Christian Book Illumiunation* (London, 1977), pl.17.

[16]   R. Ettinghausen, *Arab Painting* (Geneva, 1962), pp. 68–9.

[17]   Weitzmann, *Book Illumination*, pl. 15.

[18]   A. Grabar, *Byzantine Painting*, tr. S.Gilbert (Geneva, 1953), p. 179.

[19]   Grabar, *Byzantine Painting*, p. 184.

[20]   D. Talbot Rice, *Kunst aus Byzanz* (Munich, 1959), Pl. XL.

[21]   Ibid., pl. 190.

Let us now examine, in a little more detail, the first stage mentioned earlier: close dependence on the classical or Byzantine model. It is well illustrated by a frontispiece in an early 13th-century Arab version of the *De Materia Medica* of Dioscorides, dated 1239, now in Oxford (pl. 3).[22] The Greek physician is depicted as a standing figure shown in profile, facing left, silhouetted against an overall monochrome dull red ground enclosed by a shouldered segmental arch. This latter detail is a recognisably Islamic feature, and the same might be said for his turban, the triangular thumb-piece of the book, the colour of the background and the senatorial patches on the robe, as well as the harshly linear treatment. But iconographically this figure is firmly anchored in the familiar image of the standing Byzantine evangelist portrait: such features as the halo, profile mode, book, and the exclusive focus on this one figure, all point in that direction (pl. 4).[23]

The rather more ambitious Dioscorides manuscript of 1229 in Istanbul belongs in this same category (pl. 5).[24] Arguably, indeed, it is the closest that an Islamic painter of the period got to copying a Byzantine original. And yet even this image is far from an exact copy. Admittedly the matter cannot be proved with legal exactitude, but there are enough Evangelist portraits of Middle Byzantine date to encourage the belief that some such sacred image, as well as the Greek Dioscorides, was in the Muslim artist's mind when he Islamicized the Greek physician. Technically, the 1229 image is neither the one thing nor the other; not a simple copy of an Evangelist portrait because it is not a self-contained picture – indeed, it only makes sense as a double frontispiece, with the students deferentially approaching their master – and yet not a simple copy of a Romano-Byzantine Dioscorides portrait either, because (perhaps for reasons of Islamic respectability) the female figure Heuresis ("Inspiration") has disappeared,[25] as has the all-important book he should hold, and just as the dog has been omitted from the mandrake image.[26] We have here, in fact, a typically Islamic conflation of two separate sources. That is perhaps the most Islamic feature of the whole image – for the segmental arch under which he sits, or the turban that he wears, are merely cosmetic. They function as allusions to an Arab milieu, and are powerless to dispel the overwhelmingly Byzantine impression created by the gold background, the type of robes he wears and their drapery technique, the

---

[22]   Soucek, "Byzantium and the Islamic East," p. 402.
[23]   See Grabar, *Byzantine Painting*, p. 172.
[24]   See note 16 above.
[25]   She is there in the Vienna Dioscorides (Weitzmann, *Book Illumination*, pl. 17).
[26]   Compare the Vienna Dioscorides (see the previous note) with the Arabic version of the same text in Istanbul (Ettinghausen, *Arab Painting*, p. 71).

chair he sits in, the footstool and his sandalled feet, and above all the thoroughly Hellenized grasp of modelling shown in his face and hands.

The intention behind this close copying of Byzantine forms may be partly to underline the continuing connection which the Arabs cherished with the scientific knowledge of ancient Greece, but partly also to indicate that this knowledge is being passed on to future generations – of Arabs. Hence his distinctively Greek appearance while his students wear Arab dress. But in a distinctively Islamic sense Dioscorides is also validating – giving his seal of approval or *ijaza* to – the text which the students (or should one say "disciples"?) proffer to him. He is thus more than the author of the book; he embodies intellectual authority.[27] Thus Islam has inherited the mantle of Greek science. Our picture is a visual metaphor of that entire cultural process.

Incidentally, while the sequence of four royal and author portraits in the Vienna Dioscorides of *c.*512 does not recur in this Islamic version, the 1229 manuscript nevertheless possesses an image of the physician with the mandrake root in addition to the double frontispiece. The Byzantine idea of a whole series of frontispiece images in close succession, found not just in the Vienna Dioscorides but also in the 9th-century *Homilies of St. Gregory Nazianzus* and in the 11th-century *Homilies of St John Chrysostom*,[28] is therefore not entirely forgotten, though it was destined to have no future in Islamic painting.

Quite another kind of response to the classical heritage, but one still marked by very close dependence and thus belonging to the first category proposed above, is provided by several versions of the theme of the group portrait of philosophers or physicians. The Vienna Dioscorides of *c.*512 shows how the late antique artist handled the theme.[29] He shows his figures almost floating, each occupying his own space, seated on a slab or a rock (pl. 6). Seven such figures, each depicted in a different pose, are loosely scattered all over the page. Muslim painters responded to this general prototype in several quite distinct ways, but in every case they imposed a symmetrical design on natural disorder. In the Paris *Kitab al-Diryaq* of 1199 the corresponding picture – not, incidentally, a frontispiece – retains something of the freedom of gesture and movement inherited from the antique, but nevertheless shows these figures in adjoining box-like compartments and

---

[27]   The process whose culmination is depicted in these two paintings is described by J.Pedersen in *The Arabic Book*, tr. G.French, ed. R. Hillenbrand (Princeton, 1984), pp. 24–32.

[28]   H. Omont, *Miniatures des manuscrits grecs de la Bibliothèque Nationale* (Paris, 1929).

[29]   Weitzmann, *Book Illumination*, pl. 16.

maintaining an overall uniformity of pose (pl. 7).[30] In a slightly later version of the same text, the painter has valiantly attempted to ring the changes on what is essentially one image – that of the scholar kneeling or seated cross-legged on the ground, with a throne as a backdrop.[31] Accordingly, the figures are shown frontally, in three-quarter view or in profile; turning to the left or to the right and holding a book open or shut, and wearing a range of headgear (pl. 8). There is just enough mileage in these visually trivial variations on a theme to stave off monotony. But there can be no doubt that the pattern-making urge of Islamic art is predominant. Each figure is placed within a roundel so that the instant visual effect is of three columns of three circles apiece. Each circle, moreover, contains an upper tympanum defined by the throne and filled with the haloed head of the scholar. Regimentation on this scale is totally foreign to the late antique model.[32]

A copy of al-Mubashshir's *Choicest Maxims and Wisest Sayings*, datable to the early thirteenth century and preserved in Istanbul, illustrates a parallel development (pl. 9).[33] Taken individually, these figures are respectable copies of a classical original, even if a somewhat unclassical vein of consistent exaggeration and barely suppressed excitement can be detected in their popping eyes, craned necks, and explosive gestures. It is worth enquiring *why* these changes have been introduced. Underlying the whole picture is a firm commitment to the primacy of the spoken word. That is why all six figures are so plainly talking, even shouting, at each other. Sophisticated sign language is employed to suggest different means of communication – the head cocked upwards at an abrupt angle, the hand to the mouth not just to denote speech but also to amplify sound, the vivid chopping motion of the hands to make a point in an argument, the body eagerly hunched forward to suggest intense concentration. Clearly a lively debate is going on, and agreement is nowhere in sight. A tightly executed diagonal design emphasizes the reciprocal nature of the discussions among these scholars, the active exchange of ideas. They seem to ricochet back and forth across and up the page. One can almost hear the words reverberating, finally to be broadcast to the outside world. In a very real sense, these authors have become figures of speech. And they have the last word, too – for a double finispiece of a design almost identical to that of the frontispiece rounds off the book.

In comparison with this furious energy, the bubbling, immediate intellectual activity of this group seminar, the Byzantine author portrait seems curiously

---

[30]   B.Farès, *Le Livre de la Thériaque. Manuscrit arabe à peintures de la fin du XIIe siècle conservé à la Bibliothèque Nationale de Paris* (Cairo, 1953), un-numbered colour pl. 4.

[31]   J.R. Hayes (ed.), *The Genius of Arab Civilization. Source of Renaissance* (Oxford, 1978), p.147.

[32]   See, however, a page from ms grec 74 in Paris (Grabar, *Byzantine Painting*, p. 158).

[33]   Ettinghausen, *Arab Painting*, p. 75.

remote and muffled. The Evangelist reads a book to himself, but these are people who declaim the text of their work to us. We, the readers, are involved as the spoken word is passed on to us. It is a living tradition – another form of certification or *ijaza* in fact.

Islamic taste makes an equally dramatic intrusion in the elaborately knotted framework within which these figures are confined. Here Islamic abstract pattern collides with classical illusionistic techniques. For all the surface classical detail of the figures, the ornamental framework betrays a decisive change in the underlying spirit. It denies the real space which the accomplished illusionism of the figures demands, and which the Byzantine artist of the Vienna Dioscorides evoked with such effective economy.[34] It also suggests an intellectual discipline which controls their animated dialogue, physically imposing an overall control on all the people within it. It is not just a lifeless piece of geometry, a typically Islamic pattern. In this particular context it is susceptible of meaning, for in an obvious visual sense it keeps the argument within bounds. All these scholars obey the same rules; the geometrical framework suggests an intellectual one. But it allows ample freedom of speech. Finally, the links between this pattern and Qur'anic illumination leap to the eye.[35] Such implied Qur'anic embellishment of a secular text speaks a very Islamic language.

One might add that the type of Islamicization operating in these group portraits was not only decisively different from the merely cosmetic changes applied to the 1229 Dioscorides portraits but was also much more radical. It changed the whole nature of the inherited image.

This brings us to the second stage – the moment when the Islamic artist experiments more boldly and laterally than before with the tradition he has inherited. A good example is the double frontispiece to a completely Islamic text, *The Epistles of the Sincere Brethren*; the manuscript, which is in Istanbul, is dated 1287 (pl. 10).[36] The double frontispiece here is used not as simple repetition to secure greater emphasis, as in the *Theriaca* of 1199 or *The Choicest Maxims and Wisest Sayings* of al-Mubashshir, but to create a theatrical mise-en-scene which sets two complementary themes against each other.[37] On the left,

---

[34] Weitzmann, *Book Illumination*, pl. 16.

[35] See the succession of double geometric frontispieces in the Qur'an of Ibn al-Bawwab, made in Baghdad and dated 391/1000–1, especially ff. 8v–9r and 284v – 285r: D.S. Rice, *The Unique Ibn al-Bawwab Manuscript in the Chester Beatty Library* (Dublin, 1955), pls. II-IV.

[36] For a detailed discussion of this double frontispiece, see R. Hillenbrand, "Erudition Exalted: The Double Frontispiece to the Epistles of the Sincere Brethren," in *Beyond the Legacy of Genghis Khan*, ed. L. Komaroff (Leiden and Boston, 2006), pp. 183–212.

[37] Ettinghausen, *Arab Painting*, pp. 98–9.

the sages discuss; on the right, they contemplate. The double frontispiece acts as a visual reminder that both activities are a necessary part of intellectual life. It also expresses in immediate visual form the multiple authorship of the text. Their mental exertion finds physical outlets, as in their knotted foreheads, frowning with concentration. In the upper storey of the building, a student devours his book while to the right one author scribbles at top speed as his colleagues hold an animated discussion or just sit there thinking. The entire image evokes – by thought, by writing, by reading, by speech – what medieval books and learning were all about, from the heroic figures of the philosophers engaged in public disputation before an enraptured audience, some of whom crane from balconies for a better view, to the humble attendants who wield a fan – or even those who sneak off in search of something better to do.

Another *locus classicus* for the second stage in the gradual transformation of the author portrait is to be found in the frontispiece of the Schefer Hariri of 1237 – a turning point in the all-too-brief history of the author portrait in Islamic painting (pl. 11).[38] It exemplifies the two distinct strands in contemporary frontispiece design and shows them co-existing in precarious harmony.[39] As it happens, this moment of balance seems to have been transitory; at all events, no other comparable example survives. But subsequent manuscripts show clearly enough that the current of fashion was running against the author portrait and that the royal frontispiece was much more in tune with Islamic taste. Yet in the 1237 *Maqamat*, in a brilliantly simple solution to the knotty problem of conflicting emphases, both author and patron are allocated ttheir rightful place in the sun. A double frontispiece is all it takes. It was a familiar device in Byzantine book painting, but had curiously enough been reserved for royal images; the notion of combining author and patron in such a double frontispiece seems not to have struck Byzantine artists. A unity of layout, colour and ornament ensures that the two images of the 1237 manuscript make a natural pair. But, as in *Animal Farm*, equality is a relative concept. Within the general conceptual and physical unity the artist has deposited numerous clues to indicate the pre-eminence of the ruler image, and in that sense this frontispiece foreshadows

---

[38]   For a detailed discussion of this theme, see E.R. Hoffman, "The Author Portrait in Thirteenth-Century Arabic Manuscripts: A New Islamic Context for a Late-Antique Tradition," *Muqarnas 10. Essays in Honor of Oleg Grabar contributed by his students* (Leiden, 1993), pp. 6–20; E.R.F. Hoffman, *The Emergence of Illustration in Arabic Manuscripts: Classical Legacy and Islamic Transformation* (unpublished Harvard University PhD thesis, 1982); and, in more general vein, E. Hoffman, 'Pathways of Portability: Islamic and Christian interchange from the tenth to the twelfth century', *Art History* 24 (2001), 17–50.

[39]   For an illustration (mis-captioned), see Farès, *Livre*, 16–17, figs. 3–4 (the order is reversed from that of the original).

later developments. These clues include the location of the ruler image on the right, nearer the front of the book and therefore in the place of honour, as well as various nuances of iconography encompassing pose, attributes, and colour. There is no space to rehearse these here,[40] but two specific aspects of the author portrait do deserve brief notice. One concerns the type of scene being depicted. For the royal personage, it is a standard audience scene with the ruler surrounded by, and dominating, his courtiers. For the author portrait, though, the term "audience" has a much more literal significance. His pose and gesture show that he is communicating with them. Here, then, is a singularly appropriate image for the text of the *Maqamat*, which is all about Abu Zayd haranguing crowds. Moreover, that word *maqamat* means "assemblies," and an assembly is precisely what is being depicted here. Visual puns are far commoner in Islamic painting than is generally recognized.

The other aspect of this author portrait has wider repercussions, for it bears on the re-use of a standardized iconography in unfamiliar and sometimes downright inappropriate contexts. A couple of examples will make this clear. Despite the ostentatiously relaxed poses of the figures in the left frontispiece of the *Rasa'il Ikhwan al-Safa* of 1287, it is plain enough that the skeleton of the design is that of an enthroned ruler flanked by scribes and attendants – the kind of image that occurs repeatedly in the Rashid al-Din manuscript.[41] Even more daring is the celebrated depiction of childbirth in the Schefer Hariri itself, where one may perhaps detect a certain black humour in the way that the throne has become an obstetric stool, the attendant courtiers have turned into midwives and the gorgeously apparelled king is replaced by a half-naked Indian woman in the throes of parturition. This basic layout is caricatured above in the male realm where the distracted father, safely removed from the action, is flanked by astrologers.[42] These two cases show clearly enough the inherent flexibility of the archetypal enthronement iconography so popular in this period.

Returning now to the Hariri frontispiece, we may note that the author is undergoing the kind of heroization traditionally reserved for the monarch himself. He is seated not on a chair, like the physician Dioscorides in the manuscripts of *c.*512 and 1229 alike, but on a throne. He is raised above the level of his audience. Most tellingly of all, he is flanked by winged figures – either angels or *jinns*, but ultimately derived from classical personifications of victory

---

40   For a detailed analysis, see R. Hillenbrand, "The Schefer Hariri. A Study in Islamic Frontispiece Design," in A. Contadini (ed.), *Arab Painting: Text and Image in Illustrated Arabic Manuscripts* (Leiden and Boston, 2007), pp. 117–34.
41   D.T. Rice, ed. B. Gray, *The Illustrations to the 'World History' of Rashid al-Din* (Edinburgh, 1976), pp. 168–79.
42   Ettinghausen, *Arab Painting*, p. 121.

– which at this period were a common attribute of royalty. All the royal images from the *Kitab al-Aghani* have them.[43] Before our very eyes, then, the author is beginning to take on the attributes of a monarch. One might say that he is promoting himself out of a job.

It may be worth noting that the author portrait used as a frontispiece seems to be totally unknown in Persian painting. Clearly the Mediterranean influences so strongly marked in thirteenth-century Arab painting struck no responsive chord in Iran. Instead, it was there that the royal theme was developed most consistently in frontispiece design. That is a subject in itself, involving as it does such factors as the increasing role of narrative, the inter-relationship between the two halves of a double frontispiece, the development of secondary themes and so on. Authors are, as it happens, depicted in some manuscripts, and in *Shahnama*s this is frequently near the front of the text. But the trigger for such an image is not the frontispiece but an episode in the text itself, as in the case of Firdausi and the rival poets in Ghazna,[44] and Sa'di and the youth in the *Gulistan*.[45] The emphasis is therefore a narrative one; there is no attempt to recreate the formality and timelessness of the author portrait proper.

But the most striking development of the author portrait was still to come. This, the third and most radical stage in the three-part pattern that was mentioned earlier, adopted a quintessentially Islamic solution to the problem. The author disappeared altogether. He was replaced by his name, and the physical book which had earlier been shown in his hands was similarly reduced and abstracted to its mere title. Some vestiges of the high profile formerly enjoyed by the author portrait still remained: these verbal references still occupied the opening page or the first double opening of the manuscript. They were not upstaged by competing visual images; they had that space to themselves. Moreover, the importance of the author and his book was generously acknowledged by the setting devised for his name and for the title of his book. Typically, a large roundel comprising complex geometrical interlace enclosed these words and blazoned them forth with lavish application of blue and gold. A whole series of manuscripts produced around 1300 attests this new development – the Morgan Bestiary, the *Kalila wa Dimna* of 1333, the *Athar al-Baqiya* of al-Biruni (pl. 12),[46] the *Jami al-Tawarikh*

---

43   D.S. Rice, "The *Aghani* Miniatures and Religious Painting in Islam," *Burlington Magazine* (April, 1953), 128–35.

44   J.V.S. Wilkinson, *The Shah-nama of Firdausi* (London, 1931), pl. II.

45   R. Hillenbrand, "The Message of Misfortune. Words and Images in Sa'di's *Gulistan*," in *Silk and Stone. The Art of Asia*, ed. J. Tilden (London, 1996), p. 33.

46   For a colour plate, see R. Hillenbrand, "Images of Muhammad in al-Biruni's *Chronology of Ancient Nations*," in *Persian Painting from the Mongols to the Qajars. Studies in Honour of Basil W. Robinson*, ed. R. Hillenbrand (London, 2001), pl. XII.

of Rashid al-Din. None of them, incidentally, has a frontispiece with a ruler image. Thus the powerful tendency towards abstraction which is always – at the very least – latent in Islamic art, manifests itself again.

What was the source of this idea? It seems so simple, so inevitable when one encounters it; but for an imagination nourished on Byzantine, Jacobite or classical manuscripts it was nothing of the kind. A clue to the ultimate inspiration at work may be detected in the opening page of the so-called Schefer Hariri of 1237 – the page that precedes its double frontispiece. The design here is modest, with no pretensions to dominating the page. An oblong *'unwan* placed in the top one-third of the page gives the title – *al-Maqamat al-Hariri* – in white *naskhi* letters set aginst a broad band richly illuminated in gold.[47] The obvious parallel that springs to mind here is the *sura* heading of a typical contemporary Qur'an, even to the detail of the horizontal palmette projecting into the text.[48] Indeed, it seems likely that such a Qur'an affords not merely an intriguing parallel but was the actual source of the idea. From a tentative borrowing of this kind it was surely no major step to adopt the frontispiece of a Qur'an, or the opening folio of a *juz'*, and to employ a similar layout for the title of a secular book and the name of its author. Later still, it was similarly a small step to extend the function of such inscribed roundels to include the name of the patron, and indeed to give such an *ex libris* a page to itself. Thus image becomes epigraph. Once this idea had caught on, of course, it fell subject in its own turn to various transformations. Thus the separate chapter headings of a book might each receive their own roundel, creating a scheme whereby a constellation of such medallions wheels around the central *shamsiya*, with angels in the corners to drive home the heavenly associations of the design.[49] Or, to take a Mamluk example, the royal name of Qa'it Bay occupies the central band while formal benedictory mottoes flank it above and below.[50] Thus epigraphy, geometry and floral ornament merge seamlessly and they definitively shut out the human image. It is a triumphantly Islamic response to the classical heritage – at once intellectual, abstract and religious – and there was no turning back.

---

[47]   Hillenbrand, "Schefer Hariri," fig. 2.

[48]   D. James, *The Master Scribes. Qur'ans of the 10th to 14th centuries AD* (Oxford, 1992), pp. 43, 57 and 85.

[49]   This detail recalls the association of rulers with winged figures in royal frontispieces; here the ruler's place has been taken by inscriptions. See D. Stewart, *Early Islam* (repr. Weert, 1975), cover illustration.

[50]   D. James, *Islamic Art. An Introduction* (Feltham, 1974), 25.

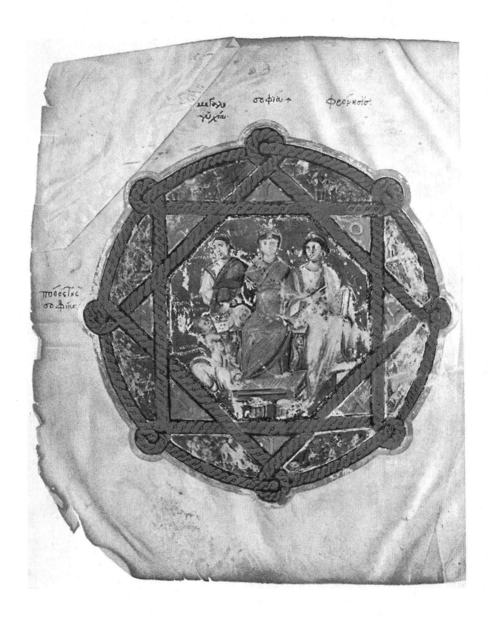

Plate 1   Frontispiece of the Vienna copy of Dioscorides, *De Materia Medica*, 512 (after Weitzmann)

Plate 2   Frontispiece of the *Homilies of St John Chrysostom*, 1078 (Paris, B.N. Coislin 79) (after Grabar)

Plate 3   Frontispiece of Islamic Dioscorides manuscript, 1239 (Oxford, Bodleian Library) (after Evans and Wixom)

Plate 4   Byzantine Evangelist portrait, 12th century (after Grabar)

Plate 5   Double frontispiece of Islamic Dioscorides manuscript, 1229 (Istanbul, Topkapı Saray Library) (after Ettinghausen)

Plate 6   Classical scholars from the Vienna Dioscorides manuscript, 512
                 (after Weitzmann).

Plate 7   Islamic scholars from the *Kitab al-Diryaq*, 1199 (Paris, BN) (after
Farès).

Plate 8   Islamic scholars from the *Kitab al-Diryaq*, *c*.1250 (Vienna) (after Hayes)

Plate 9   Islamic scholars from al-Mubashshir's *Choicest Maxims and Wisest Sayings*, early 13th century (courtesy Dr E. Lambourn)

Plate 10   Islamic scholars from *The Epistles of the Sincee Brethren*, 1287
             (Istanbul, Suleymaniye Library) (after Ettinghausen)

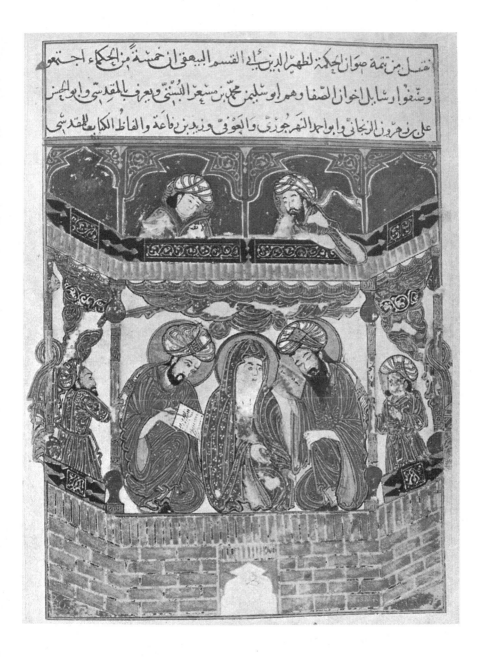

Plate 11   Author and ruler in the double frontispiece of the *Maqamat* of
                al-Hariri, 1237 (Paris, BN) (after 'Azzawi)

Plate 12   Title page of *Al-athar al-baqiya* by al-Biruni, 1307 (Edinburgh University Library) (after Hillenbrand)

Chapter 5

Alfonso I and the Memory of the First Crusade: Conquest and Crusade in the Kingdom of Aragón-Navarre

Jennifer Price
Seattle University

Either in late December 1122 or early in January 1123, when he was negotiating a truce with the rulers of León-Castile on his western frontier, Alfonso I of Aragón-Navarre (1104–1134) established a confraternity at the recently captured city of Belchite in the Ebro River Valley.[1] The king, known as the Battler, commissioned the brothers "to fight in defense of Christian people and the service of Christ."[2] Those who joined the confraternity at Belchite were promised a remission of penance, the amount of which was determined by the length of time spent providing military service. A brother who served with the confraternity for one year would receive the same remission of sins due to those unarmed pilgrims who "marched to Jerusalem," while a brother who devoted the rest of his life to serving the confraternity would be "absolved of all sins as if he were entering upon the life of a monk or hermit."[3] The grant of spiritual privileges to members

---

[1]   B.F. Reilly, *The Kingdom of Léon-Castilla under Queen Urraca, 1109–1126* (Princeton, 1982), pp. 171–173; A. Ubieto Arteta, *Historia de Aragón. La formación territorial* (Saragossa, 1981), pp. 157–159; J.M. Lacarra, "La conquista de Zaragoza por Alfonso I (18 diciembre 1118) in *En la España medieval. Estudios dedicados al profesor Don Juio González González* (Madrid, 1984), pp. 74–75; C. Stalls, *Possessing the Land. Aragon's Expansion into Islam's Ebro Frontier Under Alfonso the Battler, 1104–1134*, The Medieval Mediterranean: Peoples, Economies and Cultures, 400–1453 No. 7 (Leiden, 1995), pp. 35–36, and 46–48.

[2]   J. Goñi Gaztambide, *Historia de la bula de la cruzada en España* (Vitoria, 1958), pp. 75–77; P. Rassow, "La Confradia de Belchite," *Anuario de Historia Español* 3 (Madrid, 1926), pp. 200–226.

[3]   Even more temporary commitments were welcomed. If anyone wished to make a pilgrimage elsewhere, but instead "serves God in battle" the reward usually granted for the pilgrimage "would be doubled." Goñi Gaztambide, *Historia*, pp. 75–77; Rassow, "La Confradia de Belchite," p. 224. For confraternities in general see *Dictionnaire de droit*

of the Belchite Confraternity was confirmed by the king, Archbishop Bernard of Toledo, Archbishop Diego Gelmírez of Compostela, five bishops from León-Castile and six from Aragón.[4] Alfonso and the Spanish bishops rewarded the pursuit of an activity so worldly in nature by granting spiritual benefits usually reserved for the pilgrim or the spiritual battles of the regular clergy because the struggle against the Murabitun undertaken by the brothers fit into an established pattern of wars fought on God's behalf.[5] It was known, said the council, that

> with a similar indulgence the Lord's Sepulchre, Majorca, Saragossa, and other lands were rescued from captivity; likewise, with God's favor, the route from here to Jerusalem shall be opened and the Church of God that is still held in captivity shall be made free.[6]

Here we have one of the earliest descriptions by contemporaries of the activity now known to historians as "crusading." Those involved in the establishment of the Belchite Confraternity believed the First Crusade, the Balearic Crusade undertaken by the Pisans and Catalans in 1114, and Alfonso I's conquest of Saragossa in 1118 to be similar in form and purpose. Each of the aforementioned expeditions was remembered as having succeeded in liberating Christians and Christian territory from non-believers, which is precisely what the Battler was in the process of doing in the Ebro River Valley. The Belchite Confraternity would play an important role in this royal project by protecting the sparsely populated plain around Belchite from the advances of the Murabitun.[7] The conquest of the Ebro basin was orchestrated to meet very specific goals, the most significant of which was the opening of the pilgrimage route to Jerusalem. In recovering major cities like Lérida and Fraga, Alfonso I was not just extending boundaries of Aragón and frustrating the designs of his nearest Christian rivals, but he was also following the trail left by another group of Latin Christians who had set out towards in the Holy Land in 1096. Only a year previously, Pope Calixtus II had

---

canonique, contenant tous les termes du droit canonique, avec un sommaire de l'histoire et des institutions et de l'état actuel de la discipline, ed. R. Naz, et al., 7 vols. (Paris, 1935–65), 4, pp. 128–44.

[4]   Rassow, "La Confradia de Belchite," pp. 225–226.

[5]   The Murabitun or Almoravids were the major power in North Africa in the eleventh century. They arrived in al-Andalus in 1086 at the behest of the *taifa* kings of Seville, Granada, and Badajoz who hoped the Murabitun would help them check Leonese-Castilian expansion. They would remain and eventually absorb the *taifa* kingdoms. See Jacinto Bosh Vilà, *Historia de Marruecos: los Almoravides* (Teután, 1956).

[6]   Goñi Gaztambide, *Historia*, pp. 75–77; Rassow, "La Confradia de Belchite," p. 225.

[7]   The Murabitan will attack Belchite in 1123 in an attempt to relieve the pressure Alfonso was placing on Lèrida. Stalls, *Possessing the Land*, p. 49.

granted an identical remission of sins as that promised to those crusading in the East to those who took up the cross in defense of the Spanish Church.[8]

From 1121 until 1134, the conquest of the Ebro region was undertaken by armed pilgrims from Aragón and beyond, emblazoned with crosses, struggling on behalf of all Christians for the defense of Christendom. By directly invoking the memory of the First Crusade the king of Aragón-Navarre successfully translated what had been a personal and dynastic war into an international conflict of interest to all Christians. The application of the model provided by the First Crusade to the Aragonese conquests of the 1120s and 1130s marks the first step in the gradual extension of the idea and mechanisms of crusading to the pre-existing conflicts between Muslims and Christians in the Iberian Peninsula.

The significance of this achievement should not be underestimated. It was by no means inevitable that the crusade became "an all-purpose holy war" as it eventually would over the course of the twelfth century.[9] In November 1095 at the Council of Clermont, Pope Urban II had called on the knights of Europe to liberate Eastern Christians from the "yoke" of the "Turks."[10] However, this task was not presented as a typical military expedition. Instead, Urban commanded that the soldiers engaged in this task embark upon a penitential pilgrimage. He linked the remission of penance granted to these new variant of pilgrims and the symbol associated with the vow asked of these pilgrims, the cross, directly to the pilgrimage to Jerusalem.[11] In other words, the activity introduced by Urban II at Clermont was place and task specific. With the fall of Jerusalem to the crusade army in July 1099 the purpose, so to speak, of the crusade evaporated. At the same time, however, its success against all odds demonstrated to contemporaries that God approved of this novel activity, the armed pilgrimage. Might it be possible to continue to offer the laity this opportunity to gain salvation? Might this be the way in which to combat the enemies of Christ and the Church wherever they were to be found?

---

[8] *Bullaire du Pape Calixte II, 1119–1124*, ed. U. Robert, 2 vols. (Paris, 1891), 2, p. 454. This letter has been dated to April 1121–24. Most likely this version was composed in 1123 as Calixtus II makes the same proclamation about those who have taken the cross, but not completed their vow as is contained in the canons of the First Lateran Council held in April 1123. An earlier letter, dated to 1121, no longer exists. "The Venetian Crusade of 1122–24," *I Communi italiani nel regno latino di Gerusalemme*, eds. B.Z. Kedar and G. Airaldi, (Genoa, 1986), pp. 345–346.

[9] J.A. Brundage, *Medieval Canon Law and the Crusader* (Madison, 1969), p. 193.

[10] Baldric of Bourgueil, "Historia Jerosolimitana," in *RHC Oc.*, 4, pp. 14–15.

[11] Orderic Vitalis, *Historia Æcclesiastica*, ed. and trans. M. Chibnall, 6 vols. (Oxford, 1969–80), 5, pp. 16–18.

A number of clerical authors writing soon afterwards suggested that they believed this activity might be duplicated elsewhere, displaying, a "tendency to transfer the ideas and extravagant language" of the crusade to other conflicts.[12] In either 1107 or 1108 a Flemish cleric appealed to the clergy of the provinces of Mainz and Cologne, the county of Flanders and the duchy of Lorraine, asking them to urge the knights under their care to take up arms against the pagan Wends, "the enemies of Christ."[13] The Slavic church was identified as "our Jerusalem, which from the beginning was free" but lately had been made a slave. For the author of this letter, Christians had a solemn duty to liberate this "Jerusalem" just as they had the actual city where Christ lived and died.[14] The memory of the First Crusade and its earthly goal was used here to inspire Christians to protect the Church, just as it would be in Aragón a decade later.

It is one thing to apply the language of crusading to other conflicts; transferring the mechanisms of crusading – specifically, the cross and the vow for which it stood, as well as the spiritual and temporal privileges associated with the cross – was an entirely different matter. For one thing, of course, these mechanisms are the purview of the papacy and thus, any extension of the crusade must have papal approval. Even with papal approval, though, evidence suggests that both the clergy and the laity were initially reluctant to transform pre-existing conflicts (such as those being fought against the Muslims of al-Andalus) into crusades. The reason for this hesitation rests upon the contemporary understanding of what the activity associated with the cross entailed.

The connection Urban II made between the assumption of the cross and the completion of a pilgrimage to Jerusalem served as an obstacle to the immediate and widespread expansion of the crusade as the prevailing model of religious violence outside the Holy Land. Thus, even as Urban himself argued that it was "no virtue to rescue Christians from the Saracens in one place, only to expose them to the tyranny and oppression of the Saracens in another [Spain]," he did not suggest that people take up the cross for the liberation of the Spanish

---

[12]   J. Riley-Smith, *The Crusades. A Short History* (New Haven, 1987), p. 88; W. Wattenbach, "Handschriftliches," *Neues Archiv* 7 (1882), pp. 624–626; *The Crusades: Idea and Reality, 1095–1274*, trans. L. and J. Riley-Smith, Documents in Medieval History 4 (London, 1981), pp. 75–77. For an interpretation of this charter see G. Constable, "The Place of the Magdeburg Charter of 1107/08 in the History of Eastern Germany and of the Crusades," in *Vita Religiosa im Mittelalter. Festschrift für Kaspar Elm zum 70. Geburtstag*, ed. F. J. Felten, *Berliner Historische Studien* 31: Ordensstudien 13, (Berlin, 1999), pp. 283–299.

[13]   Wattenbach, "Handschriftliches," pp. 624–626; *Crusades: Idea and Reality*, pp. 75–77.

[14]   Wattenbach, "Handschriftliches," p. 626; Constable, "Magdeburg Charter," pp. 293–294, and n. 52.

Church.[15] Rather, he urged a number of Spaniards who had taken the cross for the liberation of Jerusalem to remain at home and aid in the recovery of Tarragona *instead*. Count Guillem Ramon of Cerdaña, Count Fernando Díaz of Asturias, and Pedro Gutiérrez refused to commute their vows, choosing to fulfill their crusade vows by completing a pilgrimage to the Holy Sepulchre.[16] While they expected to fight along the way, crusaders regarded the completion of a pilgrimage to Jerusalem to be the essential part of their duty as soldiers of Christ and the action that purged them of their sins.[17] When Urban's successor, Paschal II, turned back Castilian crusaders from their pilgrimage to Jerusalem in 1101 so that they might fight Muslims in Spain, he found it necessary to ask their "compatriots not to deride [these crusaders] for not fulfilling their vows," because, while they may not have completed the pilgrimage to Jerusalem, "in using all their strength to fight the Moabites and Moors they carry out their penance."[18] If one hoped to apply the mechanisms of crusading to other conflicts this assumption would have to be taken into consideration, if not addressed explicitly.

The explicit approach was the path taken by Bohemond of Antioch who wished to launch an attack on Alexius I. According to contemporary reports, "the emperor of Constantinople was at that time strongly opposed to our people. By trickery or open violence he thwarted or tyrannized over the pilgrims going to Jerusalem by land or by sea."[19] Bohemond was not, therefore, attacking Alexius for personal gain as it might seem at first glance, considering his particular history with the Byzantine Empire. Instead, he was helping to liberate the pilgrimage route to Jerusalem from the hands of a tyrant. Rather than attempt this feat on his own, Bohemond sought and received permission from Paschal II

---

[15]   Urban II to the counts of Besalú, Empurias, Roussillon and Cerdaña and their knights, *c.*January 1096 – 29 July 1099 in *Papsturkunden in Spanien. I Katalonien*, ed. P. Kehr (Berlin, 1926), pp. 287–288; *Crusades: Idea and Reality*, p. 40.

[16]   A. Ubieto Arteta, "La participación navarro-aragonesa en la primera cruzada," *Principe de Viana* 8 (1947), pp. 357–383.

[17]   The most coherent contemporary statement regarding the substance of the crusade vow is found in book ten of Orderic Vitalis, *Historia Æcclesiastica* 5, pp. 228–233.

[18]   Paschal II, "Epistolae et Privilegia," *Patrologiae Cursus Completus. Series Latina*, comp. J.P. Migne, 217 vols. and 4 vols. of indexes (Paris, 1841–64), p. 45. Amongst those whom Paschal II, a former legate in Spain, convinced to commute their vow was King Pedro I of Aragón who "accepted the cross to go to the region of Jerusalem" in 1100. In February 1101 Pedro is observed in front of Saragossa "with the banner of Christ." *Colección diplomática de Pedro I de Aragón y Navarra*, ed. A. Ubieto Arteta (Saragossa, 1951), p. 113, n. 6 and 115, n. 9.

[19]   Fulcher of Chartres, *Historia Hierosolymitana (1095–1127)*, ed. H. Hagenmeyer (Heidelberg, 1913), p. 521.

to undertake this expedition as a crusade. It meant he could gather a much larger host than what he may have been able to cobble together from his own domains. Accompanied by the papal legate, Bruno of Segni, Bohemond tirelessly canvassed Italy and the regions of Gaul in the spring and summer of 1106 to encourage knights to take the cross.[20] According to one chronicler, "Many were kindled by his words and, taking the Lord's cross, left all their belongings and set out on the road to Jerusalem like men hastening to a feast."[21] As this as well as the crusaders' behavior once they arrived in Asia Minor attests, the ultimate goal for those who participated in Bohemond's crusade was Jerusalem not Constantinople.[22] The expedition that sailed from Brindisi on 7 October 1107 so neatly conformed to the model of crusading presented at Clermont that an observer described it as "the third expedition from the West [to] set out for Jerusalem."[23]

What about expeditions undertaken with similar goals of liberating Christians and Christian territory, but perhaps physically removed from the pilgrimage route and Jerusalem itself? Could they too be classified as crusades? The answer given by Urban II's successor as pope appears to have been "yes" – although this was qualified somewhat by Paschal II's expectation that any expedition associated with the cross continue to take the form of a penitential pilgrimage. In 1113, the archbishop of Pisa asked the pope to bless a campaign upon which he and his flock were about to embark. The Pisans wished to free Christian prisoners held on the Balearic Islands from their Muslim captors. Led by the example of the archbishop, those Pisans who planned to participate had made a solemn vow, placing "the sign of God's army" on their shoulders prior to meeting with the pope. Though the expedition had not originated with the pope, Paschal II seems to have felt no compunction in granting his permission and blessing the cross. The pope also extended a spiritual privilege similar to that which had been granted to those participated in the First Crusade.[24] The

---

[20]   R.B. Yewdale, *Bohemond I, Prince of Antioch* (Princeton, 1924), pp. 107–109; J.G. Rowe, "Paschal II, Bohemond of Antioch and the Byzantine Empire," *Bulletin of the John Rylands Library* 49 (1966), pp. 165–202.

[21]   Orderic Vitalis, *Historia Æcclesiastica*, 6, pp. 70–2.

[22]   Robert Dalmace of Collanges was "taking the road to Jerusalem" and Joscelin of Lèves was able to get a contribution towards his "march" there from the monks of St. Peters in Chartres. *Le Cartulaire de Marcigny-sur-Loire*, ed. J. Richard (Dijon, 1957), pp. 79–80. Fulcher of Chartres, *Historia*, pp. 524–525. Anna Comnena, *Alexiade (règne de l'empereur Alexis I Comnène, 1081–1118)*, ed. B. Leib, 3 vols. (Paris, 1937–76), 3, p. 118.

[23]   Orderic Vitalis, *Historia Æcclesiastica*, 3, pp. 182–183. Despite its appearance, Brett Edward Whalen argues in this volume that the expedition was, in fact, not a crusade.

[24]   "On account of so great an act," Paschal II granted that those who died on this expedition would be forgiven of all their sins. *Liber Maiolichinus. De Gestis Pisanorum Illustribus*, ed. C. Calisse, Fonti per la Storia d'Italia 12 (Rome, 1904, repr. Torino, 1966),

Pisans were later joined by the count of Catalonia, Raymond Berenguer III, and a group of Catalan nobles who received the cross from the archbishop.[25]

While this expedition fits squarely into an older "pre-Crusade tradition of Pisan campaigns in the western Mediterranean," there can be little doubt that it was also a crusade, and regarded as such by the papacy, its participants and by those, like Alfonso I, who looked upon it in retrospect.[26] This would be the first time those who took up the cross did so without explicitly referencing Jerusalem.[27] Nevertheless, the Balearic Crusade shared in common with the First Crusade the goal of liberation and the form of a pilgrimage. Participants in the Balearic offensive are described as pilgrims, even though they did not make a pilgrimage in the way those traveling to and fighting in the East did; there does not appear to have been any specific pilgrimage site to which the Pisans and Catalans went to fulfill their vow. Pilgrimage here was clearly understood in the sense of exile and renunciation – as an act of penance. During the winter of 1114–15 the Majorcans managed to burn one of the siege engines because the crusaders assigned to guard them were overcome by sleep or wine. Their negligence caused the leadership of the crusade to rail against the troops. They were called cowards and accused of breaking their vow of holiness by being drunk.[28] The crusaders had taken a vow that not only reflected the importance placed on the act of liberation, but also signaled their status as penitents – presumably promising to act in a more sober manner than the maligned crusaders had.[29] Fortunately for these delinquent crusaders, the expedition to Majorca was ultimately a success. The pilgrim army captured the major cities of the islands and freed the Christians living there from Muslim rule.[30] Evidently their votive obligation was discharged; soon after celebrating Easter in 1115, the Pisans and Catalans collected the spoils they had won and returned home.[31]

Notwithstanding the transitory nature of the crusaders' victory – there was no attempt by crusaders to maintain a permanent Christian presence on the islands

---

ll. 39–48, 71–87, and 2224–2228. Also see Appendix 1 for the agreement between the Pisans and Ramon Berenguer III, pp. 137–139.

[25]   *Liber Maiolichinus*, ll. 1151–1153; *Documentos de Jaime I de Aragon*, ed. A. Huici Miranda and M.D. Cabanes Pecourt, 3 vols. (Valencia, 1976–8), 1: doc. 186.

[26]   G.B. Doxey, *Christian Attempts to Conquer the Balearic Islands, 1015–1229*, PhD Dissertation (Cambridge, 1991), p. 95. See also, H.E.J. Cowdrey, "The Mahdia Campaign of 1087," *English Historical Review* 92 (1977), pp. 1–29.

[27]   Doxey, *Balearic Islands*, pp. 71–72, and 78–82.

[28]   *Liber Maiolichinus*, ll. 2445–2477.

[29]   *Documentos de Jaime I de Aragon*, 1: doc. 186.

[30]   *Liber Maiolichinus*, ll. 907–916, 2724–2729, 2751–2753, 2761–2764, and 3520–3526.

[31]   Ibid., ll. 3520–3526.

until 1229 – the Balearic Crusade is significant for the history of the crusades because it set a precedent for the future.[32] The expedition to Majorca suggested that it might not always be necessary to link the cross with the completion of a pilgrimage to the Holy Sepulchre. As long as the expedition took the form of a penitential pilgrimage and was intended to free Christians or Christian territory from the tyranny of those opposed to Christianity or the Church, the pope might be willing to grant the remission of penance associated with the cross to participants. Those who understood the crusade in this way would be in the minority in the first half of the twelfth century.[33] The more common perception of the crusade, and the one embraced by Alfonso I of Aragón-Navarre, was founded on the memory of the First Crusade as a penitential pilgrimage to Jerusalem.

From the mid-eleventh century the rulers of Aragon had pursued an aggressive policy of expansion into the region surrounding the Ebro River. Their long-term goals were the conquest of the major cities of the Ebro basin – Tudela, Huesca, Lérida, and Saragossa.[34] Alfonso continued to execute this policy from the moment he took the throne in 1104. Though the enemies against whom the king and his followers fought had not changed, the participants in the conquest of Saragossa would be granted a remission of penance in 1118. Soon after, between 1121 and 1123, the mechanisms of crusade were imported into Spain with the blessing of the pope and the nature of Alfonso's war against his Muslim neighbors transformed. From this moment until his death in 1134, Alfonso I engaged in battle as a crusader. It is important to understand not only how the king of Aragón-Navarre was able to transform a pre-existing conflict into a crusade, but also to understand why he would want to do so. The key to both rests upon the memory of an armed pilgrimage to Jerusalem.

Alfonso I of Aragón-Navarre did not originally conceive of his effort to gain control over the Ebro Valley as a crusade. This was not because he was unfamiliar with the concept of the crusade. His brother, Pedro I, assumed the cross in 1100, with the intention of accompanying his former brother-in-law, William IX of

---

[32]   "Chronica Latina regum Castellae," ed. L.C. Brea, in *Chronica Hispania Saeculi XII. Pars I*, ed. E. Falque, J. Gil and A. Maya, CCCM 71 (Turnholt, 1990), pp. 98–99.

[33]   The crusade eventually came to be defined by what it did rather than where it was fought thanks in no small part to St. Bernard of Clairvaux who detached the concrete goal of liberating the city of Jerusalem from the activity associated with the cross. For Bernard the crusader's pilgrimage was figurative; a spiritual journey that could be carried out anywhere that God "puts himself into a position of necessity or pretends to be in one" or where a crusader might "defend his Lord from the infamous accusation of treachery." Bernard of Clairvaux, "Epistolae," *PL* 182, pp. 565–566.

[34]   Stalls, *Possessing the Land*, p. 13.

Aquitaine, to the Holy Land.[35] In 1096, Pedro had besieged Huesca as a papal vassal, accompanied by a papal legate and several of his French vassals. Like others from this region, however, Pedro associated the cross with a very specific and unique activity, distinct from the papally approved engagements in Aragón with which he was familiar. Significantly, he believed he had incurred an obligation to travel to Jerusalem. Only upon the advice of Pope Paschal II, did Pedro I agree to commute his vow to complete a pilgrimage to Jerusalem and aid the Holy Land into a vow to attack and liberate Saragossa from her Muslim captors. In recognition of his commutation, he wore a cross into battle in February 1101.[36] Although Alfonso could not help but be aware of the similarities between the crusade and the wars being fought in Aragón, especially when starting his own offensive against the kings of Saragossa in 1110, like his brother Pedro he did not directly identify his own campaigns as a crusade until nearly a decade later.

When Alfonso I did reformulate his approach, it was a reaction to the efforts of his rival for control over the lower Ebro River Valley, the count of Barcelona, to gain papal blessing for an attack on Tortosa. Ramon Berenguer III, like Bohemond of Antioch before him, was quick to appreciate what the designation of a campaign as a crusade could mean – especially, if as it now seemed, after the success of the Balearic expedition, the form of penitential war associated with the cross might be separated from the pilgrimage to Jerusalem. A crusade was a holy endeavor, open to all Christians no matter their political loyalties with the promise of spiritual and earthly rewards.[37] Having his expedition declared an armed pilgrimage allowed the count to recruit a navy greater than he would have been able to raise on his own, especially in regions where he did not have a political foothold. Upon returning from Majorca, therefore, Ramon Berenguer set out for Italy, where he convinced the Genoese and Pisans to join him in an expedition to secure the port of Tortosa. He also gained the pope's support for this venture.[38] The same Cardinal Boso, who had accompanied the

---

[35]   A. Ubieto Areta, *Historia de Aragón. La formación territorial* (Saragossa, 1981), pp. 80–81; D. Mansilla, *La documentación pontificia hasta Inocenio III (963–1216)* (Rome, 1955), pp. 53–54; Ubieto Arteta, *Pedro*, pp. 114–115.

[36]   Paschal II, "Epistolae," p. 45.

[37]   Those who were unfit to undertake a journey to Jerusalem were asked to remain at home in 1096. Robert of Rheims, "Historia Hiersolymitana," RHC Oc. 3, p. 729.

[38]   Ramon Berenguer III asked and received papal approval for his planned attack on Tortosa. Those who participated were granted a remission of penance, but it is unknown if they took the cross. Paschal II placed the count and his possessions under papal protection and assigned Cardinal Boso, who had accompanied the crusaders on the Balearic Crusade, as legate for the expedition. Mansilla, *Documentación pontificia*, pp. 69–70; *Liber Maiolichinus*, p. 144, no. 8; "Vita Sancti Olegarii," *España sagrada. Theatro geographico-historico de la iglesia de España. Origen divisiones, y limites de todas sus provincias. Antiguedad, traslaciones, y estado*

host to Majorca, was granted the authority to recruit for the Tortosa expedition by Paschal II who assigned him to a legatine commission in Spain in 1117.[39] The crusade to be led by the count of Barcelona never took place. War broke out between Pisa and Genoa in 1118, the same year the pope died, depriving the count of much needed naval assistance and ecclesiastical backing. Paschal II's successor, Gelasius II (1118–19), was not nearly as receptive to casting the expeditions in the Iberian Peninsula as "crusades."

The purpose of Ramon Berenguer III's trip to Italy and its result was not lost on Alfonso I; both men were interested securing Lérida and Tortosa for themselves. The designation of a campaign as a crusade would have brought very real benefits to the count had the situation unfolded as planned. For one thing, his ability to recruit men was not limited to his own territory or familial relationships. With the promise of spiritual (as well as earthly) rewards Ramon Berenguer had gained the support of Genoa and Pisa. Moreover, with the help of a papal legate the count could rely on the assistance of the Church in raising men to accompany the host to Tortosa. He probably expected that Cardinal Boso would have better luck inspiring knights to join the expedition since he could offer a reward that no king or count could hope to match – the remission of sins and a chance of salvation.[40] Furthermore, the transformation of a war of conquest into a crusade put the struggle on a higher plane. Ramon Berenguer would be fighting to regain God's territory and thus, could hope to be the recipient of divine favor. Obviously, this had implications for the rivalry between the king of Aragon and the count of Barcelona. It meant that whoever was successful in transforming the conquest of the Ebro Valley into a crusade would not only have better odds for victory, but also would have the stronger claim to the territory they acquired on God's behalf.

Thus, we observe the bishop-elect of Saragossa consulting Gelasius II on Alfonso's behalf in 1118 on the matter of the forthcoming campaign to regain his diocesan church. He may have been hoping to receive the same concessions

---

antiguo, y presente de sus sillas, con varias dissertaciones criticas, ed. E. Flórez *et al.* (Madrid, 1754–1879), p. 29, and pp. 476–477; P. Kehr, *Das Papsttum und der Katalanische Prinzipat bis zur Vereinigung mit Aragon*, (Berlin, 1928), pp. 56–57.

[39]   Little is known of Boso's activity as legate while in Aragon-Navarre. P. Kehr, "El Papado y los reinos de Navarra y Aragón hasta mediados del siglo xii," *Estudios de Edad Media de la Corona de Aragón* 2 (1946), p. 151. *Cartulaire de l'abbaye d'Uzerche*, ed. J.B. Champeval (Paris, 1901), p. 1038. Boso seems to have had some success in the region: a charter from Vigeois records that four knights went to Spain. *Cartulaire de l'abbaye de Vigeois en Limousin (954–1167)*, ed. M. de Montégut (Limoges, 1907), p. 220.

[40]   R. Somerville, *The Councils of Urban II: I, Decreta Claromontensia*, Annuarium Historiae Conciliorum: Supplementum I (Amsterdam, 1972), p. 74.

Ramon Berenguer had received from Pascal II. The pope responded by absolving from penance those already engaged in freeing the bishop's see from Muslim occupation. He did not grant the bishop the authority to bestow the cross on participants. Instead, the pope offered "remission and indulgence of their sins" to those who labored in "the service of the Lord" and to those who contributed both physically and financially to the repair of the Church of Saragossa.[41] The value of the remission of sins promised by the pope depended upon the quality and quantity of service provided. Gelasius II directed the participants to their local bishops who were to decide how much penance was to be forgiven.

Some scholars have suggested that Gelasius's grant was actually a confirmation of a crusade indulgence granted by Paschal II sometime between 1116 and his death on 21 January 1118, in connection with Ramon Berenguer's plans for Tortosa.[42] The strongest piece of evidence in favor of this interpretation is that despite the failure of the proposed expedition, Cardinal Boso's legatine commission to Spain continued. When the goal of Tortosa fell through the legate may well have been convinced by the bishops of southern France and Aragón-Navarre that Saragossa was an acceptable alternative. He later would gain a reputation as the man responsible for the liberation of Majorca and Saragossa, though it is not entirely clear that the legate was present at the siege of the latter.[43] There is little to suggest from the pope's letter itself, however, that this was a confirmation or reissue of an earlier order. The grant itself is clearly addressed to those already engaged in the siege, as well as "to all the Christian faithful;" it was likely to have been intended primarily as a local recruiting tool.[44]

It remains uncertain how the siege of Saragossa should be classified. Was it a crusade or a "penitential war" of the sort blessed by Urban prior to 1095?[45] Those who favor seeing this as a crusade note that participants in the conquest were granted a remission of sins, a benefit that soldiers fighting the Muslims

---

[41]   Gelasius II, "Epistolae et Privilegia," *Patrologiae Cursus Completus. Series Latina*, comp. J.P. Migne, 217 vols. and 4 vols. of indexes (Paris, 1841–64),163, p. 508. The novelty of this grant was remarked upon by J. Goñi Gaztambide in *Historia de la bula de la cruzada en España* (Vitoria, 1958), pp. 76–77. See also, *Documentos*, 1, pp. 67–69.

[42]   M. Bull, *Knightly Piety and the Lay Response to the First Crusade. The Limousin and Gascony, c.970 – c.1130* (Oxford, 1993), p. 108; Goñi Gaztambide, *Hisoria*, pp. 68–70; Stalls, *Possessing the Land*, pp. 37–38.

[43]   *La Chronique de Morigny (1095–1152)*, ed. L. Mirot, Collection de texts pur server à l'étude et à l'enseignement de l'histoire 41 (Paris, 1909), p. 33.

[44]   Bull, *Knightly Piety*, pp. 108–09. Gelasius II wrote "*exercitui Christianorum civitatem Caesaraugustanam obsidenti, et omnibus catholicae fidei cultoribus*" in "Epistolae," p. 508; Stalls, *Possessing the Land*, pp. 39–40.

[45]   In 1089 Urban II exhorted the Catalans to rebuild Tarragona. They were granted a remission of sins. Mansilla, *Documentación pontificia*, pp. 46–53.

of al-Andalus prior to 1095 had not been awarded.[46] It is also true that the army Alfonso assembled was international in the same way crusade hosts were. Knights from France, some of whom had participated in the First Crusade, were the first to reach the walls of Saragossa in May 1118, even before the arrival of the king.[47] Whether or not their arrival there can be attributed in some part to Cardinal Boso's attempt the previous year to recruit soldiers from southern France for the expedition to Tortosa is not known for certain. What is clear is that some recruitment for the Tortosa or a comparable campaign was taking place in the border regions of France at this time. At a council held at Toulouse in May 1118 a grant of a remission of penance for those who undertook the *via Hispania* or "road to Spain" was confirmed by a number of French and Spanish bishops.[48] However, many of those who appear before the walls of Saragossa were linked with Aragon and its king by ties of kinship or political alliance, which might better explain their participation.[49] Gaston IV of Béarn, for example, was Alfonso I's cousin by marriage; Bernard Ató of Carcassone was a vassal.[50] Moreover, neither Alfonso I, nor the men who accompanied him, assumed the cross in advance of this expedition or while undertaking the siege at Saragossa; nor, so far as we can tell were they expected to do so by the pope or other senior churchmen.[51] Neither the remission of sins offered by the Council of Toulouse, nor that granted by Gelasius II required a vow of its recipients. In the case of Gelasius, the indulgence was retrospective and applied equally to those who fought at Saragossa as well as those who contributed financially to the restoration of the city and Church – a feature not yet found in the crusading

---

[46]   Gelasius II, "Epistolae," p. 508; Bull, *Knightly Piety*, pp. 70–86.

[47]   Amongst those who had participated in the First Crusade were two Gascon nobles, Gaston IV of Béarn and his brother-in-law, Centullo of Bigorre. According to the sole surviving narrative account of the conquest, dating from the sixteenth century, the French forces were in Aragon in mid May. Alfonso I reached Saragossa in late May or June when the city was already under siege. J. Zurita, *Anales de la Corona de Aragón*, ed. A.C. López, vol. 1, 2nd edn. (Saragossa, 1976), Bk 1, c. 44.

[48]   "*Tholose fuit concilium in quo confirmata est via de Hispania*" in *La Chronique de Saint-Maxient 751–1140*, ed. J. Verdon (Paris, 1979), p. 186; D.W. Lomax, *The Reconquest of Spain* (London, 1978), pp. 83–84; J. F. O'Callaghan, *Reconquest and Crusade in Medieval Spain* (Philadelphia, 2003), pp. 36–38; Riley-Smith, *Crusades*, p. 89. Cf. Bull, *Knightly Piety*, p. 109; Stalls, *Possessing the Land*, p. 37.

[49]   Bull, *Knightly Piety*, p. 93. J. De Jaurgain, *La Vasconie*, 2 vols. (Pau, 1898–1902), 2, p. 249, and 546.

[50]   Stalls, *Possessing the Land*, p. 21, and 38.

[51]   Orderic Vitalis, *Historia Æcclesiastica*, 6, p. 396.

effort.[52] It is best, therefore, to see this particular undertaking as representing an intermediary stage in the process by which the *reconquista* takes on not only the appearance and rhetoric associated with the crusade, but the actual mechanisms of the crusade as well. Nevertheless, it is important to recognize that a number of prominent participants, in particular Alfonso I, would later come to portray the siege of Saragossa as a crusade-like endeavor, if not actually a crusade.[53] That it was not a "crusade" may simply be attributable to the intransigence of Gelasius II, who while willing to grant spiritual rewards for participation in this worthy struggle, refused to recognize it as a full-fledged crusade. After all, Saragossa had nothing to do with Jerusalem.

The events of 1119 would prove differently. On the 29 January Gelasius II died. His successor, Calixtus II (1119–1124), was more receptive to the idea of a Spanish crusade.[54] In the autumn of this first year of his pontificate, pleas for aid came to both the pope and Domenico Michel, the doge of Venice, from the king of Jerusalem after Prince Roger of Antioch and a great many other Christians of the Latin Kingdom had been killed at the Battle of the Field of Blood in June. The immediate response of the pope was to urge the Venetians and others "to hasten, instructed by faith, to help the faithful of Christ."[55] News of this catastrophe also reached the Iberian Peninsula. Patriarch Gormond of Jerusalem wrote to Diego Gelmírez, the archbishop of Compostela in 1120, informing him of the dire circumstances faced by the Christians living in Outremer and asked the bishop for aid, knowing that, "you will be moved in the depths of your heart by the unrivalled burden of the knights; they are, alas, so few!"[56] It was clear to one and

---

[52]   In 1157 Pope Adrian IV was the first pope to grant an indulgence to those who provided material support for the "liberation of the Holy Land." Adrian IV, "Papae epistolae," *RHGF*, 15, pp. 681–682.

[53]   According to the author of a charter at St. Seurin in Bordeaux dated to around 1120 Amalvin de Blanquefort was "exalting the Christian faith by going against the pagans" where he and Gaston of Béarn hoped "to seize Spain." *Cartulaire de l'église collégiale Saint-Seurin de Bordeaux*, ed. J.-A. Brutails (Bordeaux, 1897), p. 40.

[54]   Four of Calixtus II's brothers had participated in the First Crusade. M. Stroll, "New Perspectives on the Struggle between Guy of Vienne and Henry V," *Archivum Historiae Pontificiae* 18 (1980), p. 105. J. Riley-Smith, *The First Crusaders, 1095–1131* (Cambridge, 1998), pp. 81–104.

[55]   Calixtus preached the crusade in the autumn of 1119. "Documents pour l'histoire de Saint Hilaire de Poitiers," ed. L. Rédet in *Memoires de la société des antiquaries de l'Ouest* (1847), p. 122, and 128; "Chronicon Altinate," ed. A. Rossi in *Archivo Storico Italiano*, 8 (Florence, 1845), p. 153; "Historia Ducum Veneticorum," ed. H. Simonsfeld, *MGH SS* 14, p. 73; Riley-Smith, "The Venetian Crusade of 1122–24," pp. 339–350.

[56]   J. Richard, "Quelques texts sur les priemiers temps de l'Eglise latine de Jerusalem," *Recueil de travaux offerts á M. Clovis Brunel* (Paris, 1955), 2, pp. 427–428.

all that Jerusalem was once again in need of assistance, though the threat from the Murabitun in Spain had not diminished.

At some point in the period between 1119 and 1123 three developments of some consequence occurred. First, Ramon Berenguer had made his intentions to take Lérida and Tortosa transparent enough that the Murabitun were paying him tribute so as to be able to focus on the threat offered by Aragón.[57] Secondly, a connection between the Aragonese conquest of the Ebro River Valley and Jerusalem was forged. In other words, the idea circulated that Alfonso's conquest of cities like Lérida and Fraga would allow Christians to liberate the pilgrimage route to Jerusalem. This grasp of geography surprises us, perhaps, though it makes sense when considering the means of travel prevalent in the twelfth century. The capture of a Mediterranean port – such as Tortosa – would allow for Spanish pilgrims to sail to the Holy Land without the expense and danger of an overland journey to such ports as Marseilles or those on the Italian coast. The purpose of the efforts to expand Aragonese control over this region was framed in religious rhetoric rather than political or dynastic terms. Alfonso I was not just conquering territory for Aragón he was opening the pilgrimage route to Jerusalem – a goal all of Christendom could get behind. The purpose of the royal expedition into the Ebro Valley was not the only thing to shift in this period; so too was the nature of the campaign itself.

In the aftermath of the Battle of the Field of Blood when Pope Calixtus II summoned the Venetians (and from, subsidiary evidence, those living in France) to take up the cross and aid their Eastern brothers, he also called upon Spanish knights to take the cross. The crusade must originally have been proclaimed in Spain prior to April 1123, perhaps at the same time (July 1121) the Venetians were encouraged to travel to the East – though our evidence is from the later date.[58] Writing to Oleguer, the archbishop of Tarragona and papal legate for the crusade in Spain, as well as to the "bishops, kings, counts, princes and other faithful of God" Calixtus II granted a remission of sins – identical to that promised to those crusading in the East – to whoever took up the cross in defense of the Spanish Church.[59] In doing so, the pope did what no pope had done previously. He called for a crusade to be fought in Spain as well as in the Holy Land, fully extending the mechanisms of crusading into the Iberian

---

57   Stalls, *Possessing the Land*, pp. 45–46.

58   *Conciliorum oecumenicorum decreta*, ed. G. Alberigo et al., 3rd edn. (Bologna, 1973), p. 192. Crusaders from other parts of Western Europe were still departing for the East in spring 1123. Cosmos of Prague, "Chronica Boemorum," ed. D. Köpke, *MGH SS*, 9, p. 125.

59   *Bullaire du Pape Calixte II*, 2, p. 454.

Peninsula for the first time.[60] His intention was confirmed on 2 April 1123 at the First Lateran Council in Rome where Calixtus "graciously grant[ed] to those fighting firmly on this expedition the same remission of sins that we conceded to the defenders of the eastern Church."[61]

That these three developments are interrelated cannot be doubted. In reaction to the threat to his plan to expand into the lower reaches of the Ebro Valley, Alfonso I was in the market for a way to gain the upper hand. Having his expedition recognized as a crusade would do just that. However, for Alfonso and others, including the previous pope, the crusade was still an activity directed towards the pilgrimage to Jerusalem. Only by tying the efforts in Spain to Jerusalem, and perhaps more importantly, to the pilgrimage to Jerusalem could the mechanisms of crusading be extended to the Iberian Peninsula. This is precisely what was achieved in the period between 1119 and (at the very latest) 1123.

It is not entirely certain whether the idea of associating the conflicts in Aragón with the pilgrimage route to Jerusalem originated with the king himself or with those who counseled him. It was unlikely to have been dreamt up by Calixtus II. Aside from the First Crusade, all the "crusades" of the early twelfth century were launched in *reaction* to lay or clerical initiatives. Paschal II, for example, gave his blessing to Bohemond's Crusade, the Balearic expedition, and to the planned attack on Tortosa. All of these expeditions were in the planning stage well before the pope came on the scene. The same was true of the crusade called by Calixtus II in 1119–21. His call to arms was made only after the king of Jerusalem had asked him for help in the aftermath of the Battle of the Field of Blood. More than likely, therefore, the pope's support of the efforts in Spain came at the behest of Alfonso I, who would have explained to the pope that his expedition was substantively similar to that being undertaken by the French and Venetians, and thus worthy of the same reward.

The fusion of the Ebro and Jerusalem may have been the brainchild of Alfonso's cousin, Gaston IV of Béarn, who had participated in the First Crusade and was part of the force that took Saragossa in 1118.[62] We know that Gaston was influential in inspiring Alfonso to establish Spanish military order at Monreal

---

[60]   For Calixtus II's vision of the crusade see Y. Katzir, "The Second Crusade and the Redefinition of *Ecclesia, Christianitas*, and Papal Coercive Power," *The Second Crusade and the Cistercians*, ed. M. Gervers (New York, 1992), pp. 3–12.

[61]   Calixtus II, *Bullaire*, pp. 266–267; *Crusades: Idea and Reality*, p. 73.

[62]   Riley-Smith, *First Crusaders*, p. 206. Alfonso I granted Gaston IV of Béarn the lordship of Saragossa. He would hold it until his death in 1130. *Documentos para el studio de la Reconquista*, 1, p. 57, and 59.

del Campo in 1128.[63] Gaston had returned from the crusade interested in promoting pilgrimage.[64] He also was inclined, most notably in the later stages of his life, to portray his efforts in Aragon as similar to those he had undertaken in the Levant. In 1127 Gaston founded the abbey of Sauvelade, before journeying to Spain "in order to subjugate the Saracens."[65]

Whoever it was who first enunciated the idea, it was someone who remembered that the penance associated with the liberation of the Holy Land had been tied to the completion of a pilgrimage to Jerusalem. As this awareness also underlies the provisions of spiritual benefits granted to the brothers of the Belchite Confraternity, the majority of which were associated with the rewards traditionally granted to pilgrims, it seems somewhat safe to assume that this conception of the impending struggle against the Murabitun was birthed at the Aragonese court after the experiences with Gelasius II regarding Saragossa. It may have been an idea brewing for some time among a group that had vivid memories of the First Crusade. The cross did not just mark one out as a soldier of Christ, but also as a pilgrim traveling to the Holy Sepulchre.[66] Thus, Alfonso ordered the knights who joined the Belchite Confraternity to wear palms rather than crosses.[67] Presumably the adoption of the palm (a symbol of the completed pilgrimage to Jerusalem) was intended a way to both associate the brothers at Belchite with the opening up the pilgrimage route via Spain to Jerusalem and yet differentiate them from other individuals involved in similar tasks.[68] After all, the brothers were not promising to travel to Jerusalem. They were vowing to serve Christ and to protect Christians in the vicinity of Belchite instead of going on pilgrimage. However, the same could not be said for Alfonso I and the Aragonese and French knights who adorned themselves with crosses in the early 1120s.

Though he had not participated in the First Crusade, the Battler embraced its memory in carrying out the conquest of the lands to his south. From 1121 until his death in 1134 Alfonso I fought a perpetual crusade against his Murabitun neighbors. In 1122 he founded the Belchite Confraternity

---

[63]   "*auxilio vice comitis Gastonis*" in *Colección diplomatica de Alfonso I de Aragón y Pamplona (1104–1134)*, ed. J. Ángel and L. Pueyo (San Sebastián, 1990), no.173.

[64]   Bull, *Knightly Piety*, pp. 100–101.

[65]   P. de Marca, *Histoire de Béarn* (Paris, 1640), p. 421. A similar idea is expressed in a charter mentioning Gaston which is dated to 1120. See, *Cartulaire de l'église collégiale Saint-Seurin de Bordeaux*, n. 40.

[66]   "Historia peregrinorum euntium Jerusolymam," RHC Oc. 3, pp. 169–170.

[67]   Orderic Vitalis, *Historia Æcclesiastica*, 6, p. 400.

[68]   Fulcher of Chartres, *Historia*, pp. 318, 322, and 334; William of Tyre, *Chronicon*, ed. R.B.C. Huygens, 2 parts, CCCM 63, 63A (Turnhout, 1986), pp. 983–984.

to protect his southeastern frontier and in 1123, frustrated in his attempt to secure Lérida, Alfonso I renewed efforts along his southern borders, between the Jiloca and Guadolope Rivers. In the winter of 1125–26 the king led a raid into southern Spain, which attempted to take Granada and Malaga. After winning a substantial victory over the Muslims at Lucena in March 1126, the king returned to Saragossa accompanied by, some contemporaries say, thousands of Mozarabic Christians whom he settled in the Ebro Valley.[69] This journey is interesting for what it tells us about how Alfonso saw his obligations as a crusader and reflects his understanding of what his vow entailed. The vows taken in 1095–96 consisted of a promise to help liberate Jerusalem and to complete a pilgrimage to the Holy Sepulchre. What is unclear about the vow taken by Alfonso I is whether or not it consisted of a promise to "open the way to Jerusalem" or to complete a pilgrimage to the same city. All we do know is that in 1125 the king, bypassing the Almoravid-controlled Teruel, Valencia, and Murcia, marched straight for the coastal fortresses of Granada and Malaga. At the latter, Alfonso sailed out in a boat, made a speech and then returned to shore. Perhaps he was showing that he had completed his vow to "open the way to the same Sepulchre of the Lord through Spain."[70]

Later events would demonstrate that Alfonso I either did not believe he had fulfilled the obligation he had assumed in 1121, or else took the cross for a second time at some later date. In 1134, when the king led his army against the city of Fraga, Orderic Vitalis wrote that the inhabitants "feared both the anger and unconquerable determination of the magnificent prince [Alfonso I] and the armies of the Christians, who wore the cross of Christ."[71] The cross obviously denoted a larger obligation than just taking the city of Fraga.[72] There is no evidence that the papacy had issued another call to crusade in Spain in this period, though that may have not been entirely necessary as the victories of 1125

[69]　*Chronique de Saint-Maxient*, pp. 188–190; Orderic Vitalis, *Historia Æcclesiastica*, 6, pp. 404–407; *Colección diplomatica de Alfonso*, pp. 138–410.

[70]　It is reported that the Christians of Granada had invited Alfonso to join them in overthrowing the Almoravids. The king set out on 2 September 1125 accompanied by 4,000 knights and 15,000 foot soldiers. Ibn Abī Zar`, *Rawd al-Qirtas*, trans. A.H. Miranda, 2 vols (Valencia, 1964), 1, pp. 316–18; Ibn Khaldūn, *Histoire des Berbères et des dynasties musulmanes de l'Afrique septentrionale*, trans. B. de Slane, 4 vols. (Paris, 1852–56), 2, p. 83; Al-Maqqarī, *The History of the Mohammedan Dynasties in Spain*, trans. P. de Gayangos, 2 vols. (London, 1840–1843), 2, pp. 303–304; Ibn `Idhār, *Al-Bayan al-Mugrib: Neuvis framentos almorávides y almohades*, trans. A.H. Miranda, 2 vols. (Valencia, 1963), pp. 160–168; *Al-Hulal al-Mawshiyya: Crónica árabe de las dinastás almorávide, almohade, y benimerín*, trans. A.H. Miranda (Teután, 1951), pp. 108–115; *Historia Compostellana*, p. 379.

[71]　Orderic Vitalis, *Historia Æcclesiastica*, 6, p. 410.

[72]　Orderic Vitalis, *Historia Æcclesiastica*, 6, p. 410.

had not lasted and so the pilgrimage route was not yet secured. It is my belief that Alfonso I, like many contemporaries, believed a crusade vow would only be complete when the crusader reached Jerusalem. That in ten years of fighting under the cross he had neither succeeded in opening up the western route to Jerusalem nor traveled to the Holy Sepulchre would, therefore, have weighed heavily on his conscience.

This supposition may go some way towards explaining the provisions of his unusual will. With no immediate heirs, Alfonso I willed that the rule of his kingdom should pass to the Templars, the Hospitallers, and to the canons of the Holy Sepulchre in Jerusalem.[73] There are many theories as to why the king did this.[74] But among them it should be considered that Alfonso I's decision to grant a portion of Aragón and Navarre to the order of Holy Sepulchre was intended as insurance in the case that he might not live to see his crusade vow completed.[75] Alfonso I's approach to the *reconquista* was original. No one – not Urban II, Paschal II or the myriad of Spaniards who took the cross for the First Crusade or were engaged in wars of conquest with their Muslim neighbors – prior to 1118 believed that they were traveling on the road to the earthly Jerusalem. The liberation of Jerusalem and the liberation of Spain were believed to be similar, but they were not the same. Alfonso used the memory of the First Crusade to show the ecclesiastical hierarchy (it is presumed by the pope's endorsement of this plan) as well as the laity, that the project whose stated purpose was to free the port cities of the Ebro River was, in fact, the *same* as the expedition which had set out for the East in 1096 and so, it was surely worthy of being designated a "crusade." As in the case of the German monk comparing the Slavic Church to Jerusalem in 1107, one campaign was compared to another. However, the similarities were more than just a rhetorical tool. Instead, the campaigns undertaken by Alfonso I actually mimicked the First Crusade by having as a goal the pilgrimage to Jerusalem. Their success in promoting this vision can be seen at a council held at Compostela in January 1125, where Archbishop Diego

---

[73]   *Colección diplomatica de Alfonso I*, pp. 356–8.

[74]   A.J. Forey, "The Will of Alfonso I of Aragón and Navarre," *Durham University Journal* 73 (1980), 59–65; E. Lourie, "The Will of Alfonso I, el Batalldor, King of Aragon and Navarre: A Reassessment" and "The Will of Alfonso I of Aragon and Navarre: A Reply to Dr. Forey" in her *Crusade and Colonisation: Muslims, Christians and Jews in Medieval Aragon* (Aldershot, 1990) III and IV.

[75]   Alfonso I drew up his will at the siege of Bayonne in 1131. Stalls, *Possessing the Land*, p. 55. For a similar understanding of how giving property in the West to orders based in the Holy Land, and especially those associated with the Holy Sepulchre, might serve as a way in which to fulfill a crusade vow see, N. Jaspert, "*Capta est Dertosa, clavis Christianorum*: Tortosa and the Crusades," *The Second Crusade: Scope and Consequences*, ed. J. Phillips and M. Hoch (Manchester, 2001), p. 90.

Gelmírez, a close friend of Cardinal Boso and a protégé of Calixtus II – but no ally of Alfonso, summoned those present, upon the orders of the pope, to take up arms against the Muslims. For,

> just as the knights of Christ and the faithful sons of the Church opened the way to Jerusalem with much labor and spilling of blood, so we should become knights of Christ, and after defeating his wicked enemies, the Muslims, open the way to the same Sepulchre of the Lord through Spain which is shorter and much less laborious.[76]

On the surface it appears to be a short-lived victory. After the deaths of Calixtus II in 1124 and Alfonso I in 1134, little effort was made to cast the struggles in the Iberian Peninsula as crusades until Alfonso-Henriques of Portugal approached Bernard of Clairvaux in 1145–46.[77] Instead, Alfonso's eventual successor to Aragón – Ramon Berenguer IV, count of Barcelona – tried another approach to counter the Murabitun advances after the Battler's defeat at Fraga. Looking for a more permanent solution, he invited the Templars to settle and hold territory in the Ebro Basin.[78] While contemporaries continued to see the battles fought by Christians in Iberia as acts of devotion comparable to the performance of penance undertaken by crusaders, those who fought in these battles did not take the cross for them. Although the premise behind pursuing the two conflicts was believed to be equal, Spaniards did not generally feel comfortable assuming the cross in connection with the battles they fought against their neighbors unless specifically urged to do so by the pope and unless they had at their end the goal of a pilgrimage to Jerusalem. There were no doubt a variety of reasons for their reluctance to wholeheartedly adopt the cross once it had made its way to Spain, but I believe chief among them was the memory of the First Crusade, and now the memory of the Battler. The way in which these events were remembered

---

[76]   *Historia Compostellana*, ed. E. Falque Rey, CCCM 70 (Turnhout, 1988), p. 379.

[77]   *De Expugnatione Lyxbonenis:The Conquest of Lisbon*, ed. and trans. C.W. David (New York, 1948), p. 78.

[78]   In 1134 the count of Barcelona and a group of Catalan nobles tried to involve the Templars in Iberian politics by promising to serve with the knights for a year and to provide equipment and land to support ten brother knights. Both the promised military service and the grant of land were in Catalonia *Colección de documentos inéditos de Archivo General de la Corona de Aragón*, 4, pp. 32–33; M. d'Albon, *Cartulaires general de l'Ordre du Temple* (Paris, 1913), pp. 53–55. The Templars displayed a real reluctance to involve themselves in the struggle against the Muslim inhabitants of Spain. As permanent "crusaders" they believed their military duties to be restricted to the environs of the Holy Sepulchre. Not until 1143 was the Temple successfully dragged into the struggle against the Moors. A.J. Forey, *The Templars in the Corona de Aragón* (London, 1973), pp. 2–16

continued to influence the way in which contemporaries imagined activities associated with the cross. Jerusalem remained a central feature of the idea of crusading. Alfonso I, therefore, succeeded in importing, but not transforming, an activity originally conceived of as an armed pilgrimage to liberate Jerusalem into a different arena. It is not until the memory of Jerusalem fades that the Iberian "crusade" will come to exist in its own right.

Chapter 6

Crucesignatus: A Refinement or Merely One More Term among Many?

Walker Reid Cosgrove
Saint Louis University

A definition of the crusades upon which all can agree still eludes historians of the crusades. Most find a home in one of two definitions: either the single-minded focus on Jerusalem of the traditionalist school, or the broader definition of the pluralist.[1] Michael Markowski attempts to more clearly define the crusades in his article "*Crucesignatus*: Its Origins and Early Usage."[2] In this article, he traces the origins and development of the term *crucesignatus*.[3] Through this term he believes that historians can more clearly and definitively define the crusades, especially those crusades which took place during Innocent III's pontificate.[4] According to Markowski, Innocent purposely relied more heavily upon the term *crucesignatus* in order to more clearly define the crusades, in comparison with those who preceded him. It should be noted that Innocent's successors would not continue this policy, but rather follow in line with Innocent's predecessors. This paper will examine Innocent III's usage of the term *crucesignatus* to ascertain

---

[1]   A classic example of the traditionalist school is Han Eberhard Mayer, *The Crusades*, trans. John Gillingham (Oxford, 1972), pp. 283–84, and 286. The greatest proponent of the pluralist school is Jonathan Riley-Smith, *What Were the Crusades?* 3rd edn. (San Francisco, 2002), pp. xi–xii, and 2–4. Giles Constable clearly lays out the various definitions of the crusades, including the above two, Giles Constable, "The Historiography of the Crusades," in Laiou, A.E. and R.P. Mottahedeh, *The Crusades from the Perspective of Byzantium and the Muslim World* (Washington D.C., 2001). Another attempt to better define the crusades with a specific focus on the papacy is E.O. Blake, "The Formation of the 'Crusade Idea'," *Journal of Ecclesiastical History*, 21 no. 1 (January 1970), pp. 30–31.

[2]   Michael Markowski, "*Crucesignatus*: Its Origins and Early Usage," *Journal of Medieval History*, 10 (1984).

[3]   In this article Markowski clearly describes lineage of *crucesignatus*, as the combination of two words, the noun *crux* and the verb *signare* to become "a person signed by the cross," Markowski, "*Crucesignatus*," 157.

[4]   Ibid., "*Crucesignatus*," 157.

his policies with regard to the crusades, and whether or not it is appropriate to focus so intently upon one term.

Markowski begins by showing that *crucesignatus* was not used to describe a crusader until the end of the twelfth century. Even so, contemporaries did not lack terms to describe crusaders and the crusades; he discusses a handful of the more common terms, especially those that appear before the twelfth century. It is well known that the earliest and most popular terms were those centered upon pilgrimage, as Urban II connected the piety of crusade with the piety of pilgrimage in his preaching of the first crusade. Pilgrimage, however, was not the only way contemporaries described the crusades. Another set of terms they utilized centered on the crusader's taking of the cross, which became increasingly more common as time passed, and which ultimately resulted in *crucesignatus*. Finally, Markowski groups together other phrases that the papacy used to describe crusaders, such as army of God, soldier of Christ, or even the "Franks." He argues that this third group of phrases is ambiguous because they could refer to other types of people, other military action, or even non-military personnel such as monks. As a result "of their ambiguity they did little to define the crusade."[5] Yet for whom do these terms "do little to define the crusades," the contemporaries or the historian writing a millennium later? This question is especially pertinent with regard to an activity as familiar to the medieval landscape as the crusades.[6]

After his review of common terms for the crusades, Markowski argues that "the terminology that employed the symbolism of the cross increased in frequency of use and culminated in the clearest of medieval terms for crusaders, *crucesignatus*." Again, it is important to note that it might be the clearest of medieval terms for the historian, but not necessarily for the contemporary. Markowski demonstrates that terminology associated with the cross was used from the beginning in Urban II's call for the First Crusade.[7] While *crucesignatus* was not yet used, terminology related to the cross became the dominant,

---

    5   Ibid., "*Crucesignatus*," pp. 157–58. To this list of terms Riley-Smith includes *bellum sacrum* (holy war), *passagium generale* (general passage), *expeditio crucis* (expedition of the Cross), and *negotium Jhesu Christi* (the business of Jesus Christ). See Riley-Smith, *What*, p. 2. Markowski also argues that the distinction between a crusader and an unarmed pilgrim remained blurred until the term *crucesignatus* came into use. See Markowski, "*Crucesignatus*," p. 157 and James Brundage, *Medieval Canon Law and the Crusader* (Madison, 1969), p. 15.

    6   Cf. Riley-Smith, *What*, p. 2.

    7   Markowski, "*Crucesignatus*," p. 158; for Urban II see *Patrologiae latinae cursus completus*, ed. J.-P. Migne, 221 vols, Paris 1844–64 (PL), p. 151: 485.

although not the only, form to describe the crusades and crusaders.[8] Markowski illustrates this growing dependence upon terminology related to the cross as subsequent popes used it to couch their call to crusade. Pope Eugenius III utilized it in order to call the Second Crusade and the Baltic Crusade. Pope Alexander III continued to utilize traditional pilgrimage terminology, but also adopted terminology of the cross. Finally, Pope Gregory VIII employed both traditional pilgrimage terms and phrases related to the cross in his call for the Third Crusade.[9] The term *crucesignatus* came into general use after the Third Crusade commenced; however, Innocent III was the first pope to use the term frequently.[10] Finally, Markowski briefly demonstrates that Innocent's immediate successors, Popes Honorius III, Gregory IX, and Innocent IV all used the term *crucesignatus* with gradually more frequency in reference to crusades in all theaters. Markowski, thus, successfully traces the development and increase in usage of the term *crucesignatus* from the onset of the crusades through the thirteenth century.[11]

The crux of Markowski's argument, however, regards Innocent's use of *crucesignatus*; that by tracing Innocent's use of the term, it is possible to more sharply define the crusades. Markowski demonstrates that Innocent often couched the Fourth, Fifth, and Albigensian Crusades in the term *crucesignatus*, while he did not rely upon it with regard to the crusades to the Baltic, the Spanish *reconquista*, or the political crusade against Markward in Sicily. Consequently, Markowski argues, Innocent refined the definition of crusade so as to remove the latter three campaigns from consideration. Before we accept, however, this word as the litmus test for crusade, a more thorough look into Innocent's correspondence is necessary to determine if it is appropriate to do so.[12]

If we are to derive a definition of crusade from papal letters, it would be prudent to consider their nature. Markowski explains that he relies upon Innocent's "official correspondence." Since, he implicitly reasons, Innocent wrote the letters they are a useful vehicle to better understand how Innocent himself

---

[8]   Markowski, "*Crucesignatus*," p. 158. James Brundage argues that terms centered on pilgrimage were still popular even after terms centered on the *crux* began to be used, Brundage, *Medieval Canon Law*, p. 31.

[9]   Markowski, "*Crucesignatus*," p. 159; for Eugenius III, PL 180: 1065, 180: 1320, 180: 1203–04, for Alexander III, PL 200: 600–01, and for Gregory VIII, PL 202: 1542, PL 204: 216.

[10]   Markowski, "*Crucesignatus*," p. 160–61.

[11]   Ibid., p. 163.

[12]   Markowski, "*Crucesignatus*," p.163; Riley-Smith argues against this notion of focusing in on one term to define the crusades when he writes, "There was no one term consistently used to describe a crusade or its participants," see Riley-Smith, *What*, p. 2.

understood crusading. The importance of these letters is not in question; however, it is also important to remember that they have their limitations. In most cases it is difficult to differentiate between letters written by the pope himself and those generated in the curia for his approval. During Innocent's pontificate an enormous number of letters were produced each year – far more than currently survive in the register. Given that level of production it is difficult to believe that the pope could have examined every word in every document. This complicates any attempt to uncover Innocent's underlying thought based on word choices since it is impossible to know if the language was his, or simply words selected by other officials in the chancery.[13] As Damian Smith writes, "Words taken out of context in a single letter can be used to distort the thought-process of the pope."[14] Of course it is unlikely that his officials and scribes would be much greatly out of tune with Innocent's own thought.[15] Yet rather than focusing on word choices in a few letters, it is crucial to examine the entire contents of all surviving letters regarding crusades during his pontificate. Such an analysis will lead to two main conclusions. First, it seems inappropriate to focus so upon one word in order to ascertain Innocent's policies with regard to the crusades. Second, high frequency of use does not necessarily mean Innocent was focusing in on one term.

Innocent first used the term *crucesignatus* by early December 1199 and by 1202 he utilized it on a regular basis.[16] Thus, it is important to look at the

---

13   Cheney argues that any well-trained curial clerk could have composed the letters, particularly those in the registers. He goes on to discuss the difficulties in distinguishing those written by the hand of Innocent, and those written by his staff when he writes, "At the same time, we must squarely face the facts that there is no positive proof of the pope's drafting of any particular letter and that we cannot hope to distinguish clearly between those which he wrote and those written by high officials of the Curia who shared his views and his intellectual background, and acted under his orders and influence," Cheney, "The Letters," pp. 28–29, and 33.

14   Damian Smith, *Innocent III and the Crown of Aragon: The Limits of Papal Authority*, Church, Faith and Culture in the Medieval West (Aldershot, 2004), p. 7. See also C.R. Cheney, "The Letters of Innocent III," in C.R. Cheney, *Medieval Texts and Studies* (Oxford, 1973). Connected with this thought, Cheney writes, "It is not always remembered that these papal letters were not for the most part set treatises on the nature of political authority or anything of that sort; they were occasional statements adapted to the correspondents and to the circumstances," Cheney, "The Letters," p. 27.

15   Smith, *Innocent III*, p. 7. Cheney discusses the importance of knowing how these letters were composed and understanding the chancery's conventions, Cheney, "The Letters," p. 27–28.

16   Markowski indicates some of the confusion regarding the dating of when Innocent first used the term *crucesignatus*. He reveals that the first time it appears in the PL is at 214: 809, but that same letter in *Die Register* and the Vatican Register of Innocent (Reg. Vat. 4, f. cciiii) both have the term split: *cruce signatos*. Markowski explains that the PL incorrectly

terminology Innocent used before December 1199 in his call for the Fourth Crusade in order to understand how he referred to his first crusade effort and as a comparison with the terminology he used later. Before Innocent utilized *crucesignatus*, he imitated his predecessors in his reliance upon various traditional terms, such as army of Christ, soldiers of Christ, or even the battle of the Lord.[17] He also used the image of defense of the Holy Land, of Christendom, or even the need to avenge the suffering of Christ.[18] While Innocent did rely upon terms associated with the cross, he did not by any means forgo the most traditional of terms: those derived from pilgrimage.[19]

Once having used *crucesignatus*, Innocent employed the term with some frequency with regard to the Fourth Crusade and the crusaders.[20] This does not imply, however, that Innocent was attempting to use *crucesignatus* in order to establish a more specific term by which to describe crusade. Rather it appears that he had a full arsenal of terms from which to draw, and that *crucesignatus* was one term among them. After his call for the Fourth Crusade in December 1199, Innocent relied most heavily upon 5 different phrases or terms which were used

---

joined the two words as *crucesignatos*. While the PL is not the most reliable collection, I still rely upon it most heavily throughout this paper because it is the collection on which Markowski bases his argument. However, there are some letters for the Spanish *reconquista* and the Baltic Crusade that are not in the PL, but can be found in other collections; these are noted below. Also, because it does not make any difference to the findings of this paper, I will consider the letter at PL 214: 809 as the first time Innocent used the term *crucesignatus*, despite the fact that this is probably wrong. Markowski, "*Crucesignatus*," p. 160, he makes reference to PL 214: 1179, 214: 1100, 215: 262, and 214: 809.

[17] *Pedes Christi* – PL 214: 308; *exercitum Domini* – PL 214: 310; *praelium Christi bellandum* – PL 214: 308; *ad militiam sacram proficiscatur* – PL 214: 375.

[18] *Vindicandam injuriam crucifixi* – PL 214: 308; *Ad defensionem terrae nativitatis Dominicae* – PL 214: 308, 214: 310; *ad expugnandam paganorum barbariem* – PL 214: 311; *Ecclesiae Dei defensione* – PL 214: 311, 214: 770. See Riley-Smith's comments about defense of the Holy Land as an indicator of crusade, above note 6.

[19] Language centered on the cross: *Cruces signaculum* – PL 214: 008, 214: 310, 214: 319, 214: 770, *assumpto crucis signaculo* – PL 214: 319, *acceptae crucis* – PL 214: 770, *signum cruces* – PL 214: 770, *nobis vivificae crucis translationem* – PL 214: 308; language centered on pilgrimage: *Fueritis peregrinationis aggressi* – PL 214: 312, *assumptae peregrinationis laborem* – PL 214: 311, *assumptae peregrinationis oblitus* – PL 214: 008. With regard to this terminology see also Brundage, 31 and Riley-Smith, 2. Innocent also provided the traditional remission of sins and the papal protection of property while the crusader was away, *Pro remissione peccatorum* – PL 214: 329, *in remissionem injungimus peccatorum* – PL 214: 385, *et in remissionem tibi injungimus peccatorum quatenus* – PL 214: 329, 214: 385; and *Sub beati Petri et nostra protectione* – PL 214: 311, *apostolicae protectionis* – PL 214: 493.

[20] *Crucesignatus* – PL 214: 809, 214: 1179, 215: 237, 215: 260, 215: 262, 215: 301, 215: 455, 215: 521, 215: 700, 215: 701, and 215: 711.

a total of 122 times in the surviving letters regarding this crusade.[21] Of these, the term *crucesignatus* occurs 20 times – about 16 percent of the time. That percentage places *crucesignatus* fourth in frequency of appearance in Innocent's correspondence. Those terms or phrases that occur more frequently are versions of "soldier of Christ" or "army of the Lord," which appear 25 times, or 21 percent.[22] Terms related to the cross, but not *crucesignatus*, occur 30 times, or 25 percent.[23] Phrases that occur most frequently are those related to the defense of the Church, which appears 32 times, or 26 percent.[24] Just behind *crucesignatus* in frequency are those terms centered upon pilgrimage, which occur 15 times, or 12 percent.[25] In many cases various terms were used interchangeably in the same letter. This suggests that the pope and/or his curia had a cache of terms from which to draw. Rather than focusing more attention on one word or phrase he drew liberally from all of them.[26]

A thorough examination of Innocent's correspondence for the Fifth Crusade – at the end of his pontificate – reveals a similar picture to that of the Fourth Crusade at the beginning. *Crucesignatus* continued to be used frequently, though it does not appear that Innocent's definition had sharpened in reference to the crusades or crusaders by the end of his pontificate.[27] Innocent utilized the same terms and phrases as the Fourth Crusade a total of 58 times for the Fifth Crusade.

---

[21]   This is true also of the other five campaigns that will be discussed below.

[22]   *Exercitum Domini* – PL 214: 829; *bellum Domini* – PL 214: 831, 215: 261, 215: 701; *Christianorum exercitus* – PL 214: 1123, 215: 235; *exercitus Christiani* – PL 214: 1124, 215: 455, 215: 510, 215: 521, 215: 522, 215: 523, 215: 699; *armis Deo* – PL 215: 454; *Christi milites* – 214: 1179.

[23]   *signum crucis* – PL 214: 829, 215: 521, 215: 711; *signum Dominicae crucis assumpserint* – PL 214: 831; *signum crucis assumant* – PL 214: 831; *crucem susceperint* – PL 214: 832; *signaculum crucis assumpserant* – PL 215: 106, 215: 146; *exercitus signatorum* – PL 215: 147, 215: 520; *crucis...assumpsisse* or *accepiunt* – PL 215: 261, 215: 301; 215: 511; *cruce signaculum assumpsissent* – PL 215: 262; *assumpserant signum crucis* – PL 215: 301, 215: 700; *signum crucis acceperent* – PL 215: 301; *exercitus signatorum acceptis* – PL 215: 105.

[24]   *Ad defensionem* – PL 214: 809, 214: 831, 215: 455, 215: 520, 215: 700, 215: 701.

[25]   *peregrinatio* – PL 215: 450, 215: 510, 215: 511, 215: 515, 215: 520, 215: 521, 215: 522, 215: 700, 215: 701.

[26]   Examples of places Innocent seems to use terms interchangeably: PL 214: 1179, 215: 262, 215: 301, 215: 455, 215: 521, 215: 700, 215: 701, 215: 711. Just as before his usage of *crucesignatus*, and similar to those who came before him, Innocent provided papal protection while on crusade, and remission of sins for participation: *Sub beati Petri et nostra protectione* – PL 214: 831, 215: 301, 215: 455, 215: 511; *in remissionem injungimus peccatorum* – PL 214: 809, 214: 831, 215: 66, 215: 107, 215: 455, 215: 522, 215: 711.

[27]   PL 216: 962, 216: 963, 216: 964, 217: 237–38, 217: 239, 217: 240. While Markowski indicates that Innocent used *crucesignatus* often in a certain letter (PL 217: 239–41), he fails to mention that Innocent used the term interchangeably with other traditional forms of

Crucesignatus was hardly used more frequently than other terms related to the cross. The former appears 24 times – 41 percent – while the latter appears 19 times – 32 percent.[28] While this is an increase in frequency when compared to the Fourth Crusade, it is important to note that of the 24 times *crucesignatus* appears in Innocent's correspondence, 20 of them occur in the same letter. Yet that is not the only term he used in that one letter. He also utilized other terminology related to the cross, which appears four times; and even referred to the campaign as a "perfect pilgrimage."[29] Again, similar to the Fourth Crusade, this one letter alone suggests that Innocent utilized these terms interchangeably, rather than an attempt on his part to focus intensely upon one over another. In addition to his use of traditional language centered upon the cross, Innocent also depended on similar terminology as he did in the Fourth Crusade to refer to this crusade and the crusaders. He relied upon language of soldier of Christ and army of the Lord four times – seven percent.[30] The most traditional terms centered upon pilgrimage were used four times – seven percent.[31] He used terms of defense of the Church seven times – 12 percent.[32] In addition to these terms, Innocent twice promised martyrdom to those who died on the crusade.[33]

According to Markowski, the Albigensian Crusade was Innocent's third official crusade. Innocent was concerned about the heresy in Languedoc from the start of his papacy. Following the murder of his papal legate, Innocent formally called a crusade against the heretics in Southern France, and those who supported them, with letters to a number of provinces and to Philip Augustus.[34] *Crucesignatus* does not appear in any of these letters. Innocent instead depended on traditional crusade terminology. These terms included the crusaders as

---

indicating a crusade or crusaders, including *crucem assumpsit* (several times), *peregrinatione*, and *Ecclesiae Dei defensionem.*

[28]   *Crucem assumpserint* – PL 216: 819, 217: 239, 217: 240, *volverint signum crucis* – PL 216: 819, *exercitus Domini cruce signetur* – PL 216: 821, *signo crucis assumpto* – PL 21⁻. 963, *signo crucis* – PL 216: 964, *triumphavit in cruce* – PL 216: 964, *crucem recipiendam accurrerent* – PL 217: 238, *crucem recusaverat* – PL 217: 238, *statim crucem accepit* – PL 217: 238. See Markowski, "*Crucesignatus*," 164, n 8.

[29]   PL 217: 239–40.

[30]   *Dominus restrinxit exercitum* – PL 216: 963, *militent Deo regi* – PL 216: 964, *ad militiam Jesu Christi* – PL 217: 239; *Ecclesiae Dei defensionem* – PL 216: 819, 217: 239.

[31]   PL 216: 963, 217: 240.

[32]   *Ecclesiae Dei defensionem* – PL 216: 819, 217: 239.

[33]   Innocent also provided the traditional remission of sin and papal protection for crusaders: *Remissionis* – PL 216: 818, 963, 217: 241; *sub beati Petri et nostra protectione* – PL 216: 819, 216: 962.

[34]   Smith, *Innocent III*, pp. 79–80; Joseph Strayer, *The Albigensian Crusades* 2nd edn. (Ann Arbor, 1992), p. 52.

soldiers of Christ, as defenders of the church and purifiers of the land of heretics. The pope also provided the customary remission of sins and privilege of papal protection.[35] In the rest of the Innocent's correspondence regarding the Albigensian Crusade, the same variety of terms and phrases to signify that the campaign was a crusade were employed a total of 97 times. Again *crucesignatus* was used often, 17 times, or 18 percent. Similar to the Fourth and Fifth Crusades, however, it was not the only term he used, nor is there any sense that the pope or his curia were attempting to sharpen the terminology for crusade through its use.[36] Innocent freely used other traditional terminology connected with the cross, which occurs 12 times – 12 percent;[37] language centered upon soldiers of Christ or the army of the Lord, which appear 23 times – 24 percent;[38] and the concept of defense of the church, which occurs an astonishing 45 times, or 46 percent.[39]

The gathering of statistics of this sort may seem a bit facile; however, one point can be clearly drawn from this analysis: that an argument built upon the frequency of word use in a medieval papal register does not amount to much. Indeed, if anything it simply confirms what anyone who has read papal correspondence from the time intuitively suspects: that Innocent relied upon a variety of terms to describe what we today call a crusade. *Crucesignatus* occurs often, yet never sufficiently to presume Innocent was attempting to define what was and was not a crusade. Rather, Innocent appears to have used it as one term

---

[35]   PL 215: 1354–58, 215: 1358, 215: 1358–59.

[36]   PL 215: 1469, 215: 1470, 216: 91, 216: 95, 216: 98, 216: 99, 216: 132, 216: 139, 216: 141, 216: 739, 216: 740, 216: 741, 216: 834, 216: 843, 216: 851.

[37]   *Christi signatis* – PL 215: 1546; *cruce signum* – PL 215: 1546, 215: 1469, 215: 1546; *exercitui signatorum* – 215: 1546, 216: 158; *accingant assumpto charactere Crucifixi* – PL 216: 97; *signatorum exercitus* – PL 216: 98; *crucis characterem assumpserunt* – PL 216: 98.

[38]   *Christi milites* – PL 215: 1355, 215: 1358, 215: 1359, 215: 1546, 216: 98; *militiae Christianae* – PL 215: 1359, 215: 1469, 215: 1546; *Christi exercitus* – PL 216: 139, 216: 843, 216: 850, 216: 851; *Dei exercitui* – PL 216: 142; *Domino exercituum* – PL 216: 704, 216: 714; *gladius Dei* – PL 216: 704.

[39]   *Expugnandam haereticum* – PL 215: 1359, 215: 1469, 215: 1546, 216: 141; *pro defensione fidei ortodoxae* – PL 215: 362, 215: 1358, 215: 1469, 216: 99, 216: 159, 216: 843, 216: 850; *contra haereticos* – PL 216: 95. Innocent also provided papal protection and a remission of sins to the crusaders: *sub protectione apostolicae sedis* – PL 215: 1247, 215: 1546; PL 215: 362, 215: 1052, 215: 1247, 215: 1248, 215: 1356, 215: 1358, 215: 1359, 215: 1545, 215: 1469, 215, 1470, 216: 98, 216: 99, 216: 153, 216: 159, 216: 160, 216: 714, 216: 740. It should be noted that Innocent briefly revoked the indulgence for the Albigensian Crusade in his call for the Fifth Crusade, see PL 216: 817–22. However, he reinstates this indulgence with the third canon of the Fourth Lateran Council, see Josepho Alberigo *et al.* *Conciliorum Oecumenicorum Decreta*, 3d edn. Consultante Huberto Jedin (Bologna: Istituto per le scienze religiose, 1973), 233–35.

among many. Given this broader picture, it is difficult to conclude that the absence of this one term in the correspondence regarding the Baltic crusades, the Spanish *reconquista*, and the Sicilian crusade suggests that Innocent believed that they were not crusades.

A look at Innocent's correspondence in reference to the Sicilian crusade reveals the paucity of language of the cross; it only appears once: when Innocent threatened to divert those who had "taken the sign of the cross" on the Fourth Crusade to fight in Sicily against Markward.[40] While one might interpret this to suggest that Innocent did not consider the Sicilian crusade as such, it seems to indicate the opposite. In diverting the crusaders, Innocent connected the campaign in Sicily with that which was headed to the East. He did so in two ways. First, Markward was described as an enemy of the church comparable to Muslims. Second, Innocent declared that for the crusaders to fight in Sicily would be for them to defend the church.[41] Thus he described those who fought against Markward similarly to other crusades – as soldiers of Christ and the members of the army of the Lord.[42] In addition, the crusaders were given the traditional remission of sins; moreover, Innocent directly equates that remission with that which they would receive if they went on crusade to the Levant.[43]

What of the Baltic crusades?[44] Terminology related to the cross occurs in only one place in Innocent's correspondence related to the Baltic. He allowed those who had taken the vow for the Fourth Crusade – and were unable to

---

[40]   PL 214: 787; Markowski, "*Crucesignatus*," 162.

[41]   PL 214: 780, 214: 787.

[42]   *Ad defensionem* – PL 214: 513, 214: 788, 214: 806, 214: 848–49, 214: 900–01, 214: 903, 214: 1073; *ad succursum fidelium in Siciliam destinemus* – PL 214: 1072; PL 214: 513–14; *Resistatis inimicis Ecclesiae* – PL 214: 514, 214: 848–49, 214: 900–01, 214: 903, 214: 1073; *inimicis crucis* – PL 214: 781, 214: 782; Markward is also given the title *perfidum Marcualdum*, or "faithless," which resembles the title Innocent gives to the Muslims at times, cf. *paganos perfidos* – PL 215: 1132 and *perfidia sarracenorum* – DP 436: 416.

[43]   PL 214: 514, 214: 782. *Per Siciliam enim subveniri poterit facilius terrae sanctae: quae si, quod absit, in Saracenorum potentiam deveniret, nulla de caetero recuperationi Hierosolymitanae provinciae fiducia remaneret.* – PL 214.782. See also Innocent's comments at the Fourth Lateran Council with regard to those who refuse to keep peace in Europe during a time of crusade. Innocent warns secular powers that if they interfere with the peace that secular power will be invoked upon them by ecclesiastical authority. *Quod si forte censuram ecclesiasticam vilipenderint, poterunt non immerito formidare, ne per auctoritatem ecclesiae circa eos, tanquam perturbatores negocii crucifixi, saecularis potentia inducatur*, Fourth Lateran Council, canon seventy-one, see Josepho Alberigo, et al. *Conciliorum Oecumenicorum Decreta*, 267–71, for the quote see 270.

[44]   Markowski, "*Crucesignatus*," p. 161–62. With regard to the particulars of the Baltic Crusade I am greatly indebted to Iben Fonnesberg-Schmidt, both in conversation at the Saint Louis University International Crusade Symposium in the Spring of 2006, but also

fulfill it – to do so with participation in crusade to the Baltic.[45] Likewise, this could be interpreted as something different than a crusade because language of the cross only occurs in this one letter as a reference to those who had already taken the cross. The opposite seems to be the case: because crusades to the Baltic were ongoing, it was a logical move on the part of Innocent to allow previous crusaders to fulfill their vow in this manner.[46]

Counting words is even less useful when we remember that there is significantly less correspondence for the crusades to the Baltic than other crusades in Innocent's pontificate. This naturally means that there is less chance that *crucesignatus* will appear in surviving documents. However, in what little we have Innocent still used the same crusader terminology and phraseology with reference to the crusades to the Baltic as he did for the Fourth, Fifth, and Albigensian Crusade. For example, he described the crusaders as soldiers of Christ, and utilized terms centered upon pilgrimage.[47] He also offered the traditional remission of sins and papal protection to those who participated which he offered to crusaders headed to the East.[48] And

---

in her new work on the papacy and the Baltic crusades. See Iben Fonnesberg-Schmidt, *The Popes and the Baltic Crusades 1147–1254* (Leiden, 2007).

[45]   PL 215: 428–29. Innocent writes, *...qui, affixo suis humeris signo crucis, voverunt Hierosolymam proficisci, in messem ipsius ad annuntiandum gentibus Jesum Christum mittere dignaremur, et nihilominus laicos, qui, propter rerum defectum et corporum debilitatem, terram Hierosolymitanam adire non possunt, permitteremus in Livoniam contra barbaros proficisci, voto in votum de nostra licentia commutato.* See also *Diplomatarium Danicum* (DD), ed. A. Afzelius et al. (Copenhagen, 1938ff), vol. 1: 3, no. 254.

[46]   Fonnesberg-Schmidt, *Popes*, p. 128. Torben Nielsen argues that because Innocent allowed the commutation of vows to the Holy Land that "Innocent III certainly likened the missionary and crusading effort in the Baltic region to the 'proper' crusades to the Holy Land...." Torben K. Nielsen, "The Missionary Man: Archbishop Anders Sunesen and the Baltic Crusade, 1206–21" in *Crusade and Conversion on the Baltic Frontier: 1150–1500*, ed. Alan V. Murray (Aldershot, 2001), p. 105.

[47]   *miles Christi* – PL 216: 117, 216: 118, and in one letter Innocent also refers to the crusaders as *servitium Jesu Christi* – PL 216: 117. For pilgrimage terms see PL 216: 117, 216: 118. When Innocent refers to the army as soldiers of Christ there seems to be an implicit reference to the taking of the cross.

[48]   *Die Register Innocenz' III.*, vol. 7, no. 139; DD vol. 1: 5, no. 61; DD vol. 1: 4, nos. 162–3; PL 214: 738–40, 216: 117, 216: 118, 216: 919, 217: 054. Another letter with reference to the indulgence can be found quoted in its entirety in Nielsen, "The Missionary Man," 102 n. 22. Tiina Kala argues that Innocent also offered crusaders fighting against the pagan Livs the same indulgences as those fighting in the Holy Land on December 29, 1215, but I was unable to confirm this report. Tiina Kala, "The Incorporation of the Northern Baltic Lands into the Western Christian World" in *Crusade and Conversion on the Baltic Frontier: 1150–1500*, ed. Alan V. Murray (Aldershot: Ashgate Publishing, 2001), p. 9. PL 214: 738–40, 216: 668, 217: 054–055. Nielsen also shows another letter where Innocent offered the privilege

he described the crusades to the Balticas a defense of the church. He took pride in his new converts and churches in the Baltic, and so it was important to describe those who fought in the crusades to the Baltic as those who fought in defense of the church.[49] This defense included protection of missionaries in the Baltic region, and protection for new Christians and churches from pagan attacks.[50] Soldiers were called to rise up in the name of Christ in order to accomplish this holy task against the pagans.[51] Like the Fifth Crusade, the crusades to the Baltic included the promise of martyrdom for those who died on it.[52]

The final crusades to consider are those in Spain. Similar to the Sicilian and crusades to the Baltic, there is a noticeable absence of the term *crucesignatus* in Innocent's correspondence. The Spanish *reconquista* is complicated because it was ongoing and without a clear beginning or end – in this way, like the crusades to the Baltic. Second, while reconquest was ongoing in Spain, various crusades occurred from time to time, much like crusade to the Levant.[53] That

---

of protection, Nielsen, "The Missionary Man," 111. Eric Christiansen argues in his work that Pope Celestine III "authorized full crusading privileges to all who took the vow to make a pilgrimage to the Dvina, and in 1198 Innocent III reiterated the offer," Eric Christiansen, *The Northern Crusades: The Baltic and the Catholic Frontier: 1000–1525* (Minneapolis, 1980), p. 94. Christiansen does not offer a source for this, and I was unable to track down a letter in which the said privileges were offered. It is key that one should note the important research of Fonnesberg-Schmidt in this area. She clearly and persuasively shows how the indulgence Innocent offered in the crusades to the Baltics was different than for any of the other crusades he called (crusade to the Levant, Italy, Languedoc, and Spain). She argues that as a result the Baltic Crusade was a lesser crusade—but still a crusade—than the others. See note 63 below for more thoughts, and Fonnesberg-Schmidt, *Popes*, pp. 96–97.

[49]   In a letter (PL 215: 512) written at the fall of Constantinople to the crusaders Innocent likens missionary success in the Baltic to bringing the Eastern Church back to the Western through the sack of Constantinople. In this letter he uses Luke's Gospel account of the miraculous catch of fish as his starting point. He describes himself as throwing the net over the edge of the boat and catching a multitude of fish, including the conversion of pagans in Livonia, for example, *ego et fratres mei, piscium multitudinem copiosam, sive in Livonia, convertendo paganos per praedicatores illuc directos ad fidem*, PL 215: 512.

[50]   *Ad defensionem Christianorum* – PL 214: 738–40, 217: 054; *contra Livoniae barbaros* – PL 215: 438–40; *ut Livonienseum episcopum, clerum, et Ecclesiam contra paganos defendant* – PL 215: 438–40; *ad exstirpandum paganitatis errorem et terminos Christianae fidei dilatandos* – PL 216: 116, 216: 117; *pugnet adversus paganos* – PL 216: 116; *persecutionem paganorum* – PL 214: 739. See also, Riley-Smith, pp. 17–18.

[51]   *in nomine Dei exercituum assurgatis* – PL. 214: 738–40, 217: 054.

[52]   PL 216: 116, 216: 117, 216: 118. For martyrdom mentioned with regard to the Fifth Crusade see PL 216: 817, 217: 241.

[53]   Joseph O'Callaghan argues first that reconquest was an idea that began with the collapse of Visigothic Spain, and was connected with later developments of reconquest

said, it seems that Innocent saw certain campaigns within the reconquest as legitimate crusade. Even though he did not use *crucesignatus*, Innocent utilized other terminology centered upon the cross.[54] He also made reference to those who campaigned as soldiers of Christ or armies of the Lord.[55] Innocent also did not hesitate to rely upon the most traditional of images, that of pilgrimage.[56] Similar to all the campaigns above, those who fought in the *reconquista* were seen to fight in defense of the church.[57] Those who died on these campaigns were described as martyrs.[58] Finally, Innocent provided the same remission of sins and papal protection as he offered to other crusaders.[59]

In conclusion, two points can be drawn with some clarity from this examination of Innocent's correspondence. First, Innocent and his curia possessed a wide arsenal of phrases and terms with which to refer to the crusades and crusaders. They did not limit themselves to one set of terms. This terminology included

---

when Christians were strong enough to fight the Muslims. Second, he argues that the reconquest in Spain was impacted by the crusades. The papacy, beginning with Alexander II and Gregory VII, transformed the Muslim wars in Spain into crusades, and supported them with indulgences and remission of sins equivalent to those given to crusaders headed to the Levant, and that the military conflicts supported by Alexander II, Gregory VII, and Urban II were actually antecedents to the First Crusade. He then argues that the members of Christian Spain embraced the ideology of crusade as a fundamental justification for their participation and support of these wars. See Joseph O'Callaghan, *Reconquest and Crusade in Medieval Spain* (Philadelphia, 2003), pp. 24–35.

[54]   *Signo crucis* – PL 216: 699–703; *in virtute crucis Dominicae prostraverunt* – PL 216: 702; *omnes in Dei nominee armati processimus* – PL 216: 702; *bellum Domini a solo Domino et per solum Dominum est feliciter consummatum* – PL 216: 702. Innocent also called the Muslims enemies of the cross, PL 214: 593, PL 216: 553.

[55]   *exercitus Domini* – PL 216: 701, 216: 704; *bellum Domini* – PL 216: 702.

[56]   For pilgrimage see, PL 216: 353, 513, 514, 553; DP 342, 470.

[57]   *Videlicet ut militaribus armis accincti contra Saracenos pro tuitione Christiani populi...*, PL 214: 590, 216: 562, 216: 701; *Ad expugnandos Saracenos* – PL 215: 666–67, DP 351: 321; *exterminandum inimicos nominis Christiani* - 216: 353, 216: 513; 216: 553, 216: 562; *Saracenos impugnant* – PL 216: 380, 216: 381; *direxit manus sui exercitus contra inimicos suos* – PL 216: 702; *expellendam hereticam pravitatem de finibus terre tue* – DP 349: 319; *eliminandas hereses* – DP 543: 503, DP 368: 344. See also, PL 216: 553, PL 216: 353.

[58]   He writes that they will be snatched away from the Muslims' grip by means of heavenly grace, *cum auxilio coelestis gratiae de Sarracenorum minibus eripueris*, PL 216: 563. *Martyres* – PL 216: 702. Regarding martyrs for the Baltic and the Fifth Crusades see above note 55. Again, the reference to martyrs seems to be another implicit reference to the cross.

[59]   *In remissionem eis omnium peccaminum injungendo* – PL 216: 353, 216: 380, 216: 513, 216: 514, 216: 699, DP 366: 342, 436: 416, 500: 470. As mentioned above with regard to the Albigensian Crusade, this indulgence was briefly taken away at the same time as that indulgence for the Albigensian Crusade when Innocent called the Fifth Crusade, PL 216: 817–22. *Recipiuntur sub protectione sedis apostolicae* – PL 214: 590, 216: 562, 216: 513–14.

some traditional terms for crusaders, such as those with reference to pilgrimage, to crusaders as soldiers of Christ, the promise of martyrdom for those who died, and encouraging the crusaders to defend the Holy Land and the church against its enemies – Muslims, pagans, political enemies, or heretics. If one had to make an argument for one set of terms that Innocent preferred – and that is not the purpose of this study – statistically the terms centered upon the defense of the church occur most frequently in Innocent's overall correspondence. Second, based upon Innocent's wide variety of terminology, there does not seem to be any effort on his part to refine the definition of the crusades through his usage of *crucesignatus*.[60] While the development of crusade terminology over time brought into usage terms with reference to the cross, and though Innocent made frequent use of these terms, including *crucesignatus*, it does not seem appropriate to attempt to understand Innocent's idea of crusade through the picking out of that term. Innocent used *crucesignatus* as one word among many, and it does not appear to be more special than other terms he used when he discussed or called crusade. This conclusion suggests that even if Innocent considered crusade to the Holy Land to be the most important form of crusading, he still considered the Baltic Crusade, the Spanish *reconquista*, and the political crusade against Markward alongside the Fourth, Fifth, and Albigensian Crusades as important crusades waged in defense and protection of Christendom.[61] The greater implication of these two points is that, while it is important for scholars to come to the clearest and most precise definition of the crusades as possible, it is not wise to base a definition solely on the appearance or lack of a single word or phrase.

---

[60] For example, see the work of Helmut Roscher, in which he argues that Innocent was responsible for much of the work in broadening the scope of the crusades by including those campaigns outside the Holy Land, which is quite the contrary to Markowski's argument, Helmut Roscher, *Papst Innocenz III und die Kreuzzuge*, Forschungen zur Kirchen- und Dogmengeschichte 21 (Göttingen, 1969).

[61] It seems quite clear from Innocent's correspondence that he set up a hierarchy of crusading; crusade to the Holy Land was the most important. Two examples of this hierarchy are as follows. First, it is most clear in the revocation of indulgence originally granted for Spain and the Albigensian Crusade, in order to promote the Fifth Crusade. Second, it is also clear in the formula for indulgence Innocent utilized for crusading in the Baltic region, as described above in the work of Fonnesberg-Schmidt, see Fonnesberg-Schmidt, pp. 111–113, and 128–29.

PART III
The Crusades and the Byzantine World

Chapter 7

God's Will or Not? Bohemond's Campaign Against the Byzantine Empire (1105–1108)

Brett Edward Whalen

University of North Carolina, Chapel Hill

Was there a crusade against the Byzantine Empire during the years 1105 to 1108, led by the Norman warlord Bohemond of Taranto (d. 1111), then prince of Antioch? According to the evaluation of many scholars, the answer is yes: there was a crusade against the Greek emperor Alexius I (d. 1118), an attack that was sanctioned by Pope Paschal II (d. 1118) and eagerly embraced by Frankish warriors who blamed Alexius for harassing Western pilgrims and betraying earlier waves of crusading armies.[1] In his 1924 work on Bohemond, which is still cited as an authority on this subject, Ralph Yewdale writes that the assault on the Greek Empire was "a real Crusade: it had received the approval of the pope and was preached by a papal legate, and the usual crusading privileges were given to

---

[1] Important works on this topic include Ferdinand Chalandon, *Essai sur le règne d'Alexis Ier Comnène (1081–1118)*, Mémoires et documents publiés par la société de l'école des Chartes 4 (Paris, 1990), pp. 242–49; Ralph Yewdale, *Bohemond I, Prince of Antioch* (Princeton, 1924), pp. 106–34; Steven Runciman, *A History of the Crusades*, vol. 1 (Cambridge, 1952–54), pp. 32–55; K.M. Setton, ed., *A History of the Crusades: The First Hundred Years*, ed. Marshall Baldwin, vol. 1 (Philadelphia, 1955), pp. 387–91; William Daly, "Christian Fraternity, the Crusaders, and the Security of Constantinople, 1097–1204: The Precarious Survival of an Ideal," *Medieval Studies* 22 (1960), 43–91; J.G. Rowe, "Paschal II, Bohemond of Antioch and the Byzantine Empire," *Bulletin of the John Rylands Library* 49 (1966–67), 165–202; and William McQueen, "Relations between the Normans and Byzantium 1071–1112," *Byzantion* 56 (1986), 427–76. See also Gerhard Rösch, "Der 'Kreuzzug' Bohemonds gegen Dyrrhacion 1107/1108 in der lateinischen Tradition des 12. Jahrhunderts," *Römische Historische Mitteilungen* 26 (1984), 181–90; and Luigi Russo, "Il viaggio di Boemondo d'Altavilla in Francia (1106): un riesame," *Archivio storico Italiano* 163 (2005), 3–42.

those who took the cross."[2] Yewdale adds that this was "the first example of the use of the Crusade for political purposes; in this sense, it is a foreshadowing of the Fourth Crusade."[3] In his popular multi-volume history of the crusades, Steven Runciman agreed with these sentiments, writing that the expedition of 1107 was no less than "a turning-point in the history of the Crusades ... The Crusade, with the pope at its head, was not a movement for the succor of Christendom, but a tool of unscrupulous western imperialism."[4] Other scholars, however, including William Daly, Marshal Baldwin, and J.G. Rowe have been more cautious. While not substantially challenging this view, they have raised questions about the precise status of the "crusade of 1107." In particular, Baldwin and Rowe have suggested that Bohemond was responsible for hoodwinking Pope Paschal by getting him to support a new crusade to the Holy Land, which the ambitious Norman leader subsequently redirected against Byzantium.[5]

The question of whether there was a crusade against the Byzantine Empire during the opening decade of the twelfth century is not as straightforward as it initially seems. Bohemond's campaign against Alexius leads us into the thorny question of what exactly constituted a crusade in the Middle Ages. I say "thorny" because the definition of crusading has been and remains a notoriously complex and contentious matter.[6] There is a great deal of debate about what gave crusading its recognizable and distinct shape: Was it papal authorization? The swearing of a crusade vow? Was it the anticipation of spiritual benefits or a sense of just

---

[2]   Yewdale, *Bohemond I*, p. 115. For a more recent restatement of this basic position, see McQueen, "Normans and Byzantium," pp. 458–67.

[3]   Yewdale, *Bohemond I*, p. 115. See also Yewdale, ibid., p. 107: "There is no question then of a deflection of the expedition from its original purpose, when Bohemond attacks Durazzo; to attack the Greek Empire from the West was the original purpose of the expedition, and everyone was aware of the fact."

[4]   Runciman, *History of the Crusades*, p. 48.

[5]   In addition to Baldwin, *History of the Crusades*, pp. 387–91, see Marshall Baldwin, "The Papacy and the Levant during the Twelfth Century," *Bulletin of the Polish Institute for Arts and Sciences*, vol. 3 (1945), 277–87, along with Daly, "Christian Fraternity," p. 58, and Rowe, "Paschal II," pp. 167–82.

[6]   There is a vast literature on this topic. Notable works include Carl Erdmann, *The Origin of the Idea of Crusade*, trans. Marshall Baldwin and Walter Goffart (1935; Princeton, 1977); Hans Eberhard Mayer, *The Crusades*, trans. John Gillingham, 2nd edn. (1965; Oxford, 1988); Jonathan Riley-Smith, *What Were the Crusades?* 3rd. edn. (1977; New York, 2002); E.-D. Hehl, "Was ist eigentlich ein Kreuzzug?," *Historische Zeitschrift* 259 (1994), 297–336; John France, "Les origines de la première croisade: un nouvel examen," in *Autour de la première croisade*, ed. Michel Balard (Paris, 1996), pp. 43–56; Christopher Tyerman, *The Invention of the Crusades* (London, 1998); and Jean Flori, *La guerre sainte: la formation de l'idée de croisade dans l'occident chrétien* (Paris, 2001).

cause? Even if we agree that crusading was defined by some combination of these characteristics, there remains the vexing question of *motivation*. What motivated Western Christians to swear a crusading vow, to believe that they could secure the remission of their sins by fighting as soldiers of Christ under papal sanction? What marked them in their own eyes, and also the eyes of their contemporaries, as the bearers of a special identity that was different both from other kinds of warriors and other kinds of pilgrims?[7]

It is with a particular eye toward the question of motivation that I wish to revisit the topic of Bohemond's campaign against the Greek Empire (*c*.1105–1108). What motivated those who sanctioned and participated in this expedition? I am above all interested in the notion that Greek religious difference from Latin doctrine and rites somehow fostered Western Christian animosity against "schismatic" members of the Byzantine church.[8] Did Pope Paschal II openly support a crusade against the Greeks, viewing them as heretical, schismatic, and disobedient to papal authority: in short, as being "bad Christians"? Did tales of Greek treachery and religious error encourage French warriors to carry out a holy war against their fellow Christians? For reasons explained below, I would argue that there was indeed a crusade during the years 1105 to 1108, but it was not a crusade against the Byzantine Empire – it was an expedition of warriors who had sworn ultimately to go to Jerusalem, following in the footsteps of those who had captured that holy city less than 10 years earlier. The papacy supported this new crusade. At the same time, these warriors were apparently willing, perhaps some of them even eager to attack the Byzantine Empire while en route to fulfilling their crusader vows. This would be neither the first nor the last example of "multi-tasking" during a crusading expedition. It seems perfectly likely that the papacy approved tacitly or perhaps openly of this planned assault against Alexius. There is no reason to assume, however, that "wily" Bohemond duped Pope Paschal, nor did papal support for this limited campaign against the Greek ruler indicate a papal declaration of "holy war" against the Byzantines.

We are fortunate that there is considerable information about Bohemond's attack on Alexius, even though it is somewhat scattered and many of the sources

---

[7]   See Giles Constable, "The Place of the Crusader in Medieval Society," *Viator* 29 (1998), 377–403.

[8]   In addition to the general theses of scholars like Rowe, Runciman, and McQueen, see the typical statement by Peter Charanis, "Aims of the Medieval Crusades and How They Were Viewed by Byzantines," *Chuch History* 21 (1952), 123–34, who declares that the crusade "became an instrument to be used by the papacy as the papacy saw fit. It might be authorized against the infidels, as it indeed was, or it might be called against schismatics as was the crusade of 1107, authorized by Pope Paschal II in order to help Bohemond in his struggle against the Byzantine emperor Alexius I."

written down well after the fact. As one of the heroes of the First Crusade, Bohemond and his exploits were of great interest to twelfth-century chroniclers, such as Orderic Vitalis, and crusade historians including Fulcher of Chartres, Albert of Aix, and William of Tyre.[9] There are also a number of minor accounts penned by more obscure figures like Bartolf of Nangis and the anonymous writers who composed crusade-related works such as the so-called *Narrative of Fleury* and *The History of the Pilgrims Going to Jerusalem*.[10] There are a number of additional short notices about the expedition in various chronicles, mostly French in origin.[11] We also, of course, have a detailed presentation Bohemond and Alexius' conflict from a Greek perspective, written by Anna Comnena, Alexius' daughter and author of *The Alexiad*.[12]

There is no need here to review the well-known details of Norman–Byzantine relations before and during the First Crusade. Bohemond was involved in his father Robert Guiscard's assault against the Byzantine Empire in the Balkans starting in 1081 and, by the time of the First Crusade, was considered something of a "public enemy number one" among the Byzantines.[13] Along with the majority of the other crusade leaders, during his passage through Constantinople, Bohemond swore an oath that he would restore recaptured imperial territories to the hands of the emperor. When the Norman warrior seized control of Antioch in 1098 during the First Crusade's march to Jerusalem, he apparently

---

[9]   See Orderic Vitalis, *The Ecclesiastical History of Orderic Vitalis*, ed. and trans. Marjorie Chibnall, vol. 6 (Oxford, 1980), pp. 69–72, and 100–105 (Latin text with facing English translation); Fulcher of Chartres, *Fulcheri Carnotensis historia Hierosolymitana*, ed. Heinrich Hagenmeyer (Heidelberg, 1913); Albert of Aix, *Historia Hierosolymitana*, *RHC Oc.* 4, pp. 620, 650–52; and William of Tyre, *Chronicon*, ed. R.B.C. Huygens, CCCM 63 (Turnhout, 1986), pp. 495–96, and 503–4. See also the crusade history by Ekkehard, *Hierosolymita*, ed. Heinrich Hagenmeyer (Tübingen, 1877), pp. 292–93.

[10]   See Bartolf Nangis, *Gesta francorum Iherusalem expugnatium*, *RHC Oc.* 3, p. 538; the *Narratio Floriacensis de captis Antiocha et Hierosolyma et obsesso Dyrrachio*, *RHC Oc.* 5, pt. 2, pp. 361–62; the *Historia peregrinorum euntium Jerusolymam seu Tudebodus imitatus et continuatus*, *RHC Oc.* 3, pp. 228–29. See also the brief notice on the attack in Baldwin III, *Historia Nicaena vel Antiocha*, *RHC Oc.* 5, pt. 2, p. 181.

[11]   See, for example, Sigebert of Gembloux, *Chronica cum continuationibus*, ed. D.L. Bethmann, *MGH SS* 6 (Hannover, 1844), p. 372, and Robert de Monte, *Chronicon*, *MGH SS* 6, p. 483. The attack even attracted the attention of Arabic chroniclers: see *The Damascus Chronicle*, ed. and trans. H.A.R.E. Gibb (London, 1932), p. 42.

[12]   For Anna Comnena, I will cite the widely available translation by E.R.A. Sewter, trans., *The Alexiad of Anna Comnena* (Baltimore, 1969), pp. 366–434. Readers should be aware here is a new critical edition of the Greek text: Anna Comnena, *Alexias*, ed. Diether Reinsch and Athanasios Kambylis, Corpus Fontium Historiae Byzantinae 50/1 (Berlin, 2001).

[13]   For a basic overview, see Rösch, "Der 'Kreuzzug' Bohemonds," pp. 428–58.

contravened the terms of that oath.[14] In 1100, Bohemond was seized and imprisoned by one of his Muslim opponents. According to several chronicles, while in captivity, he prayed that he would make a pilgrimage to the shrine of Saint Leonard in Limoges, if he regained his liberty. Once freed, Bohemond sailed to Italy in 1105 and traveled to France in 1106 in fulfillment of this vow.[15] According to Anna Comnena's colorful account, he traveled to Italy in a coffin pretending to be dead in order to avoid capture by imperial forces. His express intention at this time, Anna reports, was to destroy Alexius and the Roman (that is, Byzantine) Empire with him.[16]

Most of the Latin chroniclers who took note of Bohemond's arrival agreed that the Norman warlord incited Western Christians to come across the sea with him and fight against the emperor Alexius. The main charge levied against the Greek ruler was that he had betrayed the armies of the First Crusade and that he was assaulting pilgrims bound for the Holy Land. Albert of Aix, for example, reported that Bohemond gathered "army of Christians from the various kingdoms of Gaul and Italy" in order to assault the emperor.[17] The Narrative of Fleury agreed, describing how Bohemond assembled troops "not just from Gaul, but truly from all of the West" to attack Alexius, who had "always been opposed to those making the pilgrimage to Jerusalem."[18] Ekkehard wrote something similar, recording that Bohemond looked as far a field as Spain for soldiers

---

[14]   There has been a considerable amount of uncertainity over the precise nature of the oath taken by the leaders of the First Crusade, particularly in light of what seems to be an interpolated passage in the anonymous *Gesta Francorum* justifying Bohemond's seizure of Antioch. See *The Deeds of the Franks and the Other Pilgrims to Jerusalem (Gesta Francorum et aliorum Hierosolymitanorum)*, ed. and trans. Rosalind Hill (1962; Oxford, 1972), p. 12 (Latin text with facing English translation). On this problematic passage, see A.C. Krey, "A Neglected Passage in the *Gesta* and Its Bearing on the Literature of the First Crusade," in *The Crusades and Others Historical Essays Presented to Dana C. Munro by his Former Students*, ed. Louis Paetow (New York, 1928).

[15]   See the observations of Russo, "Il viaggio di Boemondo," pp. 6–26.

[16]   Anna Comnena, *The Alexiad*, pp. 366–68.

[17]   Albert of Aix, *Historia Hierosolymitana*, p. 620. "Bohemundo non solum Italiam sed Galliam profecto ad acquirendas vires et commovendos principes adversus Alexium regem Graecorum."

[18]   *Narratio Floriacensis*, p. 361. "innumerabilem tam equitum quam peditum multitudinem ab eis eduxit, non solum de Galliis, verum et de toto Occidente; Graecorum imperium perturbare conatus, ea videlicet occasione, quoniam imperator semper adversabatur omnibus Hierosolymam tendentibus, commissis aditibus viarum et maritimis portibus [sic] praedonibus et piratis."

to fight the "tyrant" Alexius.[19] *The History of the Pilgrims Going to Jerusalem* declared that Bohemond gathered warriors both to fight "the Gentiles and Emperor Alexius."[20] Many other minor chronicles made similar observations that Bohemond assembled warriors "from all parts of the West" intending to assault the Greek emperor.[21] It is important to note that although such sources acknowledged Bohemond's plan to attack Alexius, they did not make any blanket references to an assault against "Greek Christians" or to Greeks as "schismatic" or "heretical." The chronicles might be described as "anti-Alexian," but should not be labeled anti-Greek or anti-Byzantine in any broad sense.

There is little doubt that Bohemond receive papal support for this effort to raise troops. In one notable passage, Bartolf of Nangis recorded that Pope Paschal II had directed Bohemond "across the Alps into Gaul and parts of the West, so that he might seek aid for himself against the emperor. Paschal made him the standard-bearer of the army of Christ, and, giving him the banner of Saint Peter, sent him away in peace."[22] Many of the chronicles reporting Bohemond's activities took note of the fact that he was accompanied by a papal legate, Bruno of Segni, during his tour of France. There is an assumption among some modern historians that Paschal, unlike his predecessor Urban II, was not particularly sympathetic toward the Greek church and was easily convinced to redirect crusading activity toward the Eastern Empire. Steven Runciman, for example, states flat out that the pope instructed Bruno "to preach a Holy War against Byzantium."[23] As noted above, others do not assume that Paschal was rabidly

---

[19]   Ekkehard, *Hierosolymita*, pp. 292–93. "militiam quocumque pacto contra tyrannum prescriptum cepit congregare."

[20]   *Historia peregrinorum*, p. 228. "ex cuius scilicet itineris occasione, et ipse gentium nonnullos Gallicanarum incitaret, quatinus, secum transmare pergentes, contra gentiles et imperatorem Alexium, quibus tunc incessanter infestabantur, pugnaturi essent."

[21]   See Fulcher of Charters, *Historia Hierosolymitana*, pp. 464–67,who describes Bohemond's arrival in France looking for soldiers to accompany him "across the sea," with no mention of Alexius ("ivit Boamundus, ut de transmarinis partibus gentem secum reduceret"), although later in his chronicle (pp. 518–521) he records that Bohemond attacked Alexius, who had been molesting pilgrims en route to Jerusalem. See also Sigebert of Gembloux, *Chronica*, p. 372. "Boiamundus dux Apuliae contracto undeunde exercitu, accingitur ad invadendum Constantinopolitanum imperium."

[22]   Bartolf, *Gesta Francorum*, p. 538. "Bohemondum vero trans Alpes in Gallias et partes Occidentis, ut contra imperatorem sibi adjutoria quaereret, legavit, atque signiferum Christi exercitus eum constituit, vexillumque sancti Petri ei tradens, in pace dimisit."

[23]   Runciman, *History of the Crusades*, p. 48. See also the typical comments in the annotation to Sewter, trans., *The Alexiad*, p. 390, n. 29: "Unlike his predecessor Urban II, who followed a moderate policy in his dealings with the eastern Christians, Paschal II was already prejudiced against the emperor."

anti-Greek, but that he was tricked by Bohemond into supporting a crusade that the Norman leader appropriated for his own malicious ends.[24]

These are points that deserve careful consideration. First of all, it is worth noting that "banner of Saint Peter" (*vexillium sancti Petri*), which did connote papal sanction for a military campaign, did not exclusively signify support for what we would now call a crusading army. The same standard was given to William the Conqueror in 1066 and to Robert Guiscard in his capacity as a defender of the papacy against the German Empire.[25] Most scholars would not call those expeditions "crusades" in any meaningful sense of the word, and there seems no reason to assume that the awarding of the papal banner around 1106 immediately bestowed upon Bohemond's attack against Alexius the same emotional and spiritual appeal as a "crusading" expedition to Jerusalem. Papal support for Norman aggression against Byzantine rulers, however distasteful to modern sensibilities, was hardly unprecedented. Since the middle of the eleventh century, the ecclesiastical sanction of violence for moral ends had taken on air of unprecedented legitimacy among those who supported the reform movement in the Roman church. For Paschal to approve of an armed campaign against Alexius as a "tyrant" who was attacking pilgrims would have been in keeping with this pre-crusade tradition, which, in fact, included Pope Gregory VII's endorsement of Robert Guiscard's earlier attack on Alexius following the ouster of Emperor Michael VII (d. 1078).

Did, however, Paschal eagerly embrace a "holy war" against the Greeks, viewing such a campaign as having an equivalent legitimacy to an expedition with the goal of protecting Jerusalem itself or liberating additional territories in the Holy Land from the hands of the infidel? There is little evidence in his correspondence that he felt deep-seated animosity toward the Greek church and empire as a whole. In 1115, eight years after Bohemond's expedition, Paschal was more than willing to address Alexius in warm and diplomatic tones about improving relations between Rome and Constantinople.[26] Although he insisted that the Greeks recognize papal authority, the pope made no blanket statements about Greek heresy or schism. On the other hand, we do know that Paschal supported further expeditions to the Holy Land in support of the Latin kingdoms established there. In the aftermath of Jerusalem's capture in 1099, he

---

[24]   See, for example, the comments of Rowe, "Pope Paschal," p. 182: "Alas for Paschal. He was soon to discover that he had unwittingly given his blessing, not to a crusade, but to an act of vengeance and aggression."

[25]   See Jonathan Riley-Smith, "The First Crusade and Saint Peter," in *Outremer: Studies in theHistory of the Crusading Kingdom of Jerusalem*, ed. Benjamin Kedar and et al. (Jerusalem, 1982), pp. 41–63, along with Erdmann, *Origin of the Idea of Crusade*, pp. 182–200.

[26]   Paschal II, Ep. 437, PL 163, cols. 388–89.

eagerly celebrated the success of the crusading army in liberating the Eastern church and freeing Jerusalem from the yoke of the infidels.[27] In addition, Paschal berated those who had failed to fulfill their vows by never leaving or abandoning the army short of its goal, and he demanded that they take action to meet their obligations. The pope's desire to support the Latin states in the Holy Land was evident, as was his willingness to engage in a dialogue with the Greek church and empire. His supposed anti-Greek sentiment was not so clear. In other words, the burden of proof seems to lie on those who assert that Paschal viewed religious disagreements between Latins and Greeks as sufficient cause to sanction "crusading" violence against them.

What about the activities of the papal legate, Bruno of Segni, when he accompanied Bohemond to France? Shortly after Easter day, 1106, Bohemond was married to Constance (d. *c*.1125), daughter of the French King Philip I (d. 1108), in Chartres Cathedral. It is roundly believed that this well attended event was an occasion for Bohemond to pitch his new expedition against Alexius. We have two sources for the ceremony at Chartres, Suger of Saint Denis' *Life of Louis the Fat* and Orderic Vitalis' *Ecclesiastical History*.[28] Although writing after the fact, both men were contemporaries, and both were well positioned to known what had happened at Chartres (one or both of them might have been in attendance at the wedding). Orderic observed that the prince of Antioch was immensely popular and that crowds flocked to hear him speak. From the pulpit of Chartres cathedral, according to the chronicler, Bohemond

> related to the huge throng that had assembled all of his deeds and adventures, urged all those who bore arms to attack the Emperor with him, and promised his chosen adjutants wealthy towns and castles. Many were kindled by his words and, taking the Lord's cross, left all their belongings and set out on the road to Jerusalem (*iter in Ierusalem*) like men hastening to a feast.[29]

---

[27] See the letter of Paschal dated 28 April, 1100, Ep. 4, *Papsturkunden für Kirchen im Heiligen Lande*, ed. Rudolf Hiestand, Abhandlungen der Akademie Wissenschaften in Göttingen: Philologisch-Historische Klasse 136 (Göttingen, 1985), pp. 90–92 (PL 163: 42–43).

[28] Suger of Saint Denis, *Vie de Louis VI le gros*, ed. Henri Waquet (Paris, 1929), pp. 44–50; *The Deeds of Louis the Fat*, trans. Richard Cusimano and John Moorhead (Washington, D.C., 1992), pp. 43–46, and Orderic Vitalis, *The Ecclesiastical History*, vol. 6, pp. 69–73.

[29] Orderic Vitalis, *The Ecclesiastical History*, ed. and trans. Chibnall, vol. 6, pp. 70–71. "casus suos et res gestas enarravit, omnes armatos secum in imperatorem ascendere commonuit, ac approbatis optionibus urbes et oppida ditissima promisit. Unde multi vehementer accensi sunt, et accepta cruce Domini omnia sua reliquerunt, et quasi ad epulas festinantes iter in Ierusalem arripuerunt."

I find this passage to be ambiguous: Bohemond advocated an attack on Alexius, but the men who took up the cross set out on the "road to Jerusalem" (*iter in Ierusalem*). What did this mean? Did Orderic use the expression *iter in Ierusalem* as a convention, meaning that the expedition against Alexius would be the equivalent of an armed pilgrimage to Jerusalem? Or, and I find this more likely, did those who took up the cross at Chartres intend to go to Jerusalem to fulfill their crusader vow, dealing with Alexius en route? If we compare with Suger's description of the wedding at Chartres, he writes:

> Among those present was the legate of the apostolic Roman see, the lord Bruno, bishop of Segni. The lord pope Paschal had sent him in the company of the lord Bohemond to summon and urge people to make an expedition to the Holy Sepulcher.[30]

The following June, Suger immediately adds, Bruno held a council at Poitiers, which Suger himself attended. At this council, Bruno "conducted the varied business of the synod, but especially made sure that zeal for the journey to Jerusalem had not grown lukewarm, for both he and Bohemond aroused many of those present to make it."[31] Suger was clear that the crusade endorsed at Chartres and also at Poitiers by the papal legate was an expedition to the Holy Sepulcher, that is to say, a crusade to Jerusalem. In his chronicle, Suger did not even mention the Greek Empire or Alexius. A number of minor chronicles from around the region of Poitiers agreed that Bruno encouraged those present at the council to "hasten to Jerusalem" or "make the journey to the Holy Sepulcher."[32] This sort of testimony strongly suggests two things. One, that Bruno of Segni (and by extension, Pope Paschal) envisioned a crusade to Jerusalem *c*.1105–1106, although they were well aware that Bohemond was equally or more interested in gathering support for his own attack on Alexius. One can speculate that, rather than supporting a "holy war" against Byzantium, Bruno was in fact riding Bohemond's coat-tails to generate support for a new expedition to the Holy Land. Lending support to the Norman leader's ambitions against Alexius might have been a shrewd way to capitalize on a campaign against the Byzantine ruler that the papacy could do little to prevent. Second, it seems that Jerusalem, not a blanket hatred of the Greeks, was what inspired French warriors to take up the cross in 1106, even if they were willing to attack the Byzantine Empire in the bargain.

---

30   Suger of Saint Denis, *The Deeds of Louis*, trans. Cusimano and Moorhead, p. 45.
31   Ibid., p. 45.
32   *Chroniques des églises d'Anjou*, ed. Paul Marchegay and Émile Mabille, Recueillies et publiées pour la société de l'histoire de France (Paris, 1869), pp. 171–72, and 423.

We are fortunate that one of these new crusaders, the Viscount Hugh of Puiset, was involved in a dispute with a neighboring count, Rotrocus. Rotrocus had constructed a fortification in a township that Hugh claimed was rightfully held by one of his own vassals. According to Ivo of Chartres, the famous canonist, who wrote several letters about this dispute, Hugh claimed special ecclesiastical protection due to his status as a crusader: that is, he sought justice from the church and the pope as one who was "going to Jerusalem" (*Hierosolymum tendente, Hierosolymam eunti*).[33] This is not conclusive evidence of Hugh's intentions: perhaps these expressions were being used formulaically and meant that Hugh expected the same protections as a pilgrim going to Jerusalem. A simpler explanation, however, is that Hugh had in fact sworn a crusader vow to go to Jerusalem and sought the legal protections conveyed by that status. Given the public nature of Bohemond's intentions to attack Alexius, Hugh was certainly well aware of the plan to assault the Byzantine ruler, justifiable in light of Alexius' putative attacks on pilgrims and supposed betrayal of earlier crusading expeditions.[34] The goal of what we might anachronistically call Hugh's crusading quest, however, was the Holy Land.

Without going into the details, suffice it to say that Bohemond's campaign was a military failure. In October 1107 he and his forces crossed over from Italy to the Balkans and laid siege to Durazzo. Due to the city's defenses, the outbreak of disease, and a naval blockade of his position, Bohemond was forced to concede defeat in September 1108. Many of the Latin chroniclers record that Alexius bribed or influenced some of Bohemond's closest companions to work against him. According to Orderic Vitalis, when it became apparent that the battle was lost, the Norman warrior's companions beseeched him to desist with the following words:

> We are paying the penalty of our presumption, for we have embarked on a proud
> undertaking which is more than our birthright and beyond our strength, and have
> dared to raise a hand against the holy Empire. No hereditary right drew us to this
> bold enterprise; no prophet sent from God roused us with a message from heaven;

---

[33]   See Ivo of Chartres, Ep. 68, PL 162, cols. 170–172. "Quod audiens vicecomes quia Hierusalem iturus erat, et dominus Curvaevillae, clamorem fecerunt in auribus Ecclesie, ut justicia eis fieret, quae debebatur Hierosolymitanis et paci," and Ep. 69, PL 162, cols. 172–173. "suggestum est domino papae, sicut forsitan audistis ab Hugo vicecomite Hierosolymum tendente, quatenus super hac injuria justitiam faceret, et rem Hierosolymitani secundum sua statute defenderet." See Tyerman, *Invention*, pp. 23–24.

[34]   See Orderic Vitalis, *The Ecclesiastical History*, ed. and trans. Chibnall, vol. 6, pp. 100–01, who comments about Hugh and several others that they had "elected to fight against the Emperor [i.e. Alexius] with Duke Bohemond."

only lust to rule the dominions of another induced you to undertake the difficult task and, on our side, greed of gain lured us on to suffer an intolerable burden of toil and peril. But because God is not mocked and does not overturn justice or destroy what is just, he has lent a favorable ear to the prayers of just men who cry out to him against us in Greece and has scattered our armies, weakening them not by war but by famine, and has undermined our strength without bloodshed. So we beg you to make peace with the Emperor, before you are captured or sentenced to death and all of your followers irreparably involved in the disaster of your fall.[35]

I find this speech to be highly significant, not for what it reveals about the events of 1107, but rather for what it tells us about possible reactions to Bohemond's unsuccessful attack on the Greek Empire. Although Orderic was generally well disposed toward Bohemond in his chronicle, and seemed to feel that he was poorly served by his followers, this portion of his chronicle suggested possible criticisms of the Norman leader's enterprise (even if Orderic did not himself agree with them). Within the still forming genre of crusade historiography, a sense that the expeditions were divinely sanctioned and part of a just cause was critical for the validation of the armed pilgrimages. Here, we see an express declaration that the expedition against Alexius was not a just cause and was not favored by God. In fact, it could be argued that divine justice was on the side of the Greeks, whom the Franks had attacked for all the wrong reasons. Perhaps if Bohemond's attack had been successful, Orderic's chronicle would have never included such an indictment of the campaign, but this possibility does not change the fact that an assault on the "just men" of the "holy" Byzantine empire was open to such a charge. Although failed crusades against Muslims could be and were attributed to crusaders' sins, it is hard to imagine a Christian chronicler expressing similar sentiments after an unsuccessful battle with such "infidels."

---

35   Orderic Vitalis, *The Ecclesiastical History*, trans. Chibnall, vol. 6, pp. 102–05. "Nostrae temeritatis poenas luimus, qui ultra natales nostros et vires superbos nisus suscepimus, et contra sanctum imperium manus levare presumpsimus. Ad tantos ausus nec hereditarium ius nos illexit, nec prophetarum aliquis a Deo destinatus coelesti nos oraculo exciuit, sed cupiditas in alterius dicione dominandi ardua te incipere persuasit, et nos nichilominus appetitus lucrandi ad intolerabilem sarcinam laborum et discriminum sustinendam pertraxit. Verum quia Deus non irridetur, nec supplantat iudicium, nec subvertit quod iustum est, preces iustorum qui contra nos ad eum in Grecia clamant benigniter exaudivit, etagmina nostra non bello sed fame attenuate dispersit, viresque nostras sine sanguinis effusione abolevit. Fac igitur quesumus pacem cum imperatore antequam comprehendaris, seu morte condempneris, et omnes tui te cadente protinus deputentur inextricabilibus erumnis."

After making peace with Alexius, Bohemond's army dissolved. According to the Narrative of Fleury "part of the army went onward to Jerusalem for the sake of worship, part returned to Apulia with Bohemond."[36] *The History of the Pilgrims Going to Jerusalem* declared that part of the army, "those who were able, went to Jerusalem to pray at the Lord's Sepulcher."[37] Albert of Aix recorded that the soldiers left behind by Bohemond sought the clemency of the emperor "so that they might have leave to pass peacefully through his kingdom and continue on the road to Jerusalem."[38] William of Tyre stated that Bohemond returned to Apulia "after dismissing the crowd of pilgrims, who, obligated by their vows (*votis obligata*), endeavored to complete the road to Jerusalem."[39] This sort of testimony implies that the majority of army assembled for the siege at Durazzo had every intention of going to Jerusalem in fulfillment of their crusader vows after completing the campaign against Alexius. We know from Orderic Vitalis that Hugh of Puiset was among those who eventually did go to Jerusalem in fulfillment of his crusading vow.[40] If they had taken vows to go to Jerusalem, had received papal sanction for their activities, and enjoyed special protections due to their status, it seems reasonable to argue that the Frankish warriors accompanying Bohemond were indeed crusaders by most modern definitions: crusaders going to the Holy Land. In these terms, their continuance to Jerusalem was not an afterthought or a consolation prize. It was the essence of their crusade.

By this time, there were certainly precedents for crusaders to seize Byzantine-held territories while carrying out their crusading vows, but this did not mean that they were actually crusading against the Greeks. Even if the attack on Alexius was sanctioned by the papacy and could be declared a just war against a tyrant, this did not make it a crusade against the Byzantine Empire or a holy war against "schismatic Greeks." To the best of my knowledge there is only one source related to Bohemond's expedition against the Byzantine Empire that explicitly raised the problem of religious errors among the members of the Greek church, including their deviance from the authority of Rome. This topic

---

[36]   *Narratio Floriacensis*, p. 362. "Quibus peractis, imperatore ad sua revertente, pars exercitus Hierosolymam adorandi profiscitur gratia, pars cum Boamundo in Apulia repedat."

[37]   *Historia peregrinorum*, p. 229. "Alii autem qui cum eo iverunt, pars, qui poterant, Jerusalem ad sepulchrum Domini oraturi eunt."

[38]   Albert of Aix, *Historia Hierosolymitana*, p. 652. "Imperatoris exorata clementia, ut pacifice per regnum ejus usque in Iherusalem viam eos continuare liceret."

[39]   William of Tyre, *Chronicon*, ed. Huygens, p. 504. "Inde in Apuliam reversus, dimissa perigrinorum turba que votis obligata tenebatur iter Ierosolimitanum perficere, ipse domi, familiaribus adhuc detente curis, remansit."

[40]   Orderic Vitalis, *Ecclesiastical History*, ed. and trans. Chibnall, pp. 104–105.

was brought up in a letter written by Bohemond to Pope Paschal, shortly after the "army of God" (*Dei exercitus*) had reached Durazzo.[41] Thanking the pontiff for his support during his journey in France, the Norman leader requested that Paschal convoke a council in the near future to deliberate about "setting out on the road to Jerusalem, or obtaining justice between us and the emperor, or removing the schism, heresies, and diverse traditions that are in the church."[42] Specifically, the letter mentioned the debate over the double procession of the Holy Spirit (*filioque*), over the proper form of baptism, over which kind bread (leavened or unleavened) to use for the Eucharist, and over the propriety of clerical marriage. Bohemond knew his audience. These points of contention, some new and some centuries old, had all assumed a high profile during the previous decades since the infamous ecclesiastical confrontation of 1054.[43] This is not the place to discuss it, but the insistence of the reform-era Roman church on papal primacy and a new level of conformity on religious doctrine, as well as rites, had clearly raised the stakes in papal relations with the Greek church and empire. In the context of the "crusade of 1107," however, Bohemond's attempt to tar the Greek church with the blanket label of heresy was exceptional. None of the Latin chronicles make a similar justification for the attack, nor, as far as we know, did Paschal respond in like terms to Bohemond's rhetoric. Even in the Norman prince's letter, it is not exactly clear that he was willing or able to pitch outright his attack on the Byzantines as a "holy war." The expedition to Jerusalem, the attack on Alexius, and the problem of Greek religious error were three separate matters for Paschal's consideration, linked implicitly rather than explicitly.

Unlike observers in the early twelfth century, we are well aware that continued crusading activity would create the threat of violence or cause actual violence against Greek Christians. In 1147, during the Second Crusade, members of the French army passing by Constantinople agitated for an assault on the city, justifying this action, in part, because of Greek religious errors and deviance

---

[41] Bohemond of Antioch, Ep. 7, *Papsturkunden für Kirchen im Heiligen Lande*, ed. Hiestand, pp. 102–104. The letter is also published with commentary by Walter Holtmann, "Zur Geschichte des Investiturstreites 2. Bohemund von Antiochen und Alexios I," *Neues Archiv der Gesellschaft für ältere deutsche Geschichtskunde* 50 (1957), 270–82.

[42] Ep. 7, *Papsturkunden für Kirchen im Heiligen Lande*, ed. Hiestand, p. 103. "Hec autem esset nostra voluntas, si Deus vestro cordi inspirare dignaretur, ut cum episcopis et cardinalibus et clero Romano sive etiam concilio in proximo convocata concilium caperetis et ad expediendam iter Jerosolimanum sive ad iustitiam inter nos et imperatorum tenendam sive ad scismata et hereses et diversas traditiones removendas, quae in ecclesia de processione sancti [spiritus], de baptismate, de sacrificio, de coniugo in sacris ordinibus [existunt]."

[43] For a recent discussion of 1054 and its aftermath, see Axel Bayer, *Spaltung der Christenheit: Das sogennante Morgenländische Schisma von 1054* (Cologne, 2002).

from Rome.[44] It is important to remember, as pointed out by William Daly in his insightful piece on continued role of "Christian fraternity" in mitigating armed conflict between Latins and Greeks, that the majority of the French army in 1147 did not accept this argument and refused to assault Constantinople.[45] Whatever the hotly debated reasons for the Fourth Crusade's diversion to Constantinople, during the second assault on the city in April 1204, the clergy in the army openly preached that their attack against its inhabitants was licit due to Greek treason, the Greek rejection of Roman authority, and the Greek distain for Latin rites.[46] In this instance, due in large part to the contingencies of the situation, this justification for the assault apparently drew more support. For the first but not the last time, we see clearly a successful argument that because the Greeks were heretics and schismatic, they were legitimate targets for crusading.

It is only natural that modern scholars want to see a prelude to these events in the "crusade of 1107," confirming our impression that there was an inevitable falling out between Byzantium and the West during the era of the crusades. Upon closer inspection, however, the sources do not support this view, or at

---

[44]   The major source for these events is Odo of Deuil, *De profectione Ludovici VII in orientem (The Journey of Louis VII to the East)*, ed. and trans. Virginia Berry, Records of Civilization: Sources and Studies, (New York, 1948), pp. 57–73 (Latin text with facing English translation).

[45]   Daly, "Christian Fraternity," pp. 60–71. Recently, Jonathan Phillips, "Odo of Deuil's *De profectione Ludovici VII in Orientem* as a Source for the Second Crusade," in *The Exerpeience of Crusading*, ed. Marcus Bull and Norman Housley (Cambridge, 2003), pp. 80–95, has made the argument that Odo's account is not as uniformly "anti-Byzantine" as scholars sometimes make it out to be. In a similar vein, see also Jonathan Phillips, *Defenders of the Holy Land: Relations between the Latin East and West, 1119–1187* (Oxford, 1996), pp. 100–39, and Timothy Reuter, "The 'Non-Crusade' of 1149–50," in *The Second Crusade: Scope and Consequences*, ed. Jonathan Phillips and Martin Hoch (Manchester, Eng., 2001), pp. 150–63, which argues against the commonly held notion that there was a joint French and Sicilio-Norman proposal for a crusade against Constantinople in the wake of the Second Crusade. Reuter questions the supposed anti-Greek sentiment of the period and cautions against seeing the events of 1204 as inevitable. For a contrary view, see Giles Constable, "The Crusading Project of 1150," in *Montjoie: Studies in Crusade History in Honour of Hans Eberhard Mayer*, ed. Benjamin Kedar et al. (Aldershot, UK, 1997), pp. 67–76.

[46]   See the eye-witness accounts of Fourth Crusaders Geoffrey de Villehardouin, *La conquête de Constantinople*, ed. Edmond Faral (Paris, 1938–39), and Robert of Clari, *La conquête de Constantinople*, ed. Philippe Lauer (Paris, 1924). On the Fourth Crusade, see Donald Queller and Thomas Madden, *The Fourth Crusade: The Conquest of Constantinople*, 2nd edn. (1977; Philadelphia, 1997), and Michael Angold, *The Fourth Crusade: Event and Context* (Harlow, UK, 2003). On the contentious historiography of the Fourth Crusade, see Thomas Madden, "Outside and Inside the Fourth Crusade," *International History Review* 17 (1995): 726–43.

least, they reveal a great deal of uncertainty about the intersection of crusading and Western attitudes toward the Greeks in the early twelfth century. On the one hand, Jerusalem still possessed a place in the interior landscape of crusading that could not be so easily displaced or manipulated. It is worth remembering that this was still the case when the Fourth Crusade set out for Constantinople to "restore" the young Prince Alexius to the Byzantine throne: the crusaders were not intending to wage a "holy war" against Greeks, they were searching for funds to support their expedition to liberate the Holy Land. On the other, the association of the Byzantine Empire and its inhabitants with religious schism and heresy was not nearly so fixed in Latin minds as we might assume in the early twelfth century. Bohemond got the war that he wanted against Alexius in 1107. This was neither the first nor the last time that Franco-Norman armies fought Byzantine forces in a struggle for political dominance in the Mediterranean world. If he was selling his attack as a "holy war" against Greek Christians, however, there are signs that not everyone was buying.

Chapter 8

"Like an Ember Buried in Ashes:" The Byzantine–Venetian Conflict of 1119–1126[1]

Thomas Devaney
Brown University

When called to the aid of the Crusaders after the *Ager Sanguinis* in 1119, Doge Domenico Michiel of Venice provided a fleet to assist in the conquest of Tyre. He also seized the opportunity to further Venetian interests. On both its outbound and return voyages, the Venetian Crusading expedition raided Byzantine islands in an attempt to force Emperor John II Comnenus (1118–1143) to restore trading privileges revoked a few years earlier. This essay investigates the particulars of this conflict, which set the tone for later relations. Although tensions had existed between Venice and the Byzantine Empire before this time, they had maintained a close military and economic association, in which Byzantium was the senior partner. However, Venice's successful campaign to force John II into granting concessions established a new hierarchy in the relationship. Though later emperors sought to contain the Venetians, they would not again be able to treat them as inferior partners. Further, the conflict created an atmosphere of mistrust that would taint all future interactions.

The Venetian role in the Fourth Crusade and the conquest of Constantinople in 1204 has been the subject of much debate. Though many scholars have challenged the argument that the crusade was "diverted" by the Venetians for their own purposes, questions about relations between Byzantium and Venice remain relevant to this controversy, with Manuel I's 1171 expulsion of all Venetians from the empire commonly cited as the point of divergence for Byzantium and Venice. However, the Venetian raids in 1123–1126 marked the first open conflict between Byzantium and Venice. It is to this confrontation that one should look for the roots of later discord.

---

[1]   I would like to thank Walter Kaegi, Daniel Larison, Leonidas Pittos, Nicole Couture, and Amy Remensnyder for their comments on earlier drafts of this article.

The relationship between Venice and Byzantium was, before John II took the throne, largely positive. Although Alexius I Comnenus' (1081–1118) chrysobull of 1082 is rightly considered a turning point in Byzantine–Venetian relations, it built on earlier agreements exchanging commercial concessions for military aid. In 992, Emperor Basil II (963–1025) had offered reduced tariffs and regularized trading rights, describing the Venetians as loyal allies and outsiders (*extranei*) rather than as subjects. In return for these concessions, the emperor asked that Venice provide aid in Italy and in the Adriatic.[2] When, in 1082, a Norman invasion led by Robert Guiscard (1059–1085) captured Durazzo (Dyrrachion) on the Adriatic coast and threatened Thessalonica and Constantinople itself, Alexius therefore turned to Venice.[3] Doge Domenico Silvio of Venice (1070–1084) had his own reasons to support Alexius: the doges had considered themselves Dukes of Dalmatia since their defeat of Croatian pirates in 1000; many Venetians lived in Durazzo; and a Norman naval presence in the Adriatic could threaten the Venetian economy. Though they suffered several setbacks, the allied Byzantines and Venetians eventually repulsed the invaders. Venice paid a considerable price for their aid. Anna Comnena estimated Venetian casualties at 13,000 dead and noted that the Normans captured and mutilated many others.[4]

The Byzantines clearly appreciated the efforts of their ally. Alexius lost no time in providing the promised reward, offering substantial commercial concessions to Venice in his chrysobull of 1082: the right to trade duty-free in all parts of

---

[2]   Andrea Dandolo, *Chronicon Venetum. Andreae Danduli Ducis Venetiarum Chronica per extensum descripta aa. 46–1280*, ed. Ester Pastorello, *Rerum italicarum scriptores*, 13: 1 (Bologna, 1938), p. 193; Gottlieb L.F. Tafel and Georg M. Thomas, *Urkunden zur älteren Handels- und Staatsgeschichte der Republik Venedig, mit besonderen Beziehung auf Byzanz und die Levante*, Fontes Rerum Austriacarum 12 (Vienna, 1856), 1, no. xvii, pp. 36–9 (hereafter cited as *TTh*); Franz Dölger, *Regesten der Kaiserurkunden des oströmischen Reiches von 565–1453*, (Munich, 1924–65), 1, no. 781 (hereafter cited as *DR*); O. Tůma, "Some Notes on the Significance of the Imperial Chrysobull to the Venetians of 992," *Byzantion*, 54 (1984): 358–66; Raimondo Morozzo della Rocca and Agostino Lombardo, eds. *Documenti del commercio veneziano nei secoli XI–XII* (Turin, 1940), 1, nos. 2, 7, 11, 12, 13.

[3]   A number of sources describe the Norman invasion, including Anna Comnena, *Alexiad* 4–6, trans. Edgar R.A. Sewter, *The Alexiad of Anna Comnena*, (New York, 1969), pp. 136–216; Geoffrey of Malaterra, *De rebus gestis Rogerii Calabriae et Siciliae comitis et Roberti Guiscardi ducis fratris eius* 3, ed. Ernesto Pontieri, *Rerum italicarum scriptores*, 5: 1 (Bologna, 1928), pp. 71–82; and William of Apulia, *Guillaume de Pouille, La Geste de Robert Guiscard* 4–5, ed. Marguerite Mathieu, Testi e Monumenti: Testi 4 (Palermo, 1961), pp. 204–59.

[4]   Anna Comnena, *Alexiad* 6.5, pp. 189–90; *DR*, II, no. 1119; Dandolo, *Chronica per extensum*, pp. 196–9, 218; *TTh*, 1, no. xix, p. 40. On Venetian motives for opposing Guiscard, see Donald Nicol, *Byzantium and Venice: A Study in Diplomatic and Cultural Relations* (Cambridge, 1988), pp. 55–6.

the empire; a number of properties in Constantinople that would eventually form the Venetian Quarter of that city; the hereditary title of *protosebastos* to the doge; and numerous other honors, pensions, and guarantees. While earlier accords had facilitated Venetian trade with Constantinople, this decree paved the way for an extensive and permanent Venetian presence in the empire. It also solidified Venice's *de facto* monopoly of Byzantine trade.[5]

Relations were far from perfect, as demonstrated by the Venetian expedition to support the First Crusade. Though Venice did not initially contribute to the crusade, Vitale I Michiel (1096–1101) eventually organized a major fleet, which set sail in 1099 and wintered on the Byzantine island of Rhodes. Ignoring Alexius' warning to desist, the Venetian fleet sailed on to Myra, on the Southern coast of Anatolia, where they removed the alleged relics of Saint Nicholas after torturing the local clergy into revealing their location. On reaching the Levant, the fleet participated in the conquest of Haifa before returning home in August 1100.

Although Alexius and Vitale disagreed sharply over Venetian participation in the crusade, these tensions existed but did not outweigh the political and economic advantages of maintaining close ties. Alexius issued warnings, but took no action. For their part, the Venetians had assembled a fleet of approximately 200 vessels, the largest single contribution to the First Crusade, with great pomp and ceremony. Yet when this fleet reached the Holy Land, they consented to stay only two months and quickly returned to Venice after receiving their share of Haifa. Alexius's influence likely played a prominent role in the Venetians' quick return; they fulfilled their obligations in Syria but did not excessively offend the emperor. Similarly, though they did not hesitate to use violence in their pursuit of relics, they made sure to offer reparations to the Bishop of Myra. Although

---

5   This chrysobull has received a great deal of attention from scholars, especially concerning its date. The Latin text of the document can be found in *TTh*, 1, no. xxiii, pp. 41–54. John Cinnamus referred to the concessions offered Venice as "recompense" for their assistance, *Deeds of John and Manuel Comnenus*, trans. Charles M. Brand, Records of Civilization, Sources and Studies 45 (New York, 1976) (hereafter cited as Cinnamus), p. 210. For the dating of the chrysobull, see André Tuilier, "La date exacte du chrysobulle d'Alexis I Comnène en faveur des Vénitiens et son contexte historique," *Rivista di studi bizantini e neoellenici*, n.s. 4 (1967): 27–48; O. Tůma, "The Dating of Alexius' Chrysobull to the Venetians: 1082, 1084, or 1092?", *Byzantinoslavica* 42 (1981): 171–85; Thomas F. Madden, "The Chrysobull of Alexius I Comnenus to the Venetians: The Date and the Debate," *Journal of Medieval History* 28 (2002): 23–41. The title *protosebastos*, invented by Alexius I, ranked fourth in the court order after the emperor. The practice of bestowing imperial titles on foreign potentates was common in the later empire.

willing to ignore the emperor in pursuit of their goals, the Venetians took care to maintain a semblance of goodwill.[6]

A Venetian monk challenged this delicate balance when he arranged the theft of the relics of Saint Stephen in 1107 or 1108 and brought them to a Venetian church in Constantinople. Before they could be removed from the city, the theft was discovered and a standoff ensued, as the Byzantines would not enter the church to recover the relics by force and the Venetians could not remove them without escalating the confrontation. Although the issue had faded by 1110 when a number of prominent Venetians accompanied the relics to Venice and Doge Ordefalo Falier (1101–1118) endorsed the theft by placing them in the monastery of San Giorgio Maggiore, the incident contributed to tensions in Constantinople between resident Venetians and local citizens.[7]

Shortly thereafter, Alexius granted commercial privileges to Pisa. These concessions, while not as comprehensive as those received by Venice 30 years earlier, still posed a threat to a Venetian monopoly. Pisan merchants were granted only discounted customs duties rather than the duty-free status of Venice, but did receive a quarter and wharf in Constantinople, implying a permanent presence. Venice retained the dominant position in the Byzantine trade for the moment; however, the extension of privileges to Pisa threatened its monopoly and raised questions about the future.[8]

---

[6] *Translatio Sancti Nicolai. Monachi anonymi Littorensis*, in *RHC Oc.*, 5, pp. 255–64, 272; Heinrich Simonsfeld, ed., *Annales venetici breves, MGH SS* 14 (Hannover, 1883), p. 70; Dandolo, *Chronica per extensum*, pp. 221–2; Donald Queller and Irene Katele, "Venice and the Conquest of the Latin Kingdom of Jerusalem," *Studi Veneziani*, n.s. 12 (1986), pp. 20–26; Thomas Madden, *Enrico Dandolo and the Rise of Venice* (Baltimore, 2003), pp. 10–12.

[7] Dandolo, *Chronica per extensum*, p. 227; Luigi Lanfranchi, ed., *San Giorgio Maggiore* (Venice, 1968), 3, no. cxliv, pp. 504–5; Heinrich Kretschmayr, *Geschichte von Venedig* (Gotha, 1905), 1, p. 222. Madden questions Dandolo's version of the journey to Venice, noting that there was no reason for so many prominent merchants to travel on the same ship, *Enrico Dandolo*, p. 13, n. 89.

[8] Franz Miklosich and Joseph Müller, eds., *Acta et Diplomata graeca medii aevi sacra et profana*, (Vienna, 1865), 3, pp. 9–13; Giuseppe Müller, ed., *Documenti sulle relazioni delle città Toscane coll'oriente cristiano e coi Turchi fino all'anno MDXXXI* (Florence, 1879), p. 43; *DR*, 2, nos. 1254, 1255; Georgije Ostrogorsky, *History of the Byzantine State*, trans. Joan Hussey (New Brunswick, NJ, 1969), p. 367; Ralph-Johannes Lilie, *Handel und Politik zwischen dem byzantinischen Reich und den italienischen Kommunen Venedig, Pisa und Genua in der Epoche der Komnenen und der Angeloi (1081–1204)* (Amsterdam, 1984), pp. 69–76; and *Byzantium and the Crusader States: studies in the relations of the Byzantine Empire with the Crusader States in Syria and Palestine between 1096 and the Fourth Crusade in 1204*, trans. J.C. Morris and Jean E. Ridings (Oxford, 1993), pp. 87–91.

Uncertainty over Dalmatia was another source of friction. Venetian doges had claimed the title *dux Dalmatiae* since freeing the coastal towns from the depredations of Croatian pirates in 1000. The region remained under the titular authority of the Byzantine Emperor, a claim renewed by Alexius in his chrysobull to the Pisans. As long as the province remained peaceful and Adriatic shipping was uninterrupted, the situation was tolerated in Venice. In the early twelfth century, however, Hungarian expansion threatened these territories. Having brought Croatia under his control, King Kálmán of Hungary (1095–1116) moved south, threatening to close the Adriatic and thus stifle the Venetian economy. This development also concerned Alexius. With his military stretched too thin, he sought a diplomatic solution and, in 1105, arranged the marriage of his son and heir John to Piroska of Hungary.[9] This produced a temporary solution for the empire, but Venice continued to view Hungary with concern. The Doge sent an embassy to Alexius in 1112 for the dual purpose of requesting support for a planned invasion of Dalmatia and of scouting Pisan activity in the city. Since Alexius had recently restated Byzantine claims to Dalmatia, he could not have been pleased by this appeal. However, not wanting to alienate his Venetian allies, he chose to agree in principle but offer no aid at that time. This satisfied the Venetians, who did not invade until 1116.[10]

Despite these concerns, the Venetian presence in Constantinople, though not yet the defined quarter that would develop later in the twelfth century, expanded in the decades after Alexius' chrysobull.[11] Though a precise count is difficult due to the nature of the extant sources, the available evidence points to a significant number of Venetians in the Byzantine capital. For example, Dandolo claimed that, in 1110, 72 prominent Venetians were available to accompany the relics of Saint Stephen to Venice, suggesting that a much larger number were in Constantinople at the time. These Venetians, members of the

---

[9] John the Deacon, "Giovanni Diacono, Cronaca veneziana," in Giovanni Monticolo, ed., *Cronache veneziane antichissime*, (Rome, 1890), 1, pp. 155–60; *TTh*, 1, nos. xix, xxiv, pp. 40, 54–5; Dandolo, *Chronica per extensum*, p. 217; Jadran Ferluga, *L'amministrazione bizantina in Dalmazia* (Venice, 1978), pp. 201–4; Nicol argues that Dandolo may have exaggerated or invented Alexius' concessions in Dalmatia, *Byzantium and Venice*, p. 63.

[10] *TTh*, 1, no. xxxv, pp. 75–6; Dandolo, *Chronica per extensum*, p. 229; Ferdinand Chalandon, *Jean II Comnène (1118–1143) et Manuel I Comnène (1143–1180)* (Paris, 1912), p. 155; Lilie argues that Alexius agreed because he hoped for Venetian naval support in an assault on Antioch planned for 1113, *Byzantium and the Crusader States*, pp. 91–3 and *Handel und Politik*, pp. 362–3.

[11] On the development of the Venetian Quarter in Constantinople, see M.E. Martin, "The Chrysobull of Alexius I Comnenus to the Venetians and the Early Venetian Quarter in Constantinople," *Byzantinoslavica* 29 (1978), pp. 19–23, and "The Venetians in the Byzantine Empire before 1204," *Byzantinische Forschungen* 13 (1988), pp. 201–14.

leading families of Venice, were in Constantinople to trade goods ranging from textiles and foodstuffs to mastic and alum. Commerce remained brisk through the end of Alexius' reign and into that of John II. Shortly before he died in 1118, Alexius offered his son some bits of wisdom for his coming reign but neglected to mention Venice. He may have assumed, based on the success of his Venetian policy, that relations between Byzantium and Venice would remain stable.[12]

However, when Doge Domenico Michiel (1118–1129) sent envoys to John II to congratulate him on his succession and request that he renew Venetian privileges, he was rebuffed. John refused, considering it within his rights to withdraw Venetian privileges at any time. Chrysobulls issued by one emperor were not necessarily binding on his successors as they were neither treaties nor contracts but unilateral acts of the emperor that could be altered at his discretion. Venetian merchants, therefore, were entitled to their privileges only so long as they met their obligations as the emperor's loyal subjects. To John, their behavior in the empire proved that they were not doing so.[13]

The chrysobulls of 992 and 1082 had led to immense riches for Venetian merchants in the empire and left them largely outside the control of civil authorities. Merchants in the nascent Venetian Quarter fell under the *de facto* jurisdiction of the Doge and his representatives while technically subject to the laws of the city.[14] To the Byzantines, the behavior of these resident Venetians, such as the theft of the relics of Saint Stephen, demonstrated that they considered themselves to be above the law in Constantinople. Further, they showed contempt for Byzantine citizens and even senior officials:

> They used to treat the citizen like a slave, not merely one of the general commonality, but even one who took pride in the rank of *sebastos* [which denoted

---

[12]   *TTh*, 1, no. xxxii, pp. 67–74; Dandolo, *Chronica per extensum*, pp. 227, 232; Madden, *Enrico Dandolo*, p. 12; Morozza della Rocca and Lombardo, *Documenti*, 1, nos. 19, 24, 33, 41, 42, 45, 46; Paul Magdalino, *The Empire of Manuel I Komnenos, 1143–1180* (Cambridge, 1993), pp. 27–34.

[13]   Cinnamus, p. 210; *TTh*, 1, no. xxxix, p. 78; Heinrich Simonsfeld, ed., *Historia Ducum Veneticorum*, MGH SS 14 (Hannover, 1883), p. 73.

[14]   The Chrysobull of 992 placed Venetian traders under the jurisdiction of the Logothete of the Dromos, a senior Byzantine official. Only he would have the authority to inspect Venetian ships, levy fines, or judge disputes between Venetians and Byzantine citizens. The purpose of the provision seems to have been to facilitate trade by dispensing with bureaucratic formalities. There is no mention of the Logothete of the Dromos in the Chrysobull of 1082; however, this does not mean that Venetian traders were now outside of his jurisdiction. See Nicol, *Byzantium and Venice*, pp. 41, 79; Horatio F. Brown, "The Venetians and the Venetian Quarter in Constantinople to the Close of the Twelfth Century," *Journal of Hellenic Studies* 40 (1920), pp. 69–72; Angold, *Byzantine Empire*, p. 185.

a connection by blood or marriage to the emperor] and who had advanced to some greater position among the Romans' grand offices ... Therefore they inflicted blows on many of the well-born who were related to the emperor by blood, and generally insulted them savagely. Even in the time of Emperor Manuel, they no less continued the same practices, taking for themselves Roman wives and dwelling like other Romans in their houses outside the residential area granted them by the emperor.[15]

The presence of large numbers of Venetians resident in Constantinople, rich on the proceeds of privileges granted by the emperor and condescending in their treatment of local citizens, led to tensions on the street. Their resistance to physical and social boundaries while in the city contributed to the problem.

Other considerations may have influenced John. His father had taken care to maintain close ties with Venice because he needed naval aid to counter the ever-present danger of Norman invasion. During the first years of John's reign, however, the Norman threat appeared to have dissipated and he may have judged that Venetian assistance was not worth the infringement on his sovereignty posed by privileges granted to Venetian troublemakers in his capital. The question of control over Dalmatia remained a point of contention. Though Venice had established a measure of authority in Dalmatia by occupying a number of towns, the common argument that John refused to ratify Venetian privileges solely in response to their pretensions in Dalmatia does not stand up well to scrutiny.[16] Though Venice had re-occupied Dalmatia, Doge Michiel, unlike István II of Hungary (1116–1131), remained willing to recognize the emperor's nominal sovereignty over the province. John showed no inclination at the beginning of his reign to attempt the re-conquest of the northwestern Balkan territories occupied by Hungary and Venice. Relations with Hungary remained cordial at this time, due to Alexius' policy of diplomacy.[17] John would eventually go to war with Hungary, but not until 1128 and then only in response to attacks on the frontier. John's foreign policy at this time focused on continuing his father's Anatolian strategy by leading campaigns in 1119 and 1120 to recover areas of the Maiander valley around Sozopolis that had been lost in the preceding years. Even

---

[15] Cinnamus, p. 210.

[16] For example, Magdalino, *Manuel I Komnenos*, pp. 34–5; Lilie, *Handel und Politik*, p. 367. These arguments are based in part on Alexius' claim to Croatia, Dalmatia, and Durazzo in his chrysobull of 1111.

[17] They were not, however, as close as they had been. Alexius' decision to endorse Venetian attacks on Hungary had cooled relations. See Ferenc Makk, *The Árpáds and the Comneni: Political Relations between Hungary and Byzantium in the 12th Century*, trans. György Novák (Budapest, 1989), pp. 18–21.

had Venetian claims in Dalmatia offended John, he would not have alienated an ally until he was ready to enforce Byzantine sovereignty by occupying the region. Similarly, growing Venetian ties with the Crusader States may have irritated John. However, as he showed no inclination at this time to pursue his claims in Antioch and elsewhere, there was no reason for him to break with Venice over this issue.[18] Arguments that economic concerns motivated John II to dissolve the connection to Venice are likewise questionable.[19] Little evidence supports this claim and John's dealings with other powers offer no comparable actions. Legal prerogatives, ideology, and military necessity were the main concerns of John II's foreign policy. Venetian abuses in Constantinople were a challenge to imperial authority. John needed to re-establish Byzantine superiority over the Venetians to remind them that the riches gained through trade came with an obligation to serve the emperor faithfully.

John II refused to ratify the chrysobull of 1082 mainly because of Venetian behavior in the capital. Explanations that attempt to fit this decision into a picture of grand strategy in either the Balkans or the Crusader States fail to take into account the timing. Heavily committed in Anatolia, John would have seen no purpose in alienating Venice over territorial claims until he was prepared to pursue his objectives in those regions. As a newly crowned emperor who had recently weathered an attempted coup, however, John may have been particularly sensitive to challenges to his authority, especially at home.[20] Venetian merchants in Constantinople did just that and he dealt with them summarily. If the situations in Dalmatia or the Levant influenced him, it was not because he was prepared to reclaim the province, but because they provided further evidence of Venetian arrogance. In severing ties with Venice, John's attitude reflected the changing fortunes of the empire. In 1082, faced with invasion from both east and west, Alexius I had no choice but to seek aid from Venice; in 1119, at the helm of a reconstituted empire facing no dire threats, John II looked to re-establish control over these troublesome foreigners.

In response to the loss of Venetian privileges, Doge Michiel again sent envoys to Constantinople, but met with no success. Venetian merchants remained in the empire through 1121, though now required to pay customs duties and

---

[18]   For Venetian trading privileges in the Crusader States, see *TTh*, 1, nos. xxvii, xxx, xxxi, xxxvii, pp. 64–6, 77–8; Brown, "Venetians," 72.

[19]   For example, Ostrogorsky, *Byzantine State*, p. 377: "John tried without success to sever the link which bound the Empire to Venice and strangled Byzantine trade."

[20]   John's sister, Anna Comnena, had intrigued against him with the hopes of putting her husband, Nicephorus Bryennius, on the throne. Angold, *Byzantine Empire*, p. 183; Ostrogorsky, *Byzantine State*, pp. 376–7.

trade under less favorable conditions.[21] Given the peaceful resolution of past disagreements, it is possible that Venice and Byzantium would have reached an accord had external developments not changed the context in which negotiations took place. In 1119, Atabeg Ilghazi of Aleppo (1107–1122) invaded Antioch and, at the *Ager Sanguinis* (Field of Blood), defeated a Crusader army. In the aftermath of this defeat, Baldwin II (1118–1131) of Jerusalem appealed for aid to the pope and Venice. Pope Calixtus II, preoccupied with other concerns, added his voice to Baldwin's by sending 10 papal *nuntii* to Venice in 1120. Doge Michiel summoned the citizens of Venice to answer the call and earn glory and wealth.[22] Michiel succeeded in gathering a significant fleet, though details of its size and composition are unclear. An estimate of 15,000 crew and passengers loaded on 72 vessels seems most appropriate.[23]

Significantly, the Doge did not mention the difficulties with Byzantium when appealing to the people. Whatever else it might do, the main purpose of the expedition was to aid the Crusaders, not to wage war against Byzantium. If possible, however, he intended also to seize the opportunity to advance Venetian interests. The situation in Dalmatia had destabilized; a number of towns had rebelled in favor of István II, who had opened negotiations to obtain imperial recognition of Hungarian claims in Dalmatia. Just as Venice had allied with Byzantium against the Normans to prevent a hostile power from holding Dalmatia and gaining the ability to control shipping in the Adriatic, so it would move to prevent Hungary from attempting the same. In August 1122, the fleet reasserted Venetian control in rebel towns as it sailed along the Dalmatian coast.

---

[21]   Morozzo della Rocca and Lombardo, *Documenti*, 1, nos. 41, 42, 45, 46.

[22]   William of Tyre, *Chronique* 12.9–12, ed. Robert B.C. Huygens. CCCM 63–63A (Turnhout, 1986), 1, pp. 556–62; Fulcher of Chartres, *Fulcheri Carontensis Historia Hierosolymitana (1095–1127)* 3.3.2–4, ed. Heinrich Hagenmeyer (Heidelberg, 1913), pp. 621–3; *TTh*, 1, no. xxxviii, p. 78; Dandolo, *Chronica per extensum*, p. 232; *Historia Ducum Veneticorum*, p. 73; *Translatio Isidori*, in RHC Oc., 5, pp. 322–3; Runciman, *History of the Crusades*, 2, pp. 149–52; Queller and Katele, "Venice," p. 29.

[23]   William of Tyre, *Chronique* 12.22, 1, p. 573–4; Fulcher of Chartres, *Historia Hierosolymitana* 3.15.2, pp. 656–7; Dandolo, *Chronica per extensum*, pp. 232–3; *Historia Ducum Veneticorum*, p. 73; *Translatio Isidori*, p. 323; *Annales*, p. 71. See also John Pryor, " 'Water, water everywhere, Nor any drop to drink': Water Supplies for the Fleets of the First Crusade," in *Dei Gesta per Francos: Etudes sur les Croisades dédiées à Jean Richard*, ed. Michel Balard, Benjamin Kedar, and Jonathan Riley-Smith (Aldershot, 2001) p. 24, and "Byzantium and the Sea: Byzantine Fleets and the History of the Empire in the Age of the Macedonian Emperors, c. 900–1025 CE" in *War at Sea in the Middle Ages and the Renaissance*, ed. John Hattendorf and Richard Unger (Woodbridge, UK, 2003), pp. 85–6; Queller and Katele, "Venice," pp. 30–31 and n. 60.

With the Dalmatian situation in hand for the moment, Michiel attacked the Byzantine island of Corfu.[24] He had a number of motives for doing so. Attempts to reach a diplomatic accord with John II had failed. By negotiating with István II to recognize Hungarian claims in Dalmatia and by denying Venetian privileges, John now threatened Venetian trade, the life-blood of the city, in two ways. Although Venice might hope eventually to reach an accord with John over trading privileges, the recall of all merchants to serve with the fleet rendered the issue less pressing. However, Venice could not permit an enemy power to control Dalmatia. John's treatment of his former ally proved to the Doge that he was ungrateful for Venetian service against the Normans. Venice had fought Robert Guiscard to regain Corfu for Byzantium and lost many men and ships. It was only just that John would lose the island if he would not respect his obligations. In addition, Corfu, located at the mouth of the Adriatic, allowed an occupying power to control the Adriatic trade; for these reasons, Guiscard's forces had occupied Corfu even before their main assault on Durazzo.

Michiel had another pressing motive for choosing Corfu. After leaving Venice on August 8, the fleet spent some time in Dalmatia; at their slow pace, they could not hope to reach Acre before winter storms would force the fleet into port.[25] Fulcher of Chartres explains their slow pace:

> And because it was necessary, in order that they advance simultaneously and not haphazardly, and also the breeze varied now and then, they controlled their journey with forethought lest they quickly get separated one from another. Therefore, sailing in short stages, by day and not by night, they daily landed through necessity at the ports they frequently discovered, that both themselves and their horses not be burdened with thirst, suffering want of fresh water.[26]

---

[24] Lilie argues that the Doge delayed preparations for the expedition in order to strike Corfu at the most opportune moment, *Handel und Politik*, pp. 370–1.

[25] Pryor has estimated that the average continuous cruising speed of this fleet was 0.8 knots, based on the length of time it took to travel from Corfu to the Holy Land in the spring of 1123, "'Water, water everywhere,'" p. 23. Therefore, assuming it arrived off Corfu in late September or early October 1122, the fleet could not have reached Acre until midwinter, by which time Mediterranean storms would present a dire threat to galleys with shallow draft and low gunwales.

[26] Fulcher of Chartres, *Historia Hierosolymitana* 3.15.4, p. 658: "*et quia necesse erat, ut simul nec sparsim incederent, flabris etiam interdum alternantibus, nisi provide iter suum modificarent, alii ab aliis cito discreparent, propterea diebus [dietis] brevibus die non nocte velificantes, portibus frequenter inventis necessario cotidie applicabant, ne recentis aquae penuriam patientes tam ipsi quam equi siti gravarentur.*"

Michiel needed to spend the winter somewhere; Corfu offered an opportunity both to address the needs of the fleet and to strike a blow at Byzantium. He may not have intended aggression at this point, simply hoping to winter peacefully at Corfu; in fact, unaware of hostilities, Fulcher assumed that such was the case, writing, "[the Venetians], having come from their own land the preceding year, passed the winter on an island called Corfu, awaiting an advantageous season for sailing."[27] However, when the Byzantine authorities on Corfu denied permission to land, the Venetians attacked.

Similar attacks had occurred during the First Crusade. A Pisan fleet, possibly as large as 120 ships, sailed for Syria in 1098. En route, they attacked several Byzantine islands. John Pryor has argued that the Pisans intended to winter on the Ionian islands and, when denied permission, had no choice but to attack, being unable either to return to Pisa or carry on to Syria before winter. They met refusal either because they failed to acquire permission in advance or because the fleet was too large for these ports to accommodate them. The Byzantine response to these raids was aggressive and effective as Alexius organized a fleet that set sail in April 1099 and defeated the Pisans later that year.[28]

The Venetians found themselves in a similar situation in 1122. However, they had alternatives; the fleet could return to Venice and set sail in spring or could forge ahead beyond Corfu to winter on another Byzantine island. Neither offered much advantage. A return to Venice would waste several months and the smaller islands were less strategically relevant and less able to provide provisions than Corfu. Given the tensions between Venice and Byzantium, it is unlikely that Venice would have sought or been granted permission to winter on Corfu; the Venetians had to control the island by force in order to stay. Unlike Pisa in 1099, Venice did not have to worry about an effective Byzantine naval response. By this time, the empire's ability to defend its borders on land had improved while its maritime defenses had deteriorated. John's policy of imposing a centralized tax instead of levying conscripts for the navy from coastal provinces played a role in weakening naval defenses as officials diverted this money to pay other expenditures. Heavily committed on land through the early part of his reign, John could not amass a fleet to resist the Venetians.[29]

---

[27]   Fulcher of Chartres, *Historia Hierosolymitana*, 3.14.1, pp. 655–6: "*qui anno praecedenti de terra sua egressi, in insula, quae Curpho nuncupater, tempus exspectantes opportunum navigandi hiemaverunt.*"

[28]   Anna Comnena, *Alexiad* 11.10, pp. 360–2; Bernardo Maragone, *Annales Pisani*, ed. Michele Lupo Gentile, *Rerum italicarum scriptores*, vol. 6, part 2 (Bologna, 1936), p. 7; Pryor, "Water, water everywhere," pp. 23–4.

[29]   On the Comnenian Navy, see Lilie, *Handel und Politik*, pp. 613–43; Hélène Ahrweiler, *Byzance et la mer: la marine de guerre, la politique et les institutions maritimes de*

Alexius had counted on naval aid from Venice or, after 1111, from Pisa to augment his inferior navy in times of need. However, neither Pisa nor Genoa, the other potential source of naval aid, was available to assist Byzantium in 1122. Venice's two maritime rivals, both of whom might relish an opportunity to improve their standing with the Byzantine Empire at the expense of Venice, were fighting over the rights to Corsica. Alexius I may have issued his chrysobull to the Pisans with the potential of strife with Venice in mind. Once the conflict materialized, however, this foresight came to naught, as the Byzantine navy could not hope to oppose Venice alone and could hope for no foreign support.[30]

John II might have overcome these difficulties had he adopted an energetic defense against the Venetians and used all available resources to assemble and equip a fleet. However, he was fresh from campaigns in Anatolia and hard pressed to retain effective control over the Balkans. In 1121 and 1122, as the Venetian fleet was making ready, Petchenek nomads from the Russian steppe crossed the Byzantine frontier in the Balkans, raiding Thrace and Macedonia. John personally led the campaign against the Petcheneks, defeating them decisively. He then moved against the Serbs to ensure the security of his Balkan provinces. Though successful, this campaign occupied the emperor and the greater part of his armed forces from 1122 through late 1123 or early 1124.[31] The Venetians, however, were unable to dislodge the Byzantine garrison on Corfu and wintered on the island. Early in 1123, messengers arrived from Jerusalem, reporting that Baldwin had been captured and imploring Venice to hurry to their aid. The fleet left Corfu in March 1123 and arrived off the coast of Acre in May. On the way, they may have raided the islands of Chios, Rhodes, and Lesbos to secure water supplies.[32]

Byzance aux VIIe-XVe siècles, Bibliothèque Byzantine, études 5 (Paris, 1966), pp. 175–297.

[30] Lilie, *Handel und Politik*, pp. 364–5.

[31] Niketas Choniates, *O city of Byzantium: annals of Niketas Choniatēs*, trans. Harry Magoulias (Detroit, 1984) (hereafter cited as Choniates), pp. 10–1; Cinnamus, pp. 16–7; Ostrogorsky, *Byzantine State*, pp. 377–8.

[32] The sources disagree on the order of events. Cinnamus mentions the raids on these islands before he notes the fleet's arrival at Tyre but implied that the attacks took place on the homeward voyage, p. 210. Fulcher of Chartres has the Venetians stopping at Methone and Rhodes, logical places for the fleet to water and provision; he does not mention hostilities, *Historia Hierosolymitana* 3.15.3, p. 657. Dandolo, *Chronica per extensum*, p. 233 and the *Historia Ducum Veneticorum*, p. 74, mention these raids only after their accounts of Tyre. Queller and Katele argue that they raided Rhodes and Chios on both the way to and the way from the Holy Land, "Venice," pp. 31, 38. Chalandon claims that the fleet stopped at Methone, Rhodes, and Cyprus but says that it is unclear if these stopovers were marked by hostilities, *Jean II Comnène*, p. 157. Other scholars, including Madden, *Enrico Dandolo*,

The Venetian Crusade lasted more than a year and contributed to the successful conquest of Tyre.[33] There is no extant evidence regarding diplomatic contact between Venice and Byzantium during this time and, when the fleet sailed for home late in the summer of 1124, it was in a state of undeclared war. The situation was similar to that of 1122, with no hope of reaching Venice before winter. The expedition would have to winter along the route; all the likely locations were in Byzantine territory.[34] Although John had not prepared his naval defenses or begun to assemble a fleet, he had ordered Venice to be treated as an enemy. The Doge's decision to leave the Levant at this time indicates that, having accomplished the goals of the crusade, he now wanted to put further pressure on John II. Rumors that John had detained Venetians remaining in Constantinople would have strengthened his resolve. In the event, the doge chose to sail to the Byzantine island of Rhodes, arriving in October 1124.[35]

The *Historia Ducum Veneticorum* claims that "when [the Venetians] came to Rhodes and went among the citizens peacefully to buy supplies at the market, the Rhodians were unwilling to sell them provisions or concede to their entreaties, but rather they began to reproach them as enemies." Andrea Dandolo's version of events is similar: "He landed on Rhodes and sought provisions from the inhabitants, and when they refused he invaded their city, stole their property and shared it out."[36] Implying that the Doge had no intention of further raids on Byzantine territory after his unsuccessful siege of Corfu, these accounts claim that it was only after this rebuff on Rhodes that he chose to renew his conflict with the emperor. The fleet would have needed to stop for water, and Rhodes

---

p. 16; Nicol, *Byzantium and Venice*, p. 79; and Lilie, *Handel und Politik*, p. 371, argue that the Venetians sailed directly from Corfu to Syria.

[33] Fulcher of Chartres, *Historia Hierosolymitana* 3.14–41, pp. 655–761; Dandolo, *Chronica per extensum*, pp. 233–5.

[34] The main sea route ran along the coast of Anatolia, across the Aegean Sea, around the Peloponnesian peninsula, and thence to Italy. See Lilie, *Handel und Politik*, p. 243; and *Byzantium and the Crusader States*, p. 98.

[35] Several scholars interpret the decision to end the crusade in this way, including Nicol, *Byzantium and Venice*, p. 79: "They had in fact other business to do. Corfu had resisted them. They would take their revenge on the Byzantine Emperor elsewhere;" and Madden, *Enrico Dandolo*, pp. 16–7: "There remained, however, the pressing problem of John II's refusal to honor the promises of his father to Venice's merchants." Cf. Queller and Katele, who argue that the allies dispersed and the Venetian fleet sailed with its task completed, "Venice," p. 37.

[36] *Historia Ducum Veneticorum*, p. 74: "*Cum autem Rodum venissent et marcatum accepturi pacifice ad cives intrassent, noluerunt eis Rodenses alimenta precio vel precibus dare, sed eos pocius ut hostes exprobare ceperunt.*" Dandolo, *Chronica per extensum*, p. 234: "*Rodum aplicuit, et incolis alimenta peciit, quibus renuentibus, urbem invadit, opes abstulit, et aceptas dividit.*"

was a logical choice. It was an important port of call on the sea route from Syria to Italy, one familiar to Venetians; the fleet they sent to join the First Crusade had spent the winter of 1099–1100 on Rhodes. However, recent events offered Michiel no reason to believe that his fleet would be received peaceably. Moreover, provisioning a fleet of more than seventy vessels with fifteen thousand sailors was a major undertaking; arrangements were customarily made in advance. While the Venetians could reasonably request water without prior arrangement, food or naval stores presented a problem, even if relations between Byzantium and Venice had been positive.[37] Michiel likely used the refusal of provisions as a pretext to attack.

After sacking Rhodes, the fleet sailed north along the Anatolian coast and plundered Kos and Samos before wintering on Chios, locations north of the main sea routes and unlikely spots to seek provisions:

> At that time it was made known to us that the Venetians, returning to their homeland after the capture of Tyre, had violently seized the islands of the emperor through which they passed, namely Rhodes and Methone, also Samos and Chios and, in like manner, destroyed the walls. They took the boys and girls into wretched captivity and carried away various properties with them. But because we cannot change this on hearing of it, we grieved piously in our deepest hearts.[38]

The following spring, the Venetians used Chios as a base from which to plunder Lesbos and Andros before setting sail on March 29. They left with great stores of plunder, including the relics of Saint Isidore the Martyr, and many prisoners. The fleet arrived in Venice in June 1125 to popular accolades. Venice had risen to the aid of the Christians in the East, earning material rewards and trading concessions in the process. In the same voyage, the city had punished the Byzantine Empire for reneging on its promises and reclaimed Dalmatia from the depredations of the Hungarians.[39]

---

37   Pryor, "Water, water everywhere," pp. 23–4.

38   Fulcher of Chartres, *Historia Hierosolymitana* 3.41.1, pp. 758–60: "*Tunc temporis usque ad nos divulgatur Veneticos post Tyrum captam in repatriate suo insulas imperatoris, per quas praeteribant, Rhodum videlicet et Mothonem, Samum quoque et Chium violenter comprehendisse pariterque moenia diruisse, puberes et puellas miserabiliter captivasse, pecuniam multimodam secum asportasse. sed quoniam emendare hoc nequivimus, in visceribus, intimis hoc audientes pie condoluimus.*"

39   Dandolo, *Chronica per extensum*, pp. 234–5; *Translatio Isidori*, pp. 323–4; *Historia Ducum Veneticorum*, p. 74; *Annales*, p. 71; Pietro Giustiniani, *Venetiarum historia vulgo Pietro Iustiniano Iustiniani filio adiudicata*, ed. Roberto Cessi and Fanny Bennato, Monumenti storici, n.s. 18 (Venice, 1964), pp. 106–7; Cinnamus, p. 210; Chalandon, *Jean II Comnène*, pp. 157–8; Lilie, *Byzantium and the Crusader States*, pp. 97–9.

The raids had not succeeded, however, in forcing the emperor to submit to Venetian demands. John remained obstinate, assuming that, with the Crusading fleet disbanded, the attacks had ended. Attitudes on both sides had hardened. Reports reached the Doge that John II had ordered the Venetian quarter in Constantinople burned in retribution. Michiel was so enraged, Dandolo tells us, that he ordered all Venetians to shave their beards so they would not resemble Greeks. In 1126, Michiel sent a force to attack Byzantine possessions in the Ionian Sea, including Cephalonia, adding the relics of Saint Donatos to Venice's growing collection of Greek saints.[40]

John now faced two choices: build a fleet or renew the privileges. Assembling a naval force would have required not only building ships but also training and paying skilled crews; requiring money that could be spent strengthening land forces in the Balkans and Anatolia. Compromise, on the other hand, would end the threat to Byzantine coastlines and islands. Accordingly, John sent emissaries to inform the Doge that he would negotiate. In August 1126, he met with a Venetian delegation dispatched to Constantinople and conferred on Venice all the rights granted in the chrysobull of 1082.[41]

John had refused to ratify Venetian privileges in 1119 because he wanted to re-establish Byzantine superiority over Venice – as Donald Nicol has put it, to "restate the fact that Byzantium was the senior partner in the arrangement."[42] Although forced to renew them, John did not relent on this issue in his chrysobull. He began by reminding the Venetians of their loyalty and friendship to the Byzantine Empire and passing over their recent offences:

> It is often the case that former good faith and good will conceals and destroys later ill will, when masters and friends are overcome by the memory of earlier kindness from their subjects and friends. Just as now has happened in the case of the Venetians. For I, the Emperor, recall their former goodwill and good faith, which they always showed towards the memorable and most beloved father of the emperor, when they single-mindedly exposed themselves to dangers to defend Romania, and fought without hesitation and with energy against our enemies, who had at that time led out an army against that land, and have not given thought to the evil deeds that they have recently done.[43]

---

[40] Dandolo, *Chronica per extensum*, p. 236.

[41] The chrysobull of 1126 survives only within the text of the chrysobull issued by Manuel I (1143–1180) in 1147. *TTh*, 1, no. xliii, pp. 95–8; Dandolo, *Chronica per extensum*, p. 237; *DR*, 2, no. 1304.

[42] Nicol, *Byzantium and Venice*, p. 78.

[43] *TTh*, 1, no. xliii, p. 96: "*Solet multociens antiquior fides atque beniuolentia posteriorem maliuolentiam contegere ac delere, uictis dominis et amicis memoria prioris subjectorum et*

He confirmed all of the details of Alexius I's chrysobull. In return, the Venetians were required to resume their former role as the servants and allies of the emperor:

> At the same time they have agreed in writing and on oath to perform some particular services to my empire and Romania, and their agreement has a wider application to these matters, just as though it had been made by Papal officials ... And yet the Venetians must preserve whole and uncorrupted by an oath to my empire what was promised by their emissaries in an agreement made in writing.[44]

Venice did not just agree in general terms to support the empire but took on specific obligations not included within the chrysobull itself. Unfortunately, the text of these obligations does not survive, making it difficult to analyze the terms of the chrysobull of 1126 completely.[45] However, John did not bow completely to intimidation; the Venetians had to behave appropriately to continue receiving the favor of the emperor and the benefits that accompanied it. In successfully forcing the emperor to grant concessions, however, Venice had established its ability to dictate terms. The Venetian delegation, familiar with the tone of imperial decrees, did not protest the tone or requirements of John's decree. It did not suit their purposes to endanger their privileges again by insulting the emperor's dignity.

This outcome was a humiliation for Byzantium and a great victory for Venice. When Doge Michiel died in 1130, he was lamented by his fellow Venetians as a hero, not only for his victories in Syria or Dalmatia, but also for bringing the intransigent emperor to terms. An inscription on his tombstone, added some time after his death, reads:

---

amicorum bonitatis; uelut nunc quoque in Veneticos contigit. Reminiscens enim Imperium meum antiqueeorum beniuolentie et fidei, quam erga semper memorabilem Imperatorem et dilectissimum patrem eius ostenderunt, obicientes se periculis toto animo pro Romania,et cum strenuitate indubitanter certantes contra inimicos, qui tum exercitum eduxerant contra eam, que paulo ante ab eis male gesta sunt, non reputauit."

[44]   *TTh*, 1, no. xliii, pp. 97–8: *"simul autem et propria quedam seruitia per scriptum et jusjurandum conuenientes seruire Imperio meo et Romanie, uelut facta ab apocrisiarijs eorum symphonia latius de his tractat.. Verum tamen debent et Venetici eam, que per factam scripto conuentionem a legatis eorum promissa sunt, jurejurando Imperio meo firma seruare incorrupta."*

[45]   It is not until Isaac II Angelos (1185–1195, 1203–1204) confirmed all Venetian privileges in 1187 that a detailed account of Venetian obligations survives. *TTh*, 1, no. lxxii, pp. 195–203; Lilie, *Handel und Politik*, p. 20.

Here lies the terror of the Greeks and the glory of the Venetians, Domenico Michiel whom Manuel fears; a doge honest and steadfast, whom the whole world honored; prudent in diplomacy and the greatest in intellect. The capture of Tyre and the destruction of Syria and Hungary prove his manly deeds; he made the Venetians abide in peace, for while he flourished he made his country safe.[46]

The financial rewards of victory followed shortly thereafter. Though documentary evidence is scant, Venetian merchants resumed trading in the empire. Later in his reign, John even expanded Venetian privileges by granting them the right to trade freely on Crete and Cyprus. By 1147, the number of Venetians in Constantinople had grown so much that they appealed to Emperor Manuel I (1143–1180) for an expansion of their properties.[47]

Though both sides appeared content with this settlement, the conflict had fostered suspicion and contempt. To Venetian eyes, Greeks were untrustworthy and weak; John's ingratitude and disloyalty were seen not as a personal failing, but as a Greek trait. Byzantium's inability to defend its coasts and capitulation in the face of aggression bred Venetian disdain for the empire. Byzantine authors expressed similar contempt for Venice: "The nation is corrupt in character, jesting and rude more than any other, because it is filled with sailor's vulgarity."[48] Trade resumed and even expanded after 1126, but animosity remained. Byzantium and Venice, though still allies, were no longer partners. The first major test of their renewed alliance, a combined effort to dislodge Norman invaders from Corfu in 1147, illustrates the changed nature of their relations. As had been the case during Alexius' reign, a Norman presence on this island threatened both Venetian and Byzantine interests. Now, however, rather than bringing them together toward a shared goal, military cooperation revealed the fragility of the alliance.

When Manuel I called on Venice to assist Byzantium as it had in the past, Doge Pietro Polani (1129–1148), facing opposition to Byzantium at home, first insisted that Manuel confirm Venetian privileges before he would agree to send

---

[46]   Sanudo, *Le Vite dei Doge*, pp. 194–5: "*Terror Graecorum iacet hic et laus Venetorum, Dominicus Michael quem timet Hemanuel, Dux probus et fortis, quem totus adhuc colit orbis, prudens consilio summus et ingenio. istius acta viri declarat captio Tyri, interitus Syriae moeror et Ungariae; qui fecit Venetos in pace manere quietos; donec enim viguit, patria tuta fuit.*" See also Madden, *Enrico Dandolo*, p. 19, n. 1.

[47]   Morozzo della Rocca and Lombardo, *Documenti*, nos. 53, 54, 56, 57. The first of these documents dates from 1129, but there is no reason to assume that Venetian merchants waited until that time to resume trade.

[48]   Cinnamus, p. 210. He wrote his history much later, probably between 1180 and 1182.

aid. With Normans holding Corfu, Manuel lost no time and granted Venice concessions under the same terms as 1126. He also confirmed Venetian rights to free trade on Crete and Cyprus.[49] Alexius I had needed only to promise Venice great rewards in 1081; he issued his chrysobull only after a Venetian fleet had sailed. Venetian distrust of Byzantine motives had fallen so low that Polani felt he must have documents in hand before taking action. Anticipating a successful campaign, Manuel renewed the privileges and expanded the Venetian Quarter of Constantinople. Even then, the Doge had to overcome the objections of influential Venetians before sending aid. The Patriarch of Grado, Enrico Dandolo, gathered a following of supporters to protest the alliance with the "unrepentant schismatics" of Byzantium. Though the doge quickly silenced the Patriarch and his supporters, this opposition speaks to a growing hostility toward Byzantium. No such problems had arisen in 1081 to complicate or delay Venetian aid.[50]

The siege of Corfu began poorly. Norman artillery killed Grand Duke Stephen Constostephanus, the Byzantine commander, and the besiegers had difficulty attacking the well-designed-and-sited citadel. Only with the collusion of the island's inhabitants had the Normans succeeded in taking it with such ease the year before. Even after Manuel arrived in spring 1149 to take charge, the siege progressed slowly. After several months, animosities that had developed between the Venetian and Byzantine troops began to erupt into violence. An argument broke out amongst a group of sailors in the agora and quickly turned into a deadly brawl. In describing the clash, Niketas Choniates argued that this was more serious than the brawling that was to be expected among bored troops:

> the discord was not merely a matter of light banter exchanged by both nations, nor of vulgarities wherein whatsoever was spoken was also heard, nor did they engage in mutual ribaldry, nor did the disputants engage in clever taunts, nor did they hurl insults and heap scorn on one another, but they took up arms and doubtful battle reared its head.[51]

---

49   *TTh*, 1, no. xlix, pp. 107–9, no. li, pp. 113–24 (wrongly dated as October 1148; it should read October 1147); *DR*, 2, nos. 1356, 1365; Dandolo, *Chronica per extensum*, p. 242; Nicol, *Byzantium and Venice*, pp. 85–6; Lilie, *Handel und Politik*, pp. 22–4; Chalandon, *Jean II Comnène*, pp. 321–2.

50   Cinnamus, pp. 76–8; *TTh*, 1, no. l, pp. 109–13; *DR*, 2, no. 1373; Dandolo, *Chronica per extensum*, p. 242; *Annales*, p. 71; Madden, *Enrico Dandolo*, pp. 29–31; Martin, "Venetian Quarter," pp. 73–5. The Patriarch of Grado held the highest ecclesiastic office in Venetian territory.

51   Choniates, p. 50.

Once the fighters were dispersed, a number of Venetians returned to their ships and sailed south from Corfu to attack Byzantine vessels between Ithaca and Cephalonia, including Manuel's imperial flagship. On it, they dressed an Ethiopian in the imperial vestments and staged a burlesque procession to mock the emperor, known to have a dark complexion. As Choniates relates:

> They stole the imperial ship, adorned the imperial cabins with curtains interwoven with gold thread and with rugs of purple, and placed on board an accursed manikin, a certain black-skinned Ethiopian. They acclaimed him emperor of the Romans and led him about in procession with a splendid crown on his head, ridiculing the sacred imperial ceremonies and mocking Emperor Manuel as not having yellow hair, the color of summer, but instead being blackish in complexion like the bride of the song who says, "I am black and beautiful, because the sun has looked askance at me."[52]

Manuel, although angered, was not in a position to exact revenge – he needed Venetian aid to subdue Corfu; he did not have the resources to fight both the Normans and the Venetians. Therefore, Choniates relates, he chose to reconcile with the Venetians but did not forget the insults directed personally at him.

> The emperor immediately wanted to punish the barbarians properly, but he feared these vulgar displays would lead to internecine war and so dispatched certain of his kinsmen to offer the Venetians amnesty for their lawless acts against him and for their crimes against the Romans, for he perceived that requiting vengeance had its dangers and that other, more pressing, needs required his immediate attention. Though he swallowed his anger for the one day, yet he nursed rancor in his heart like an ember buried in ashes until the opportunity came for him to kindle it.[53]

Manuel succeeded in restoring a semblance of harmony and led the siege to a successful conclusion. But after the surrender of Corfu, the alliance began to dissolve and each party eventually reached a separate peace with the Normans.[54]

The slow progress of the siege and the close proximity of Venetian and Byzantine sailors might have created an atmosphere of frustration in which

---

[52] Choniates, pp. 50–1.

[53] Choniates, p. 51. The "proper time" was 1171, when Manuel orchestrated the arrest of all Venetians within the empire.

[54] Ibid., pp. 51–2; Cinnamus, pp. 80–2; Dandolo, *Chronica per extensum*, p. 243; *Historia Ducum Veneticorum*, p. 75; Nicol, *Byzantium and Venice*, pp. 86–7.

a trivial incident set off a major confrontation. However, tensions existed between the Byzantine and Venetian contingents from the start; on arriving, they anchored their fleets in separate locations "to avoid squabbles between the two nations." Donald Nicol calls the brawl a "racial conflict," noting that the Venetians "despised" the Greeks, a general hostility reminiscent of Doge Michiel's command, in 1125, that all Venetians shave their beards.[55] The Greek sailors nursed their own grievances. Most sailors in the Byzantine navy were levied from coastal areas, including the Ionian and Aegean islands. Though surely some hailed from Constantinople where they may have resented arrogant and disruptive Venetian merchants, those from the islands would remember the atrocities committed during the 1120s. Forced now to co-exist with allies from Venice, they would have welcomed an opportunity to exact revenge for past transgressions.

The rift between Byzantium and Venice only widened as further quarrels set Byzantium and Venice on divergent paths. Manuel turned to Venice's rivals, Pisa and Genoa, for aid against the Normans. Venetian merchants resented this competition. When, in 1170, Manuel granted trading rights and properties in Constantinople to Genoa and Pisa, the Venetians in the city took matters into their own hands. They rioted and looted the new Genoese quarter, leaving it in ruins. Manuel ordered them to return stolen goods and pay restitution, but "the Venetians did not wish to do any of these things and threatened to work harm on the Romans, reminding him [Manuel] of what they had done while emperor John was still alive." The Venetian refusal reminded Manuel of the impunity with which they had dictated policy to John II and gave him an opportunity to take revenge for the insults of 1149. He arranged that all Venetians in the empire be arrested and their property confiscated. Doge Vitale II Michiel (1155–1172) launched a fleet to exact revenge but accomplished little before plague forced him to return in spring 1172. It was not until late in the 1180s that Venice saw its privileges renewed and its merchants return to Constantinople in large numbers.[56]

The brawling and burlesque mockery of Manuel I in 1148 and Manuel's arrest of Venetians in the empire in 1171 are often viewed as critical points of divergence

---

[55]   Choniates, p. 46; Nicol, *Byzantium and Venice*, pp. 87, 91. See also Sally McKee, *Uncommon Dominion: Venetian Crete and the Myth of Ethnic Purity* (Philadelphia, 2000).

[56]   Cinnamus, pp. 211–4; *Historia Ducum Veneticorum*, p. 78; Dandolo, *Chronica per extensum*, pp. 250–3; *DR*, 2, nos. 1376, 1401, 1402, 1488, 1495, 1497, 1498, 1499, 1500; Nicol, *Byzantium and Venice*, pp. 94–5. Choniates explicitly linked Manuel's actions here to the mockery in 1149: "Buffeted by a series of villanies, one worse than the other, the emperor now recalled their offensive behavior on Kerkyra [Corfu] and turned the scales against them," pp. 97–8; *TTh*, 1, no. lxxii, pp. 195–203.

in Byzantine–Venetian relations, ultimately resulting in Venetian participation in the Fourth Crusade. This perspective, however, neglects to explain the origins of this hostility. During Alexius I's reign, the Byzantine Empire faced challenges to its traditional role as the dominant Christian power in the East. Norman invasions and the First Crusade forced Byzantium to re-evaluate its relations with Western Europe. Even so, Alexius' offer of a permanent and favored role in the empire for Venice was unprecedented. Alexius spent his later years attempting to establish sovereignty over those Crusader conquests that once belonged to Byzantium. In doing so, he sought to restore the empire's traditional boundaries and limit Byzantine dependence on the West. John II devoted much of his reign to pursuing this vision. He severed connections with the West and maneuvered within the traditional borders of the empire in campaigns in Anatolia and the Balkans. John also succeeded in gaining some control over Syria. His refusal, early in his reign, to ratify Venetian privileges was in keeping with this grand strategy. He judged that he no longer needed Venetian assistance and chose to end a relationship that infringed on his sovereignty without offering tangible benefits.

In doing so, he ignored Venice's new wealth and power, gained through the exploitation of nascent commercial opportunities in the East. Despite this growth, Venice was not self-sufficient and, to survive and flourish, needed to protect its sea-lanes and trading rights. Doing so often required a balance of diplomacy and force. Though willing to maintain the fiction that they were servants of the empire, the Venetians could not relinquish the trading privileges on which their economy depended. John II miscalculated when he denied the Venetian embassy in 1119. He had hoped to humble the merchants causing trouble in his capital. Instead, they forced him to grant the concessions and established, in fact if not in name, a new hierarchy in the relationship. Though later emperors sought to contain the Venetians, as Manuel I did in 1171, they would not again be able to treat the Venetians as an inferior partner. More importantly, the repeated confrontations left their mark, creating an atmosphere of mutual suspicion and mistrust that would taint all future Byzantine–Venetian interactions.

Chapter 9

John II Comnenus and Crusader Antioch

David Alan Parnell
Saint Louis University

John II Comnenus is an enigmatic figure. Although he was a powerful monarch and wielded important influence in the Near East, his reign has often been considered a temporary interlude between the more widely-studied reigns of Alexius I and Manuel I. John has been alternately portrayed as a military warlord unable to control his temper and a cynic who could not contain his overwhelming ambitions, cheerfully breaking treaties in order to achieve them. For example, Ralph-Johannes Lilie has argued that John was willing to break a previous treaty in order to gain control of Antioch.[1] Likewise, Paul Magdalino has accused John of having a temper, insisting that the emperor entered Syria in 1142 motivated by "a strong desire for revenge."[2] More recently Jonathan Harris has argued the opposite, claiming that John was only interested in recognition of his imperial status and not the extent of his empire's territory.[3] These diverse assessments do not easily square with the evidence provided by contemporaries. John was a soldier-emperor, more comfortable in camp than in Constantinople, and although he harbored ambitions to increase the territorial extent of his empire, it seems that he was careful to strive toward those ambitions only in a way he thought reasonable and in keeping with his empire's best interests.[4] Nowhere is this more apparent than in his dealings with the crusader Principality of Antioch.

Though busy with other frontiers during his reign, John devoted significant time and resources to the situation in Antioch. His policy toward the principality is important not only for Byzantine history, but also for the history of the

---

[1] Ralph-Johannes Lilie, *Byzantium and the Crusader States 1096–1204*, trans. J.C. Morris and Jean E. Ridings (Oxford, 1993).

[2] Paul Magdalino, *The Empire of Manuel I Komnenos, 1143–1180* (Cambridge, 1993).

[3] Jonathan Harris, *Byzantium and the Crusades* (London, 2003).

[4] John has widely been considered a soldier emperor in modern accounts of his reign. For the most authoritative and exhaustive treatment despite its age, see Ferdinand Chalandon, *Jean II Comnène et Manuel I Comnène* (Paris, 1912), p. 10.

crusader states in general. Time and again the princes of the Latin East sought Byzantine assistance, and at no other time was the possibility of cooperation with Byzantium more unlikely than in John's reign. The relationship between the empire and the Principality of Antioch was precarious at best at the time of John's accession in 1118. Antioch had been captured by the crusaders following an intense siege in 1098, after they had already sworn oaths to Alexius to restore to him cities that had formerly belonged to the empire.[5] Bohemond of Taranto took control of Antioch and his subsequent disputes with Alexius led him to invade the empire in 1107. Bohemond's defeat resulted in the Treaty of Devol in 1108, which explicitly nullified all previous agreements between Bohemond and Alexius. A remarkable document preserved only by Anna Comnena, the Treaty of Devol made Bohemond a vassal of the emperor. The emperor received the direct rule of Cilicia, but Bohemond was allowed to retain control of Antioch for his lifetime, received 200 pounds of gold a year, and was further deputized to make conquests to the east of the city. After Bohemond's death, his entire principality, save Edessa, was to revert to the empire.[6] Unfortunately for Alexius, Bohemond did not return to Antioch, and the treaty was never implemented there. Alexius, however, believed the treaty should be enforced and expended some effort toward the end of his reign to have it recognized.[7] Alexius was unsuccessful in this, and bequeathed to John a legacy of a powerful claim to Antioch based on a legal treaty that had been ignored by the principality.

The period immediately following the death of Alexius and the accession of John was one of inactivity in the relationship between Constantinople and Crusader Antioch. The fact that John paid little attention to Antioch for 20 years suggests that it held a low priority in his foreign policy. His actions during this period were apparently more concerned with maintaining the vulnerable frontier zones of the empire he had inherited; conquest and expansion were understandably secondary goals. John fought a desultory war with Venice before reconfirming its trade privileges, and he had to fight against both the Pechenegs and Hungarians in Europe. These, however, were primarily defensive actions. In contrast to this relative reluctance to fight in his European provinces, he was active in the empire's eastern provinces, conducting offensives to stabilize their troubled frontiers, first against the Turks of Caria and later the Danishmends.[8]

---

[5]   On the oaths, see Lilie, *Byzantium and the Crusader States*, pp. 13–28.

[6]   Anna Comnena, *Alexias*, trans. E.R.A. Sewter (London, 1979), XIII.12.

[7]   Lilie outlines Alexius' relationship with Antioch after 1108 and convincingly posits that the emperor was attempting to arrange a coalition against the principality to forcibly attain the rights he had gained at Devol (pp. 83–95).

[8]   For a brief account of John's wars with the Pechenegs and Hungarians and advances against the Turks of Anatolia, see Warren Treadgold, *A History of the Byzantine State and*

That John campaigned so tirelessly in Anatolia suggests that he regarded it an important avenue for expansion. The large and rich city of Antioch was a logical component of any plan for expansion in Anatolia for several reasons. First, the city had been under Byzantine control as recently as 1085 when it was lost in the disintegration of Anatolia under Turkish pressure.[9] Second, Antioch was still claimed by the empire. The Treaty of Devol of 1108 stipulated that Antioch should have been given over to the empire after Bohemond I's death in 1111.[10] Finally, the fact that the treaty had not been implemented meant that the city was in technical rebellion, which the emperor could not tolerate indefinitely. With these considerations, it is unsurprising that by 1137, when he finally felt able to devote himself to it, John proved very interested in forcing a settlement with the principality.

A number of events occurred in the years leading up to 1137 that served to remind John of the claim to Antioch that he had inherited from his father. In 1135, the Antiochenes apparently sent an embassy to John proposing that one of his sons should marry Princess Constance, daughter of the deceased Bohemond II and heiress of the principality.[11] John probably favored the proposal. However, the offer was soon revoked by the nobles at Antioch, and Constance was hurriedly married to Raymond of Poitiers. The story of this tantalizing but short-lived offer is only reported directly by John Cinnamus, though William of Tyre indirectly corroborates it by saying that the emperor was "very indignant that without his knowledge or command they had presumed to give the daughter of their lord in marriage and, without consulting him, had dared to transfer the city to the rule of another."[12] In addition to this marriage issue, during the years leading up to 1137 the Armenian Prince Leo and Antioch fought over possession of Cilicia.[13] John must have viewed this with displeasure, since his father Alexius had militarily disputed control of Cilicia with Antioch. While these recent events no doubt caught John's attention, the campaign of 1137 was not carried

---

Society (Stanford, 1997), pp. 630–632.

[9]   This Byzantine control was admittedly tenuous, Antioch having been held by Philaretus Brachamius since 1071, who from 1081 on was only nominally loyal to the imperial government. Treadgold, *A History*, p. 616.

[10]   See note 6 above.

[11]   John Cinnamus, *Historiarium*, ed. J.P. Migne (Patrologia Graeca 133, 1864), trans. Charles Brand (New York, 1976), p. 22.

[12]   William of Tyre, *Chronicon*, ed. R.B.C. Huygens, CCCM 63 (Turnhout, 1986), p. 662. "Multum indignans quod absque eius conscientia et mandato aut domini sui filiam nuptui collocare presumpserant aut civitatem alicuius dicioni eo inconsulto ausi fuerant mancipare."

[13]   Lilie, *Byzantium and the Crusader States*, p. 105.

out in a rash of anger at the situation in Cilicia or the rejection of an imperial marriage. The campaign was meticulously planned and its importance chiefly determined by the empire's previous claims to Antioch.[14]

John's expedition of 1137 was a major campaign. Emerging from the western side of Cilicia at the head of a large army, John first moved to reconquer the entire plain, which was held partly by the Armenians and partly by Antioch. The emperor captured Tarsus, Adana, Mamistra and Anazarbus.[15] That his army was large and dominant is evident from the fact that no army, either Armenian or Antiochene, seems to have attempted to oppose him in the open field. After capturing the important cities of the Cilician plain, John moved his army south to Antioch and encamped before the city. Raymond of Poitiers, who, through his marriage to Constance, had recently become Prince of Antioch, was not prepared to fight John. After a brief siege, Raymond sued for peace. In reporting the negotiations, Cinnamus records that the emperor initially refused categorically to allow Raymond to remain in control of Antioch.[16] But John must have soon realized that such intransigence was counter-productive. There is no doubt that the emperor wanted control of Antioch, but he did not necessarily want to destroy the power of the Latins living there, as the treaty he was about to conclude would make clear. Therefore, he and Raymond negotiated the Treaty of 1137. John, like Alexius at Devol in 1108, showed remarkable restraint in pressing his claims to Antioch. He probably feared the likely consequences from the West that an outright assault and capture of Antioch might have entailed.[17] The exact details of the Treaty of 1137 are more elusive than those of the Treaty of Devol, because neither Cinnamus nor Nicetas Choniates describe it. The fullest account of the agreement is given by William of Tyre, who, without providing the actual text, at least gives key details. First, Raymond swore allegiance and fealty to John. It was also decided that

> He should take a solemn oath that whenever the lord emperor desired to enter Antioch or its citadel, either in anger or peace; he should not deny him a free and peaceful entrance. If the lord emperor should peacefully restore Aleppo, Shaizar, Hama, and Homs to the prince, as had been stipulated in the treaty, then he was

---

[14]   As Lilie observes, John's preparations were carefully laid: the emperor prepared his way diplomatically by encouraging war between the Normans of Sicily and the Germans, as well as with embassies to Venice and Pisa (pp. 113–117).

[15]   William of Tyre, *Chronicon*, pp. 662–663.

[16]   John Cinnamus, *Historiarium*, p. 24.

[17]   Lilie, *Byzantium and the Crusader States*, p. 121, is correct to make this point. If the fall of Edessa could elicit the Second Crusade seven years later, certainly the fall of Antioch in 1137 would have elicited a similar outraged response.

to rest content with these cities and others near by, and without contest restore to the lord emperor the city of Antioch to be held by right of ownership. In return for the fealty shown to him, the lord emperor should agree that if, by the aid of God, he succeeded in taking Aleppo, Shaizar, and all the adjacent region, he would allow the whole to be given to the prince without trouble or diminution and that the latter and his heirs should hold it in peace by perpetual right, but in benefice, which is commonly called in fief.[18]

Thus John sought direct imperial possession of Antioch, but only if he could receive it peaceably from the Latins, and receive it complete with a subject Latin principality surrounding it to the east and south as a buffer state to ward off the Muslims. Harris mistakes John's intentions when he declares that the emperor did not wish to have "physical domination" of Antioch.[19] John clearly wanted just that, but he wanted that dominion to be surrounded by Latin buffer states. Like Alexius' Treaty of Devol, the terms of the Treaty of 1137 were never to be fully realized. The agreement is, however, extremely useful as an illustration of the vision John had for the Latin East. He imagined an extension of Byzantine authority into Antioch with a concurrent expansion of a subordinate Latin buffer state to separate Byzantine territory from Muslim-held Syria.

Upholding his side of the Treaty of 1137, in the following year John led his army (with contingents from Antioch and Edessa) in an assault on Shaizar and its neighboring cities.[20] Again, the Greek sources are of little help. Choniates merely records that the emperor advanced against Shaizar without offering any

---

[18] William of Tyre, *Chronicon*, p. 671. "Prestito corporaliter sacramento, quod domino imperatori, Antiochiam ingredi volenti vel eius presidium, sive irato sive pacato liberum et tranquillum non neget introitum, et si dominus imperator ei Halapiam, Cesaram, Hamam, Emissam, sicut pactis erat insertum, principi restitueret quietas, quod his et aliis circumadiacentibus contentus urbibus Antiochiam domino imperatori sine difficultate restituat iure proprietatis habendam, dominus vero imperator in recompensationem exhibite fidelitatis principi concedat; quod si auctore domino eum contigerit Halapiam, Cesarum et omnem circumadiacentem regionem sibi adquirere, totum principi sine molestia et diminutione accrescat et iure perpetuo sibi et heredibus suis, tamen in beneficio quod feodum vulgo dicitur, tranquille possideat."

[19] Harris, *Byzantium and the Crusades*, p. 81.

[20] Although the Arabic sources are of little help in describing the relationship between Byzantium and Antioch in detail, they do provide important evidence for campaigns such as this. Ibn al-Qalanisi, in *The Damascus Chronicle of the Crusades*, trans. H.A.R. Gibb (London, 1932), records that John's army captured the castle of Buza'a before advancing on Shaizar (p. 249). John Cinnamus corroborates this event (p. 24). It should not therefore be assumed that the whole campaign was doomed from the start. Indeed, it only seems to have foundered before the walls of Shaizar.

explanation for the decision.[21] William of Tyre provides a more detailed account of the siege of Shaizar, blaming Raymond of Poitiers and Joscelin of Edessa for behaving frivolously during the siege and not doing their utmost to assist John. It seems likely that the two princes wanted John to fail. If John were to succeed at this city and at others, they would be forced by the treaty to surrender Antioch to him and Raymond would have to move to Aleppo. By failing to contribute to the siege of Shaizar, Raymond helped to ensure that would not happen.[22] The emperor would ultimately abort the siege and return to Antioch, where he was personally admitted to the city while his army remained encamped outside.[23] He then demanded that the citadel of Antioch be handed over to him and that his troops be admitted into the city as well. Did this request violate the Treaty of 1137? William of Tyre seems to regard this as entirely in keeping with the recent treaty, writing that "there was no one who could doubt that this had been included in the agreement of the lord prince."[24] It should be noted that John did not demand the dissolution of the principality or even the abdication of Raymond, but only that he be allowed to base the imperial army in Antioch. Nevertheless, Raymond probably feared that if he accepted such conditions John would eventually take Antioch by force. According to William of Tyre, to avoid this development Joscelin stirred up a riot in the city, which forced John to withdraw his demand and exit Antioch. He accepted the abject apologies of Raymond who promised, perhaps insincerely given that he had just striven to avoid this, that he would "abide by the terms of the treaty and, if permitted, transfer the city with the citadel into the hands of the emperor."[25] Having received this promise, the emperor correspondingly pledged to return to carry out his side of the treaty, presumably referring to the conquest of Aleppo and Shaizar. Then John decamped with his army and returned to Constantinople.

John did not forget about Antioch. Within four years he was ready to begin a second Syrian campaign. The emperor and his army moved swiftly through Cilicia, which remained in Byzantine hands, and then appeared suddenly in

---

[21] Nicetas Choniates, *Historia*, ed. John Aloysius Van Dieten (Berlin, 1975), trans. Harry Magoulias (Detroit, 1984), p. 17.

[22] As Treadgold, *A History*, notes, Raymond and Joscelin "preferred keeping Antioch to making conquests instead of it" (p. 634).

[23] William of Tyre, *Chronicon*, pp. 674–676. William attributes the raising of the siege to John's anger at Raymond and Joscelin, but Lilie plausibly points out that it is much more likely that John had underestimated the defenses of the Muslim cities of North Syria and realized that he could not actually take Shaizar with the army he had (p. 128).

[24] Ibid., p. 678. "Iterum id pactis domini principis insertum nemo erat qui dubitaret."

[25] Ibid., p. 681 "Paratus est... in finibus stare pactorum et, si liceat, urbem cum presidio in manus imperii transferre."

crusader lands, apparently causing quite a surprise. The motives for John's second campaign are unclear, since the sources report them differently. Cinnamus writes that the emperor intended for Antioch to be granted with Cilicia and Cyprus to his son Manuel as his own province.[26] Choniates reports that John "had always had a burning desire to unite Antioch to Constantinople" and set out with the explicit intention of annexing the city.[27] William of Tyre, on the other hand, asserts that when John arrived at Antioch he demanded, "in accordance with the principle of the agreements formerly concluded between them, that the city with the citadel and all the fortifications of the town without exception be surrendered to him, in order that he would be able to wage war upon the neighboring cities of the enemy as from a convenient nearby base."[28] If William of Tyre's version of the Treaty of 1137 is accepted, his explanation of the emperor's demand here in 1142 is entirely plausible. John had not promised a new principality to the Latins of Antioch because he had to do so, but because he wanted to see them established around Antioch when that city fell to his direct possession. The campaign of 1138 perhaps made John feel that the attempt to capture those cities could only be successful if he had full use of Antioch as a base. It is also likely that Raymond would have felt more inclined earnestly to assist operations against Muslim Syria if he knew Antioch was occupied by the emperor. Moreover, William of Tyre's explanation for the expedition does not necessarily contradict either Cinnamus' or Choniates'. The reports of these Greek sources that John wished to annex Antioch fit in with this, for Antioch would be annexed formally after John had conquered the Muslim cities prescribed by the Treaty of 1137. Lilie's contention that John's demand for entry and access to the city violated the treaty is unsupported by the main source, William of Tyre.[29] William states that earlier, in 1138, Raymond had promised to surrender the citadel to John whenever he needed it, and now William seems to regard it as proper for the emperor to demand the city, writing "it had been agreed between them that he [Raymond] should surrender the city without difficulty."[30] Choniates also argues

---

[26]   John Cinnamus, *Historiarium*, p. 26.

[27]   Nicetas Choniates, *Historia*, p. 22.

[28]   William of Tyre, *Chronicon*, p. 701. "Mandat ut, iuxta pactorum legem inter se prius initam, urbem ei cum urbis presidio et omnibus indifferenter civitatis munitionibus resignet, ut inde finitimis hostium civitatibus guerram possit inferre quasi de vicino commodius."

[29]   Lilie, *Byzantium and the Crusader States*, p. 136, argues that John's demand violated the treaty because he had not yet captured Shaizar, Aleppo, Hama, and Homs before demanding Antioch for himself. He may be right, but without the actual text of the treaty it cannot be proven. In the absence of additional evidence, the argument proposed here seems just as likely.

[30]   William of Tyre, *Chronicon*, p. 702. "Inter eos convenerat, ut premisimus, ut ei civitatem sine difficultate traderet."

that John's demands were just, explaining that the terms of the treaty gave him the right to enter the city.[31] However, Raymond and his nobles were reluctant to surrender the city to John. The nobles claimed that Raymond did not have the authority to surrender Antioch, and therefore John's demand was refused on behalf of the patriarch and "all the citizens." William states that John was incensed by this refusal, and he himself calls it a "far from laudable act."[32] John seems to have determined to attack Antioch in reprisal, but as the season was too far advanced he withdrew his army into winter quarters in Cilicia. Before he could take any further action against Antioch, he died in a hunting accident on April 8, 1143.[33]

Whether John would have seized Antioch by force cannot be known. Lilie argues that the Antiochene refusal to hand over the city in 1142 convinced the emperor to break completely with his former policy, abandon the Treaty of 1137, and begin open hostilities with Antioch. John decided to break the treaty he had concluded several years before because it was no longer convenient for him.[34] The obvious problem with this argument is that our major source for John's relationship with Antioch (William of Tyre) appears to exonerate John from blame and instead suggests that there was nothing problematic with the emperor's request. In an extensive appendix on the subject, Lilie seeks to avoid this problem by positing that either William's version of the Treaty of 1137 or his estimate of the events is faulty. Lilie concludes that the record of the treaty is correct, but that William presented the events of 1138 and 1142 incorrectly out of a desire to malign Raymond.[35] Lilie sets forth two options insisting that one must be correct. It is possible, though, that neither are correct, for a third possibility exists. If William recorded the Treaty of 1137 correctly and correctly interpreted the events of 1138 and 1142 then John's demand for the use of Antioch did not violate the treaty.[36] In fact, according to a literal reading of the

---

[31]   Nicetas Choniates, *Historia* p. 23.

[32]   William of Tyre, *Chronicon*, p. 702. "Factum minus commendabile."

[33]   The preponderance of evidence suggests that the death was an accident. The possibility of a conspiracy for murder does exist and is raised by Robert Browning, "The Death of John II Comnenus," *Byzantion*, 31 (1960), pp. 229–235.

[34]   In short, "Only when [John] realized that he could not fulfill the obligations he had voluntarily undertaken was he ready, in 1142, for open conflict" (Lilie, p. 139).

[35]   Lilie, *Byzantium and the Crusader States*, pp. 307–308.

[36]   This argument relies upon William of Tyre and credits him with an accurate and reasonably balanced understanding of John's relationship with the principality. Lilie's questioning of William's accuracy and bias in searching for moral explanations for historical events is appreciated (pp. 284–297), but gives the archbishop too little credit for his personal knowledge and experience. William's experience with Byzantium was extensive. He had been to Constantinople on diplomatic missions twice, in 1168 and 1179, and had treated with

sources as shown above, John was not demanding the annexation of Antioch, but merely the use of it as a military base for a new campaign into Muslim Syria.

In conclusion, it may be helpful to contemplate John's intentions after he was turned back from Antioch in 1142. Choniates, recording John's last speech, has the emperor say, "I have not, O Roman men, according to my great expectations, taken Syria; I had hoped to perform deeds more glorious than heretofore; to bathe without fear in the Euphrates."[37] It is interesting to note that Choniates uses Syria and the River Euphrates to indicate a broader geographical area than Antioch alone and it is possible that he was alluding to John's promise to take cities in Muslim Syria to give to the Franks. William of Tyre records a similar sentiment, stating that when moving into Cilicia for the winter John "promised and purposed in his heart that in the following summer he would accomplish in the regions of Syria something great and worthy of remembrance forever."[38] This could be evidence that John was planning, even in 1143, to continue with the conquest of Muslim Syria as was proposed in the Treaty of 1137, even if he first had to take Antioch by force to give himself a firm base. John's death rendered such plans moot, and the accession of Manuel brought an abandonment of his policy.

It seems evident, then, that John followed a more active policy against Antioch than did Alexius. John twice led large armies into Syria and encamped before the walls of Antioch. Yet his policy also showed a marked continuity with that of Alexius. Both the Treaty of Devol and the Treaty of 1137 provided for eventual Byzantine absorption of Antioch, while allowing for dependent Latin buffer states to exist in Syria and Mesopotamia. It appears that John's demand for entry and temporary possession of Antioch did not violate the terms of the Treaty of 1137. Even when repulsed from Antioch in 1142, it seems that John was not planning to abandon that treaty or the policy. Instead, he continued his plan to conquer Aleppo and other cities for the crusaders of Antioch, although he now demanded the use of the city as a military base. Despite John's intentions, however, his policy meant that Raymond of Poitiers was frequently afraid of attack and had to regard the empire as an enemy for much of his reign. It was left to John's son Manuel to maximize Byzantine influence in the city while also confirming the principality's security.

Byzantine envoys in Jerusalem in 1177. Although his opinion of Byzantium is admittedly ambiguous, William's understanding of Byzantium is fairly accurate and worthy of trust. Peter Edbury and J.G. Rowe, *William of Tyre: Historian of the Latin East* (Cambridge, 1988), pp. 130–140, offer a positive assessment of William's understanding of Byzantium and follow his interpretations of John's relationship to the Principality of Antioch.

[37]   Nicetas Choniates, *Historia*, p. 24.

[38]   William of Tyre, *Chronicon*, p. 703. "Estate proxime futura promittens et animo gerens magnum aliquid et perhenni dignum memoria in Syrie partibus se facturum."

PART IV
The Crusades and the World of Louis IX

Chapter 10

Saints and Sinners at Sea on the First Crusade of Saint Louis

Caroline Smith[1]

The men and women who set sail from France with the forces of Saint Louis's first crusade in the summer of 1248 were to spend a considerable length of time on board ship; a total of five months if they stayed with the king throughout his failed campaign and period of captivity in Egypt, his subsequent period in the Levant, and his homeward voyage in 1254.[2] While much scholarly attention has been paid to the logistical and technological challenges posed by the need to transport people, horses, equipment and supplies by sea in the course of the crusades, the possible demands of these voyages on crusaders unused to seafaring in emotional or spiritual terms has been relatively little studied.[3] Although it is

---

[1]   In revising this paper I have benefited from numerous comments and suggestions made to me by fellow participants in the *Crusades: Medieval Worlds in Conflict* symposium, but especially from those provided by Professor William Chester Jordan in his response to the session. I would also like to thank Professor Maryanne Kowaleski for her bibliographical advice.

[2]   Jacques Monfrin, "Joinville et la mer," in *Etudes de langue et de littérature du moyen âge offertes à Félix Lecoy* (Paris, 1973), reprinted in *Le prince et son historien. La Vie de Saint Louis de Joinville*, eds. Jean Dufournet and Laurence Harf, Collection Unichamp 55 (Paris, 1997), p. 211. (References in this paper are to the latter publication.) Monfrin's calculation includes the time the crusaders spent on board ship during their imprisonment in Egypt.

[3]   On maritime support for crusading and the crusader states in the eastern Mediterranean see John H. Pryor, *Geography, Technology and War: Studies in the Maritime History of the Mediterranean, 649–1571* (Cambridge, 1988), pp. 112–34, as well as a number of more specific studies, including: John H. Pryor, "The Venetian Fleet for the Fourth Crusade and the Diversion of the Crusade to Constantinople," in *The Experience of Crusading. Volume 1: Western Approaches*, eds. Marcus Bull and Norman Housley (Cambridge, 2003) pp. 103–23; John H. Pryor, "'Water, Water Everywhere, nor any Drop to Drink' Water Supplies for the Fleets of the First Crusade," in *Dei gesta per Francos. Etudes sur les croisades dédiées à Jean Richard* (Aldershot, 2001), pp. 21–8; John France, "The First Crusade as a Naval Enterprise," *Mariner's Mirror* 83 (1997) 389–97; John H. Pryor, "Transportation of Horses by Sea during the Era of the Crusades," *Mariner's Mirror* 68 (1982), Part I, 9–27, Part II, 103–25. Pryor has also provided important studies on naval architecture in the crusading context: John

possible that for some participants in Louis's crusade campaigns and others sea travel was little more than an uncomfortable and potentially dangerous necessity, for others, sea crossings were undoubtedly of more interest and significance. This is certainly true of the king's friend John of Joinville, whose *Life of Saint Louis* has at its core an account of Joinville's own experiences on crusade. It is here that we find the most intimate account of the trials and tribulations of the voyages of Louis's first crusade. Joinville's work is central to this study, and used alongside other material relating to the campaign and its participants it can help us understand what value might be attached to time spent at sea. The particular focus here will be on the voyages' place within the crusade as a spiritual undertaking, and as episodes which brought the contrasting themes of sinfulness and sanctity to the fore.

Fear of the sea and the physical risks associated with sea travel constituted a medieval norm evident in both Christian and Muslim societies.[4] And, if Joinville's account of Louis's first crusade is anything to go by, there was good reason to be wary of taking to the seas. Among the incidents he reported was the wrecking of a damaged ship on the outward voyage with the loss of nearly everyone on board, two instances of ships being set adrift and fleets broken up by storms or violent winds, the drowning of one of his knights during the disembarkation of the crusaders off the coast of Egypt, a storm in the harbor of Damietta in which 140 ships were broken up and all the crew on board drowned, and the grounding of the king's ship off Cyprus during the return voyage to France, in the aftermath of which the damaged ship was caught in winds so strong that it took five anchors to prevent it being thrown onto land.[5] The last of these episodes is the most

---

H. Pryor, "The Naval Architecture of Crusader Transport Ships: a Reconstruction of some Archetypes for Round-Hulled Sailing Ships," *Mariner's Mirror* 70 (1984), Part I, 171–219, Part II, 275–92, Part III, 363–86; John H. Pryor, "The Naval Architecture of Crusader Transport Ships and Horse Transports Revisited," *Mariner's Mirror* 76 (1990), 255–73. One potential spiritual danger faced by crusaders at sea has been raised by Alfred J. Andrea, "The Relationship of Sea Travelers and Excommunicated Captains under Thirteenth Century Canon Law," *Mariner's Mirror* 68 (1982), 203–9. And, in a study published soon after the initial version of this paper was presented, the significance of time spent at sea in John of Joinville's depiction of Louis IX's kingship and sanctity has been considered by Huguette Legros, "Nostre roy saint Looÿs au peril de la mer dans la Vie de saint Louis de Joinville," in *Mondes Marins du moyen-âge: actes du 30e colloque du CUER MA, 3, 4 et 5 mars 2005*, ed. Chantal Connichie-Bourgne (Aix-en-Provence, 2006), pp. 285–95.

[4]   On fear of the sea within Western Christian society see Jean Delumeau, *La peur en occident (XIVe-XVIIIe siècles): une cité asiégée* (Paris, 1978), pp. 49–62; for the Muslim world see Carole Hillenbrand, *The Crusades: Islamic Perspectives* (Edinburgh, 1999), pp. 556–9.

[5]   John of Joinville, *Vie de Saint Louis*, ed. Jacques Monfrin (Paris, 1995), §§ 625, 137, 147, 153, 182, 618–30.

famous in the history of Louis's crusade at sea, and it is one to which particular attention will be given in this study.

But how far should we trust Joinville's version of these events? A recent study by Christopher Lucken suggests we might want to be skeptical; according to his analysis Joinville had an authorial agenda – to present a "gospel" of Louis – that overrode any desire for veracity.[6] In his response to Lucken's work Jacques le Goff rejected the idea Joinville had any such plan in mind for his project; producing his book meant setting his memories down in an organized way, but without any style or genre in mind. According to this view the production of the *Life of Saint Louis* was not a literary endeavor, shaped by an aim to conform to a literary style.[7] I share the view that it is inappropriate to try to categorize Joinville's work in terms of authorial intent or style, but I do not think his remembrances can be said to be free of literary interest or influence. There are a number of passages in the *Life of Saint Louis* in which I would suggest Joinville's presentation of events owes more to literary convention than it does to his own memory.[8] The crusade at sea can provide a case in point. Joinville reported that the sight of the crusaders' ships about to set sail from Cyprus in May 1249 was a most beautiful one, because it seemed that the sea, for as far as the eye could see, was covered with the sails of ships.[9] This passage has been cited as an example of the strength and length of Joinville's visual memory, and has been said to demonstrate Joinville's simple desire to share the aesthetic impression and pleasure of this moment.[10] But the same image – that of a magnificent fleet of ships with their sails unfurled, about to set sail – appears in very similar contexts and very similar terms in numerous other vernacular narratives of this era. It is present in the histories of the Fourth Crusade by Robert of Cléry and Geoffrey of Villehardouin, and in James I of Aragon's Catalan *Crònica* when he describes the crusader fleet about to set sail to conquer Majorca in 1229.[11] These crusader-historians are likely to have been familiar with this and other *topoi* from their appearance in twelfth- and

---

[6]   Christopher Lucken, "L'Evangile du roi. Joinville, témoin et auteur de la *Vie de Saint Louis*", *Annales: histoires, sciences sociales* 56 (2001), 445–467.

[7]   Jacques le Goff, "Mon ami le saint roi. Joinville et Saint Louis (réponse)," *Annales: histoires, sciences sociales* 56 (2001), 469–477.

[8]   Caroline Smith, *Crusading in the Age of Joinville* (Aldershot, 2006), pp. 61–73.

[9]   Joinville, *Vie*, § 146.

[10]   Le Goff, *Saint Louis*, p. 477; Monfrin, "Joinville et la mer," pp. 222–3.

[11]   Robert of Clari, *La conquête de Constantinople*, ed. Philippe Lauer, Les classiques français du moyen âge 40 (Paris, 1924), pp. 12–13; Geoffrey of Villehardouin, *La conquête de Constantinople*, ed. Edmond Faral, Les classiques de l'histoire de France au moyen âge 18–19 (Paris, 1938–39), 2 vols, 1, pp. 122–3; James I of Aragon, "Crònica," in *Les quatres grans cròniques*, ed. Fernando Soldevila (Barcelona, 1971), p. 32.

thirteenth-century literary works; the impressive departing fleet motif may be found in the verse and prose versions of the *Roman de Troie*, for example.[12]

If we accept that Joinville used literary devices, we must judge how far this renders his version of events untrustworthy. Returning to his account of the grounding of Louis's ship during the return voyage to France in 1254, we are told that it was by no means only inexperienced sea travelers who felt afraid; he tells us that when they realized that they were grounded the sailors on board the king's ship cried out and pounded their hands together for fear of drowning. The crew's commander, brother Raymond of the Templars, rent his shirt and tore at his beard.[13] It may well be that Joinville used this image of a man in distress, tearing at his own hair and clothes, because it is a conventional one that his audience would have recognized, rather than because this person actually behaved in this way on this occasion. By describing him thus, Joinville suggested Raymond's despair in this situation was akin to that of the numerous characters from *chansons de geste* who were depicted assaulting themselves in the same way, having been rendered incapable of effective action or speech by distress in the face of death.[14] Joinville's use of literary devices like this one enabled him to emphasize what he saw as the significance of the moment in question, a practice common in medieval writing about the past and one that helps us appreciate that modern and medieval notions of "truth" often do not coincide.[15] In the case of the *topos* of the magnificent departing fleet, the true significance Joinville expected his audience to recognize in this image was that Louis had gathered a powerful force that was about to achieve something very impressive, while the image of the distressed Templar captain shredding his shirt and beard is a form of literary shorthand that signals that this was a situation of mortal despair.

His use of the beard-tearing *topos* in this instance reinforces the essential and fearful truth of the situation that night as Joinville saw it, and as others apparently saw it too. According to William of Saint Pathus, who was later confessor to Louis's queen, Margaret of Provence, her despair at their prospects

---

[12]   Benoit de Sainte-Maure, *Le Roman de Troie*, ed. Léopold Constans, Société des anciens textes français 87–92, (Paris, 1904–12), 6 vols, 1, p. 378, ll. 7085–92; *Le Roman de Troie en prose*, eds. Léopold Constans and Edmond Faral, Les classiques français du moyen âge 29 (Paris, 1922), p. 64.

[13]   Joinville, *Vie*, § 619.

[14]   Carine Bouillot, "La chevelure: la tirer ou l'arracher, étude d'un motif pathétique dans l'épique médiéval", in *La chevelure dans la littérature et l'art du moyen âge. Actes du 28e colloque du CUER MA, 20, 21 et 22 février 2003*, ed. Chantal Connochie-Bourgne, Senefiance 50 (Aix-en-Provence, 2004), pp. 35–45.

[15]   R. Morse, *Truth and Convention in the Middle Ages: Rhetoric, Representation and Reality* (Cambridge, 1991), pp. 90–5.

in this scenario was such that she was unwilling for her children to be woken –
she preferred that they go to God sleeping.[16] Memories of this event were passed
on to succeeding generations, and could apparently retain a strong hold on an
individual's imagination; when John of Le Vignay produced a translation into
Old French of the Latin chronicle of Primat in the 1330s he interrupted the
translation by inserting a passage of his own describing the 1254 grounding, at
which his grandfather had been present.[17] This certainly seems to have been the
occasion on which the crusaders' underlying fears of sea travel came most clearly
to the surface. Although Joinville's account of this incident suggests he was a
relatively calm observer of events, an indication of his own fear is provided by his
reported outburst at the man who brought him a coat to stop him catching a chill
– what was the point of this gesture, he demanded, when they were all about to
drown?[18] It is noticeable that John of Joinville and his knightly colleagues, who
regularly faced the horrors of the battlefield, seem to have been willing to admit
to fear and frailty much more readily in the face of the sea's dangers. Oliver of
Termes, who had proved himself a brave and skilled knight during the crusade,
refused to continue the homeward journey on Louis's damaged ship because he
was afraid that he might drown.[19]

The willingness of a man like Oliver of Termes to display or declare his fear
of the sea suggests that the danger of sea travel was perceived differently from
others which he and members of the knightly class had to face. Exposing oneself
to the risks of sea travel was not like exposing oneself to the risks of warfare
– while an experienced knight relied on his own skill and bravery to bring him
safely from the battlefield (or not), at sea he had little or no control over his own
fate. And, while one's opponents in battle were a human and therefore perhaps
a more understandable or predictable force, at sea men faced the mysterious
and untamed forces of nature. This contrast may have been particularly stark
for seafarers in the thirteenth-century Mediterranean. The weakness of the
Ayyubids and Mamluks as naval powers greatly diminished the likelihood of
facing attack at sea,[20] but the lack of a human threat meant that crusaders' fears
of sea travel were focused even more intently on the seas themselves and on God,
their creator. According to Scripture, God had formed heaven and earth out of
the chaos of the dark-covered waters, and the biblical seas were a terrifying and

---

[16]   William of Saint Pathus, *Vie de Saint Louis*, ed. Henri-François Delaborde (Paris,
1899), p. 30.
[17]   "Chronique de Primat traduite par Jean du Vignay," in *RHGF*, 23, pp. 65–6.
[18]   Joinville, *Vie*, § 620.
[19]   Ibid., § 629.
[20]   Pryor, *Geography, Technology, and War*, pp. 130–4.

repellent source of storms and floods, and the home to monstrous creatures.[21] A thirteenth-century image of the seas' wild and unfamiliar forces appears in the *Rothelin* continuation of William of Tyre's history; it digressed from its account of Saint Louis's voyage to Damietta to provide a description of sirens, fire-spewing mountains and other dangers the crusaders might have encountered.[22] While this description probably does not reflect many crusaders' actual expectations of the dangers of sea travel it is emblematic of the medieval image of the sea as an alien and fearful environment.

As well as the physical challenges of seafaring, some crusaders may have set sail with an alternative or additional wariness of the sea as a morally or spiritually dubious space. A sense that the unpredictable forces of the sea reflected or embodied the destabilizing power of sin is evident among Louis's crusading companions. In one of his model sermons for the preaching of the cross Odo of Châteauroux, papal legate on the king's first crusade, used a metaphor contrasting the steadiness of land with the shifting of the seas to distinguish faithful people from sinners. On the one hand there was "the earth [meaning] people who are strong and firm in their faith 'offering the fruits of their good works' ," while on the other there was "the sea [meaning] unsteady people, who are driven by the wind of their temptations, colliding with each other full of the bitterness of their sins."[23] In an abstract way, then, the sea could represent sinfulness in thirteenth-century minds. The possibility that the sea physically contained sinfulness and sinners comes through most clearly in contemporary attitudes towards those who spent their lives at sea. Churchmen feared for the souls of sailors, whose lifestyle meant they could not receive regular pastoral attention or make confession.[24] In a model sermon written earlier in the thirteenth century for use before an audience of sailors, James of Vitry outlined the dangers of the murky and sinful sea and listed some of the vices of which sailors were likely to be guilty. These included leaving pilgrims stranded on islands in order to steal their possessions, or selling their passengers into slavery to Muslims, as well as the more prosaic offences of spending their wages in taverns and brothels when

---

[21]   Alain Cabantous, *La ciel dans la mer. Christianisme et civilisation maritime (XVe-XIXe siècle)* (Paris, 1990), pp. 19–21. See also Legros, "Nostre roy saint Looÿs au peril de la mer," p.291.

[22]   "Continuation de Guillaume de Tyr, de 1229 à 1261, dite du manuscrit de Rothelin," in *RHC Oc.*, 2, pp. 571–3.

[23]   Odo of Châteauroux, "Sermon V," in *Crusade Propaganda and Ideology. Model Sermons for the Preaching of the Cross*, ed. Christoph T. Maier (Cambridge, 2000), pp. 172–3.

[24]   Delumeau, *La peur en occident*, p. 59.

they came to dry land.[25] According to the *life* written by Ralph of Bocking, when Saint Richard of Chichester undertook the preaching of the crusade in southern England in 1253, he saw sailors as being in particular need of salvation through the cross:

> He strove to place the untamed necks of sailors under the yoke of the Cross and, having shown them the abomination of their sins and the torments which would punish them, he set about moving his hearers to tears and contrition and thus he placed upon them the saving sign of the Cross like the mark of Tau.[26]

Our sources indicate that Louis went to considerable lengths to counteract the often haphazard religious observance among seafarers by establishing a familiar and regular pattern of religious life on board his ship.[27] This routine was one that acknowledged their special circumstances, for example by performance of Masses for seafarers at key moments like the disembarkation at Damietta,[28] but most strikingly by taking measures to ensure the spiritual security of the ship's crew. Given their poor reputation, it is perhaps not surprising that Louis was apparently shocked and concerned about the spiritual condition of the men who manned his ships during his first crusade. According to the Dominican friar Geoffrey of Beaulieu, Louis's confessor in later life and author of a *life* written to promote the king's canonization, Louis encouraged sailors on board his ship to listen to sermons at times when the seas were calm. Since the sailors rarely heard the word of God preached to them, these sermons covered basic spiritual concerns – the articles of faith, moral behavior and sinfulness. He also provided them with their own confessor, since it had been many years since some of them had made confession. In his effort to counteract the burden of sin that had accumulated on board he reportedly even expressed a willingness to stand in to perform menial tasks like hauling rope while a sailor made his confession.[29]

---

[25]   Unedited MS cited in Jacques Le Goff, "Saint Louis et la mer," in *L'Uomo e il mare nella civittà occidentale: da Ulisse a Cristoforo Columbo. Atti del convegno Genova, 1–4 giugno 1992* (Genoa, 1992), pp. 19–20.

[26]   Ralph of Bocking, "Life of St Richard," ed. and trans. David Jones in *Saint Richard of Chichester: the sources for his life*, ed. David Jones, Sussex Record Society 79 (Lewes, 1995), p. 134 (translation at p. 211). I am grateful to Professor William Chester Jordan for making me aware of this example.

[27]   Le Goff, "Saint Louis et la mer," p. 18.

[28]   John Sarrasin, "Lettre à Nicholas Arrode," in *Lettres françaises du XIIIe siècle. Jean Sarrasin, lettre à Nicolas Arrode*, ed. Alfred Foulet, Les classiques français du moyen âge 43 (Paris, 1924), p. 4.

[29]   Geoffrey of Beualieu, "Vita et sancta conversatio piae memoriae Ludovici quondam regis Francorum," in *RHGF*, 20, pp. 14–15, chapter 23.

While Louis seems to have had a specific concern that the sinfulness of these sailors might jeopardize the safety of his ships, John of Joinville's attitude towards professional seafarers is somewhat different. Sailors in this account do not appear as irreligious. At the moment of his ship's departure from Marseilles it is the captain and his crew who prompt the clerics on board to sing the hymn *Veni creator Spiritus*.[30] And Joinville reports that one sailor was believed to have stayed on one of the islands at which the king's ship called during the return voyage to France in order to assume the life of a hermit.[31] It is possible that the captain of the ship, who was the person who asserted that this must have been the sailor's wish, did so in order to hasten their onward journey. At another moment – when ships sent to gather provisions from the island of Pantelleria failed to reappear when expected – the crew of the king's ship were ready to leave their colleagues on board those other vessels to their fate rather than run the risks attached to waiting for them.[32] The instinct for self-preservation evident in this incident also seems to have had an impact on the religious choices made by the sailors Joinville encountered. Amid the confusion and violence that accompanied the capture of the crusade army during its attempted retreat down the Nile in 1250, Joinville learned from one of his captors that all the sailors from the ship in which he had been traveling had apostasized. In the conversation that followed both Joinville and his Muslim interlocutor agreed that there was every chance that the sailors would switch their religious allegiances again if the opportunity arose.[33] Pragmatism seems to have had a large part to play in these men's faith, as perhaps it did in their lives in general.

The impression we get of Joinville's interest in the religious life of the sailors he met, which was that of a curious observer, stands in contrast to our image of Louis, a concerned interventionist. This perhaps reflects their personalities and preoccupations more generally – while Louis approached the overall direction of the crusade at sea with pious seriousness, Joinville was able to absorb and embrace the new experiences his time at sea offered.[34] But this does not mean that Joinville was unconcerned about sin at sea. It was personal sinfulness that worried him, rather than that of his fellow seafarers. One of the anonymous songs written to celebrate Louis's taking of the cross and to promote recruitment for his crusade assured its listeners that anyone who died during the sea-crossing

---

[30]   Joinville, *Vie*, § 126.

[31]   Ibid., § 639.

[32]   Ibid., § 640–1.

[33]   Ibid., § 331.

[34]   For the contrasting attitudes and concerns of Louis and Joinville as seafarers compare Le Goff, "Saint Louis et la mer," and Monfrin, "Joinville et la mer."

would be saved.[35] Joinville does not seem to have thought the matter was so straightforward. As he described the start of his outward voyage he pointed out the folly of any man who would dare take to the sea in a state of mortal sin, as each man goes to sleep on board ship uncertain as to whether he might be at the bottom of the sea the next morning. But it was not only mortal sinners who should fear this eventuality – Joinville said that sea travel posed the same threat to those in possession of someone else's property.[36]

He was not alone in his concern about the harmfulness of setting out for the East with another's possessions. Righting such wrongs was a prerequisite for anyone who hoped to benefit from the indulgence offered to crusaders, and it is one that Louis himself had gone to great lengths to fulfill by sending out his *enquêteurs* to investigate complaints against royal officials.[37] Joinville himself had summoned his vassals to inform them of his imminent departure and to offer them the chance to raise any claims they might have against him.[38] In insisting on this aspect of their preparation Louis and Joinville acknowledged that taking the cross and joining a campaign was not in itself enough to make you a true crusader. Odo of Châteauroux stated the importance of redressing grievances in realizing the penitential value of the crusade unambiguously in the model crusade sermon mentioned earlier. It closes with a warning to would-be crusaders:

> note that Christ went to the cross and did not steal somebody else's clothes, but he left his own. This is why those who have stolen other people's things and do not pay what they owe do not take the cross in the right manner; it is better for a man "to follow the naked Christ naked" than to follow the devil with a great following and sink with his cross into hell.[39]

That Joinville chose to focus on this spiritual danger, and on the dangers of sinfulness more generally, as he recalled his first moments at sea is intriguing. It is true that he was remembering a stage in his journey at which he, a novice

---

[35]   Anonymous, "Tous li mons doit mener joie," in *Les chansons de croisade*, eds. Joseph Bédier and Pierre Aubry (Paris, 1909), p. 241, l. 7.

[36]   Joinville, *Vie*, § 127.

[37]   William Chester Jordan, "The Rituals of War: Departure for Crusade in Thirteenth-Century France," in *The Book of Kings: Art, War, and the Morgan Library's Medieval Picture Bible*, eds. William D. Noel and Daniel Weiss (London, 2002), p. 101; Jean Richard, *Saint Louis, roi d'une France féodale, soutien de la Terre Sainte* (Paris, 1983), pp. 193–4.

[38]   Joinville, *Vie*, § 111.

[39]   Odo of Châteauroux, "Sermon V," pp. 172–5.

seafarer, may have felt particularly vulnerable and prone to moral reflection,[40] but the nature of that moral reflection is revealing. It signals that to him the sea-crossing itself was a key phase in his crusading pilgrimage; one that brought the dangers of personal sinfulness to the fore and might expose the depth of each crusader's commitment to the penitential cause.

But while their sea voyages posed a spiritual challenge to Louis and Joinville, and perhaps to other of their crusading colleagues, these phases of their journeys also provided a setting in which their faith in a beneficent God could be affirmed. Here too, crusaders might have had the understanding of the seas they received from Scripture confirmed. For, as well as being a fearful space, the biblical seas were a place in which God's people could experience his power and compassion.[41] The seafarers of Psalm 107, for example, "saw the deeds of the Lord, his wondrous works in the deep"; they were exposed to God's power to raise storms and then to calm them before he brought them into safe harbor (Ps. 107.23–30). Joinville's *Life of Saint Louis* recorded a number of instances in which God was understood to have intervened, often through the agency of saints, to save the crusaders from the perils of the sea. So, when the ship on which Joinville and his companions made their outward journey to Cyprus proved unable to move out of sight of a mountain on the coast of north Africa – an episode which frightened the crew of the ship in particular, we are told – one of the priests on board suggested that holding a series of processions might solve the problem. He had found this efficacious in other situations, when God and his mother had responded to save him and his parishioners from difficulties. And God and his mother did indeed appear to come to the crusaders aid; once the first procession had been performed they left the mysterious mountain behind for good.[42] The same remedy would work to ensure the safe arrival in Egypt of Louis's brother, the count of Poitiers, whose delay raised fears that he was lost at sea.[43] On their return journey it was Saint Nicholas, a patron saint of seafarers, who was believed to have brought the crusaders through the violent storm that followed the grounding of the king's ship. At Joinville's prompting Margaret of Provence promised a votive offering of a silver ship to be delivered to the shrine of Saint Nicholas at Varangéville. When the winds dropped she announced that it was the saint himself who had saved them.[44] Later in the same voyage the Virgin Mary apparently intervened once more to help the crusaders, this time by saving a servant who had fallen overboard. Joinville was so struck by

---

[40] Monfrin, "Joinville et la mer," p. 220.
[41] Cabantous, *La ciel dans la mer*, pp. 22–5.
[42] Joinville, *Vie*, §§ 128–9.
[43] Ibid., §§ 180–2.
[44] Ibid., §§ 630–2.

this miracle, which he heard about from the rescued man himself, that he later had it depicted in wall-paintings in his chapel at Joinville and in the stained glass of the nearby church of Blécourt.[45]

Joinville's seaborne encounters with the miraculous clearly stayed with him throughout his life. But these isolated incidents did not constitute his only contact with sanctity at sea. The time spent on board ship during the six-day journey from Egypt to Acre in 1250 and the two and a half-month return voyage to France in 1254 brought Joinville and Louis into close, consistent contact. The first of these phases, during which the ailing Joinville spent all his time alongside Louis, was an important one in forming his friendship with the king.[46] The second and longer phase provided a setting for observations and conversations that would be central to Joinville's perception of his friend as a saint. The key episode here is that of the grounding of the king's ship off Cyprus. Having described the panic this accident induced among many of the ship's crew and passengers, Joinville presents a starkly contrasting image of the king; barefoot and lying on the deck with him arms stretched out in the shape of a cross. He was prostrate before the consecrated host.[47] Louis here displayed a "mystical readiness for death" that set him apart from his fellow crusaders.[48]

According to the accounts of this episode that appear in the *lives* of Saint Louis written by Geoffrey of Beaulieu and William of Saint Pathus it was Louis's actions – calmly and quickly removing himself to pray before the host that he had carefully housed on board at their departure – that ensured the ship's safety.[49] William of Saint Pathus also reported the views of the sailors on board the grounded ship, who declared that not one ship in a thousand would ordinarily escape from such danger, and that the king's prayers and merits were what had enabled them to complete the voyage.[50] For Joinville the significance of this episode as a demonstration of Louis's sanctity lay less in the fact that the ship was saved than in the king's response to the dilemma the grounding presented. Having established that the vessel was afloat but damaged, Louis had to decide whether he should abandon it as unsafe. Ignoring the advice that he should do so, Louis determined that the welfare of his people – who might otherwise be stranded on Cyprus for lack of transport and the funds to hire it – demanded that they all risk continuing the journey together. This was one of the four occasions Joinville highlighted at the start of his *life* of the king in which

---

45 Ibid., §§ 650–1.
46 Ibid., §§ 404–5.
47 Ibid., § 621.
48 Monfrin, "Joinville et la mer," p. 231.
49 Geoffrey of Beaulieu "Vita," p. 18, chapters 29–30.
50 William of Saint Pathus, *Vie de Saint Louis*, p. 30.

he demonstrated his willingness to face death for the good of his people.[51] The grounding of the king's ship was thus a key episode in Joinville's illustration of Louis's sanctity as performed in deed, and it also provided the context for one of the king's saintly pronouncements. After the grounding and subsequent storm, Louis had Joinville sit at his feet and told him that such trials as these, in which God had demonstrated his great power, were sent as warnings that any man or woman could be drowned or killed if God so desired it. In response each person should look within himself or herself for any fault that might be displeasing to God, in order to correct it.[52] Joinville repeated his account of this saying of the king in the section of his work concerning his saintly words.[53] Louis's pious admonition to Joinville probably reflects the king's interpretation of the far greater setbacks that beset the crusade as a whole.[54] It also brings us back to the idea that the seaborne phase of their crusade could be just as vital as that which took place on land in exposing, and potentially in punishing, people's moral weaknesses and errors.

As Jacques le Goff points out, Louis's meticulous preparation for his crusades yielded success at sea, even if the campaigns failed on land; his construction of a new port at Aigues-Mortes, the efficient gathering of material and financial resources and the establishment of supply-lines along which they could pass allowed his crusade at sea to function smoothly.[55] I would argue that among Louis and his fellow crusaders, including John of Joinville, there was likely to have been a sense that the seaborne stages of their crusade were a spiritual as well as a practical success, and certainly that they were integral to the crusade as a spiritual project. Louis may have seen in the successful completion of his crusade at sea a vindication of his personal efforts to lighten his damaged ship's cargo of sin. Similarly, Joinville may have interpreted his own safe landing as a sign that his efforts in not just taking the cross but becoming a true crusading penitent had been recognized and rewarded. To these individuals the sea was therefore much more than a physical obstacle to be crossed *en route* to the East; it was another testing ground of faith and as such it presented as many opportunities to Louis and his companions as it did challenges. Indeed, God seemed to smile on the crusaders' efforts at sea – intervening through his saints to assure their safe passage – in a way that had not been true of their efforts on land.

---

[51]   Joinville, *Vie*, §§ 13–16.

[52]   Ibid., §§ 634–7.

[53]   Ibid., §§ 39–40.

[54]   Le Goff, *Saint Louis*, p. 753.

[55]   Le Goff, "Saint Louis et la mer," pp. 22–3.

Chapter 11

Louis IX, Charles of Anjou, and the Tunis Crusade of 1270

Michael Lower
University of Minnesota

Shortly after Philip III ascended to the throne of France in 1270, he wrote to the abbot and monks of St Denis about the deaths of his father, Louis IX, his brother John of Nevers, and his brother-in-law Thibaut of Navarre:

> After these men, having signed themselves with the sign of the living cross, had prepared themselves with all their strength to spread and exalt the faith and had come to Africa to extirpate from the roots the errors of the infidel Saracens there, they were withdrawn from this world.[1]

Philip thus explained why all three men were in Africa in the double language of crusade (extirpating from the roots the errors of the Saracens) and of mission (spreading and exalting the faith). He did not, however, address what a curious place it was for the three to be performing such activities, since all had taken vows to crusade in the Holy Land, not Tunis. In the years following this disastrous crusade, suspicion for the diversion fell on Louis's brother Charles of Anjou, king of Sicily, who, it was rumored, wanted to punish the emir of Tunis. Others believed that Charles was more interested in Byzantium and that the decision rested with Louis himself and his desire to convert the emir and his subjects to Christianity. Modern historians have been little more conclusive, proposing a variety of reasons for the crusade's diversion, from Charles's vendettas to Louis's piety to bad cartography. In this essay I will examine the decision to crusade to Tunis in light of the larger careers and wider concerns of both men, particularly Charles's diplomatic interests and Louis's conversion policies. For the former, I look at a little-used collection of documents relating to the Tunis crusade that

---

[1]   *Epistola Philippi regis ad abbatem et monachos S. Dionysii*, in Luc d'Achéry, *Spicilegium: sive, collectio veterum aliquot scriptorum qui in Galliae bibliothecis delituerant...*, 3 vols. (Paris, 1723), 3, p. 669.

Renato Lèfevre reconstructed from the lost Angevin archives in Naples;[2] for the latter, I turn to recently discovered texts relating to Louis's missionizing efforts among the Jews of Paris in the years preceding the crusade.[3] Taken together, this evidence suggests that the conversion motive ascribed to Louis is not as idiosyncratic as scholars have tended to think.

The case for Charles's responsibility for the Tunis diversion was first made by the chronicler Saba Malaspina, who charged that "wishing to go to that country and desirous of extirpating by the force of others the serpent from his cave, Charles had acted adroitly to lead such an important army against Tunis."[4] This insinuation has had historical staying power, drawing strength from the treaty Charles negotiated to end the crusade.[5] He received assurances from the emir of Tunis, al-Mustansir, that "every enemy" of Angevin Sicily would be banished from the North African kingdom. He also obtained one third of the indemnity for war expenses that al-Mustansir paid to the crusaders and a revival of the tribute Tunis had formerly rendered to Sicily. Charles received five years of arrears and a renewal of the tribute at double the previous rate. In addition to these financial gains, crusading in Tunis prevented crusading in Egypt, where Charles nurtured peaceful relations with Sultan Baybars. Given the ways in which Charles benefited from the crusade, it is not surprising that many commentators have joined Saba in blaming the king of Sicily for directing it against Tunis.

Charles's interests in the years leading up to the expedition were geographically diverse. He ruled the county of Provence (and its great commercial center Marseilles) through marriage. He ruled Sicily by conquest, having defeated Manfred, the Hohenstaufen claimant, at Benevento in 1266. He claimed Corfu because it had been included in the dowry of Manfred's wife, who had become Charles's prisoner. He also had interests in Byzantium, which had fallen out of Latin control upon Michael Paleologus's conquest of Constantinople in 1261. In 1267, as part of the Treaty of Viterbo, Charles promised the deposed emperor Baldwin that he would recover the Latin Empire of Constantinople within six

---

[2]   Renato Lèfevre, *La crociata di Tunisi del 1270 nei documenti del distrutto archivio angioino di Napoli* (Rome, 1977).

[3]   Joseph Shatzmiller, *La deuxième controverse de Paris* (Paris-Louvain, 1994).

[4]   Saba Malaspina, *Sallae, sive rerum Sicularum, liber VI ab anno Christi MCCL usque ad annum MCCLXXVI*, in *Rerum Italicarum Scriptores*, ed. Lodovico Antonio Muratori, 25 vols. (Milan, 1723–51), 8, p. 860.

[5]   Sylvestre de Sacy, 'Mémoire sur le traité fait entre le roi de Tunis et Philippe-le-Hardi, en 1270, pour l'évacuation du territoire de Tunis par l'armée des croisés', *Histoire et mémoires de l'Institut royal de France, Académie des inscriptions et belles-lettres* 9 (1831), 448–477; de Sacy's French translation of the treaty is reprinted in Louis de Mas Latrie, *Traités de paix et de commerce et documents divers concernant les relations des chrétiens avec l'arabes de l'Afrique septentrionale au moyen age* (Paris, 1866), pp. 93–96.

years. In return, Charles would receive one third of all territory reconquered, suzerainty over the principality of Achaea, and the marriage of a daughter to one of Baldwin's sons.[6] During this time Charles also negotiated with al-Mustansir of Tunis over the lapsed tribute payments. There was a brief interruption in these discussions in 1267, when the leading Hohenstaufen supporters Frederick of Castile and Conrad Capece used Tunis as a staging ground for an attack on Sicily.[7] Although there seem to have been suspicions that al-Mustansir had supported the project, the matter was settled by 1269 and negotiations over the tribute payment resumed in May of that year.[8]

Important as the tribute may have been to Charles, in 1269 and 1270 most of his attention was devoted to planning an invasion of Byzantium. On 7 September 1269, at Foggia, Charles declared "to all the faithful of the church" his intention to give counsel and aid to Emperor Baldwin and the doge of Venice in order to recover their rights within the Byzantine Empire.[9] Venice shortly afterwards received ambassadors from the Neapolitan court, who proposed an alliance to defeat Michael Paleologus. Alliances with the Serbians, Hungarians, and Bulgarians followed shortly after. The Angevin curia ordered all its ships in Apulia to be repaired on 4 November 1269:[10] the *Saint Cecilia*, docked at the port of Brindisi, the natural launching point of a Constantinople expedition, received 88 gold ounces worth of refurbishments.[11] By 20 November, similar orders had been given to virtually all the provinces in the *Regno* – every ship should be ready to sail at a moment's notice.[12]

Preparations continued apace throughout the winter of 1269–70 and into the spring. The new year saw Charles forbidding "protonotaries, counts, sailors and mariners" to leave the *Regno* with any boats or vessels, "so that we might have them [the boats] present in the aforementioned state of readiness for our

---

[6]   Charles Perrat and Jean Longnon, *Actes relatifs à la principauté de Morée 1289–1300* (Paris, 1967), pp. 207–211.

[7]   Robert Brunschvig, *La Berbérie orientale sous les Hafsides, des origines à la fin du XVe siècle*, 2 vols. (Paris, 1940–7), 1, pp. 52–53; Steven Runciman, *The Sicilian Vespers: A History of the Mediterranean World in the Later Thirteenth Century* (Harmondsworth, 1960), p. 121, and 142.

[8]   For Angevin suspicions of al-Mustansir, see Lèfevre, *La crociata*, no. 9; document also printed in *I registri della cancelleria angioina ricostruiti da Ricardo Filangieri con la collaborazione degli archivisti napoletani*, ed. Ricardo Filangieri et al. (Naples, 1950–), 4: no. 1141. For the renewed negotiations, see Lèfevre, *La crociata*, nos. 14 (22 May 1269), 29 (18 August 1269), 84 (22 April 1270); *Registri della cancelleria angioina*, 2: no. 247, 2: no. 692, 5: no. 190.

[9]   *Codice diplomatico sui rapporti veneto-napoletani durante il regno di Carlo I D'Angiò*, ed. Nicola Nicolini, (Rome, 1965), no. 13.

[10]   Lèfevre, *La crociata*, no. 36; *Registri della cancelleria angioina*, 5: no. 226.

[11]   *Registri della cancelleria angioina*, 6: nos. 362–366.

[12]   Lèfevre, *La crociata*, no. 38; *Registri della cancelleria angioina*, 5: no. 76.

service."[13] In April 1270, Charles took Don Ferrante, the son of James I of Aragon, into his service along with 40 knights, 40 foot soldiers, and 20 artillerymen.[14] The conditions of service indicate that the goal remained the Balkans, but that Charles wished to keep his options open if unforeseen contingencies arose. Don Ferrante was to enter into Charles's service for one year, which would begin either when Charles wished, or when they entered the Latin Empire of Constantinople, or when Don Ferrante arrived in the *Regno*. Once begun, the Spanish adventurer was to fulfill his obligation in Sicily, Constantinople, or "other places."[15]

Don Ferrante's contract reveals the open-ended nature of Charles's plans. Soon a modified proposal emerged from the Angevin curia: the full scale invasion was off; a less ambitious "expeditionary force" would replace it. The announcement of the new program came on 11 May 1270:

> wishing to extend more fully and robustly the arm of our majesty and to open the hand of our power in aid of the prince of Achaea, we order that twenty-five galleys should be sailed to the coast of Dalmatia.[16]

This fleet represented a major commitment to the prince of Achaea, one which would leave Charles virtually incapable of transporting his army to Tunis in the summer.[17] The "Constantinople option" was still a priority; on 27 May 1270, he announced the marriage of his daughter Isabella to the son of the king of Hungary;[18] and as late as 10 June Charles summoned the feudatories of Calabria to set out for Achaea, although his intention was most likely to collect the *adduamentum*, a monetary contribution in lieu of personal military service.[19] Although an Angevin invasion of Constantinople did not take place, many of the resources of the *Regno* and other Angevin holdings were devoted to it, along with much of the time and energy of their ruler, far more than was

---

[13]   Richard Sternfeld, *Ludwigs des Heiligen Kreuzzug nach Tunis 1270 und die Politik Karls I. von Sizilien* (Berlin, 1896), appendix A, no. 16 (330).

[14]   Lèfevre, *La crociata*, no. 76; *Registri della cancelleria angioina*, 5: no. 160.

[15]   Lèfevre, *La crociata*, no. 76; *Registri della cancelleria angioina*, 5: no. 160.

[16]   Lèfevre, *La crociata*, no. 106; *Registri della cancelleria angioina*, 5: no. 294.

[17]   Peter of Condé, letter to Matthew, abbot of St. Denis, 21 August 1270, in Léopold Delisle, *Instructions adressées par la Comité des Travaux historiques et scientifiques...littérature latine et histoire du Moyen Age* (Paris, 1890), 73–77. "[D]ominus rex, cum exercito suo...adhuc erat in castris Cartaginis et adhuc expectabat rex ibi [suum fratrem], et miserat ei dominus rex quasdam naves quas mandaverat, quia venturus erat, ut dicebatur, cum magna multitudine armatorum."

[18]   Lèfevre, *La crociata*, no. 119; *Registri della cancelleria angioina*, 5: nos. 17–35.

[19]   Sternfeld, *Kreuzzug nach Tunis*, appendix A, no. 23 (337–338).

expended upon what actually did happen in the summer of 1270: the expedition to Tunis.

Charles's preparations for Louis's crusade were very late; they begin with a document dated 23 July 1269:

> Since King Louis, with one brother, his sons, barons, and a most powerful Christian army, has arranged to come to the port of Syracuse on the feast of St. John in the near future, [24 June 1270] God willing, from that place setting out in aid of the Holy Land, we intend to honor and swear in this magnificent passage for God.[20]

It seems that as of 23 July 1269, Charles still thought that the Holy Land was the objective of the crusade. Syracuse would be the first port of call, an excellent launching point for a Syrian or Egyptian campaign. Charles was to have ships and supplies ready to depart from there by June 1270. With that goal in mind, Louis and Charles readied themselves through the winter months of 1269 and 1270. Louis sent a carpenter, Master Honoratus, to the *Regno* to construct siege engines and artillery for the crusading army, and Charles ordered his officials to provide what the master required.[21] In March and May 1270, the Angevin curia had wheat and other foodstuffs sent from the mainland to Sicily for Louis's army.[22] The shipping orders make no mention of Charles's own preparations for the crusade, nor of his intention to participate. The order of 13 May 1270 speaks of Charles's wish "to have an abundance of victuals and other things necessary for the sustenance of the men and horses for the passage of our dearest brother Louis, king of France, overseas."[23] His role was still limited to furnishing boats, war-machines, and other supplies for his brother. Charles had not committed himself to personal involvement in the crusade, even at this late date, despite Louis having demanded that he do so at Viterbo in 1267. The one obligation he undertook in May 1270 was sending 25 galleys to the prince of Achaea.

Preparations continued in the same manner through May. On 27 May, Charles ordered wheat which had been transported to Messina to be placed at the disposal of his officials, at the same time that he announced the wedding of his daughter Isabella to the son of the king of Hungary.[24] Charles finally made crusade organization a priority in July, when he left the mainland, sometime

---

20 Lèfevre, *La crociata*, no. 27.

21 Lèfevre, *La crociata*, no. 40; *Registri della cancelleria angioina*, 5: no. 137.

22 Lèfevre, *La crociata*, nos. 65, 110.

23 Lèfevre, *La crociata*, no. 110.

24 Lèfevre, *La crociata*, nos. 118, 119; *Registri della cancelleria angioina*, 5: nos. 315, 17–35.

after 5 July, and arrived in the Sicilian capital Palermo, shortly before 14 July.[25] This move corresponds with Louis's departure from Aigues-Mortes on 2 July.[26] Only Louis's departure for Cagliari seems to have induced Charles to take his first hesitant step towards Tunis.

The first document referring to Charles's own passage across the Mediterranean is dated 20 July 1270, one day after Louis landed on the North African coast.[27] Charles requested that two ships docked in Naples be repaired immediately and sailed to the port of Trapani, from which Charles would eventually depart.[28] The first mention of Tunis in the registers comes on the following day, and the first explicit mention of Charles's participation appears on 27 July 1270, three days after Louis's army captured Carthage.[29]

Charles began to ready himself in earnest for the expedition at the end of July 1270, after Louis confirmed his presence before Tunis by letter. The Angevin administrative machine had great difficulty assembling the necessities – food, horses, men, and ships. An order of 31 July 1270 requisitioned more wheat for the expedition; and a letter of 13 August chastised the justiciar of Bari and the *secretus* of Apulia for neglecting to send the necessary supplies quickly enough.[30] These organizational troubles are understandable, considering the shortage of serviceable galleys wrought by the previous consignment of 25 to the prince of Achaea, and the late starting date of preparations – in itself testimony to Charles's lack of interest in the Tunis expedition, the half-hearted nature of his earlier preparations, and his distraction by more appealing goals. His departure

---

[25]   Sternfeld, *Kreuzzug nach Tunis*, appendix A, no. 24 (338); Lèfevre, *La crociata*, no. 162; *Registri della cancelleria angioina*, 5: no. 198.

[26]   Lèfevre, *La crociata*, 62, n. 46.

[27]   Lèfevre, *La crociata*, 63.

[28]   Lèfevre, *La crociata*, no. 166; *Registri della cancelleria angioina*, 5: no. 147.

[29]   Lèfevre, *La crociata*, no. 178. This important document has been ignored in many accounts of the expedition. "Cum karissimus frater noster et dominus Ludovicus rex Francorum illustris, sicut nuper accepimus per eius licteras speciales, cum christiano exercitu in partibus Tunicii, favente domino, applicaret e ibidem per insultum Cartaginiensium ceperit civitatem multis in ea milibus saracenorum gladio interfectis; Nos, volentes eidem regi de nostro potente extolio quod ipse eciam (postulavit) magnifice subvenire...mandamus quatenus...omnia victualia Curie nostre ubicumque sint, de pecunia curie nostre que est vel erit per manus vestras...sine mora qualibet deferre Trapanum faciatis."

[30]   Lèfevre, *La crociata*, nos. 187, 198; *Registri della cancelleria angioina*, 5: nos. 408, 97–98. The Angevin curia carefully controlled the grain trade, and for the Tunis expedition virtually the entire Sicilian crop was requisitioned. See Michel de Boüard, "Problèmes de subsistances dans un État médiéval: le marché et les prix des céréales au royaume angevin de Sicile (1266–1282)," *Annales d'histoire économique et sociale* 10 (1938), 493, 498.

on 24 August is surprising less for its lateness than for its earliness;[31] Louis after all, had been preparing for three years while Charles organized himself in just over a month.

Even before his arrival, though, Charles had made his presence felt in the crusader camp. Shortly after the crusaders landed on 18 July, Charles sent a messenger who asked them not to attack the city until he arrived. This emissary was Amaury of Roche, master of the Temple in France.[32] The crusaders heeded Amaury's request. Except for the uncontested capture of Carthage, they limited themselves to skirmishing and defensive maneuvers, with Amaury supervising the construction of fortifications around the crusader camp to prevent enemy incursions.[33] The Templar discouraged counter-attacks to the very end. On 20 August 1270, five days before Louis's death, a Tunisian raid prompted some crusaders to venture beyond the camp gates. Before they could retaliate, Amaury called them back and reminded them of Charles's request that they avoid hostilities until he joined the army.[34]

Having prevented the crusader army from destroying Tunis, Charles finally arrived on 25 August 1270, at the very moment, the chroniclers say, when Louis IX died.[35] Leaving an inexperienced Philip III as king of France, the death of Louis made Charles master of the situation. An assault on the Hafsid position on 4 September frightened al-Mustansir into beginning peace talks. Another attack on 2 October resulted in the capture and pillage of a Hafsid outpost and brought a new intensity to discussions.[36] Rather than building upon these military successes, Charles focused on achieving a settlement with al-Mustansir that would both allow the crusaders to withdraw and, if popular rumor is to be believed, fill Angevin coffers.

Charles's financial circumstances at the time do nothing to dispel these rumors. As negotiations with Tunis reached their height, he wrote to the archdeacon of Palermo that "truly, just as we have often on other occasions written to you, we are suffering a great lack of money at present."[37] Charles had borrowed heavily for the conquest of Sicily from the papacy, from Florentine, Sienese, and Roman

---

[31]   Jean Longnon, "Les vues de Charles d'Anjou pour la deuxième croisade de Saint-Louis: Tunis ou Constantinople?" in *Septième centenaire de la mort de Saint-Louis: actes des colloques de Royaumont et de Paris* (Paris, 1976), p. 195.

[32]   Primat, *Chronique de Primat, traduite par Jean du Vignay*, in *R[ecueil des] h[istoriens des] G[aules et de la] F[rance]*, ed. Martin Bouquet et al. (Paris, 1737–1904), 23, pp. 50–51.

[33]   Primat, *Chronique*, p. 55.

[34]   Primat, *Chronique*, p. 55.

[35]   Geoffrey of Beaulieu, *Vita Ludovici noni*, in *RHGF*, 21, p. 24.

[36]   Brunschvig, *La Berbérie orientale*, 1, p. 61.

[37]   Lèfevre, *La crociata*, no. 223; *Registri della cancelleria angioina*, 6: no. 85.

banking houses, from King Louis, and from Alphonse of Poitiers.[38] His first priority after Benevento was to repay these debts. High taxation of his new kingdom was the result, with the despised *subventio generalis*, originally an aid levied in exceptional circumstances, becoming an annual charge.[39] Indirect taxes and customs duties were even more profitable and to maximize this revenue Charles introduced a program of economic renewal in the *Regno*. The agricultural, industrial, and commercial resources of the kingdom were to be exploited to the full, an effort in which the royal domains took the lead.[40]

But Charles's revenue policies proved unsustainable. The taxes were burdensome and his economic initiatives failed to yield significant returns.[41] An over-regulated economy, along with an inflated idea of what the natural resources of the kingdom could provide, combined to disappoint Angevin ambitions: the outcome was a shortfall between the expenses his plans incurred and the funds he raised.

Adding to Charles's financial difficulties, Louis IX, who had lent him money for the Italian expedition, now wanted it back for his own crusade. In January 1270, Charles surrendered the revenues of the county of Anjou to the French king in order to repay a 5,000 *livres tournois* loan.[42] A policy of confiscating the goods of Conradin's supporters, motivated by political and financial considerations, was not enough to make up the shortfall.[43] Charles was still distracted by his financial problems in mid-June 1270, when he should have been preparing for the crusade. As part of the pact made between Charles and the papacy before the Italian campaign, he had agreed to pay 8,000 gold ounces in annual tribute to Rome.[44] Citing the financial burdens imposed by the anticipated arrival of King Louis and Alphonse of Poitiers in Sicily, the upcoming wedding of his daughter Isabella, and "other great and arduous affairs, [undertaken] as much for the Christian faith as for others," Charles requested a deferment of half the tribute until 1 November 1270.[45] Though almost certainly a coincidence, this deadline fell two days after Charles concluded his treaty with al-Mustansir.

The treaty gave favorable financial terms to Charles of Anjou: 70,000 gold ounces as his share of the indemnity, payment of the tribute for the past 5 years,

[38]   Runciman, *Sicilian Vespers*, p. 103.
[39]   Léon Cadier, *Essai sur l'administration du Royaume de Sicile sous Charles Ier et Charles II d'Anjou* (Paris, 1891), pp. 10, and 30–32.
[40]   Émile Léonard, *Les Angevins de Naples* (Paris, 1954), pp. 85–86.
[41]   Cadier, *Essai sur l'administration*, p. 35.
[42]   Sternfeld, *Kreuzzug nach Tunis*, appendix A, no. 16 (330).
[43]   Sternfeld, *Kreuzzug nach Tunis*, appendix A, no. 8 (325).
[44]   Runciman, *Sicilian Vespers*, p. 97.
[45]   Lèfevre, *La crociata*, no. 131; *Registri della cancelleria angioina*, 5: no. 346.

and a doubling of the tribute for the next 15 years.[46] Charles's participation, late as it was, would have been virtually impossible without the indemnity, but the truce was advantageous enough to Charles that rumors about his intentions spread as soon as it was announced to the army.[47] "The vulgar common people," reports William of Nangis, "blamed Charles of Anjou [for the truce]; they said that he had arranged the truce in order to return the tribute, which for some years before had not been paid."[48] Peter of Condé, a clerk of Louis IX who accompanied the king on the Tunis expedition and later became a Dominican, also suggested that Charles's interest in Tunis was financial.[49] In a letter to Matthew, abbot of St. Denis, Peter explained how

> the king of Sicily had asked our barons at the beginning of the war, that they should not threaten the king of Tunis until they had received his [Charles's] message. I believe this was because there were discussions about peace between [al-Mustansir] and [Charles] and about the tribute that should be collected again from the king of Tunis. I heard as much from a knight of the king of Sicily, who on this account had been sent twice to the king of Tunis, and now had come once more concerning the discussions about peace and the tribute, because the king of Tunis wished [to pay] the tribute only from the beginning of Charles's reign, while the king of Sicily was asking for the tribute in arrears from the time of Manfred and Frederick. These talks had been suspended for some time, and our army invaded the kingdom of Tunis. Once Charles had joined our army, and found his brother dead, he decided that he would carry out as if by violence, what he had taken previously by conducting negotiations.[50]

Peter suggests that Charles's aims were constant throughout earlier negotiations, the siege of the city, and concluding negotiations. He wanted Tunis saved, not sacked: destroying the city would prevent the renewal of the lapsed tribute payments; far better, once Louis had brought an army before Tunis, to use it as a negotiating tool for better terms with al-Mustansir.

---

46   Mas Latrie, *Traités*, pp. 93–96.

47   On Charles's inability to fund his expedition to Tunis without the proceeds of the indemnity, see the detailed discussion in Sternfeld, *Kreuzzug nach Tunis*, pp. 268–276.

48   William of Nangis, *Gesta sanctae memoriae Ludovici regis Franciae*, in *RHGF*, 20, p. 478.

49   Louis Carolus-Barré, "Un recueil épistolaire composé à Saint-Denis sur la croisade (1270–1271)," *Comptes rendus de l'Académie des inscriptions et belles-lettres* (Paris, 1966), 564; *Histoire littéraire de la France* 27 (1877), p. 93.

50   Peter of Condé, *Epistola Petri de Condeto, ad Matthaeum Abbatem*, in *Spicilegium*, 3, pp. 667–668.

Peter of Condé may have been recycling the rumors of crusaders, bitter because Charles denied them the chance to sack Tunis. According to the chronicler Primat, the disagreements were not only between the crusaders and the leadership. Primat notes a double division within the army: first among the councilors themselves, and then between the leadership and the fighters. The council, according to Primat, was "divided into two parties: one believed that they should kill as many Saracens as they could find and that the said city of Tunis should be destroyed with the entire country, and then they should leave everything thus destroyed," while the other thought that the truce offered by al-Mustansir "should be accepted under certain conditions."[51] Charles and Thibaut of Navarre advocated the truce, the position ultimately taken, a decision that was, according to Primat, deeply unpopular:

> And truly the common knighthood and the community of people, who deeply coveted having the spoils of the enemy, did not want in any way to consent to this arrangement; instead they wanted to go to avenge the enemies of the Christian faith and to destroy the city entirely, and declared that that would be the more honorable and more profitable thing to do. And they also blamed the king of Sicily, . . . [and said] that he had arranged for the truce to be granted, so that he could make the king of Tunis (who was terrified by fear of the French and had for several years refused to render him the tribute that he was accustomed to render him) give satisfaction for the tribute by this peace accord.[52]

The interests of "the common knighthood and the community of people," in this account, are both religious and financial: by sacking the city they could fulfill their crusade vows and gain money from the looting. These interests are opposed to the benefits of the truce, cast in financial terms, for those who advocated it: under its terms, Charles and Thibaut would earn a share of al-Mustansir's war indemnity as part of the crusade leadership while the "common knighthood" would come away empty-handed.

By negotiating the Treaty of Tunis, Charles gained a new source of revenue for his government, preserved a trading partner for his merchants, and acquired funds that partially alleviated his pressing financial needs. Sicily and Tunis were allies throughout the 1270s. The tribute was paid regularly and in 1276, a Sicilian trade center, or funduk, was established in Tunis, a permanent testimony to their peaceful relations.[53]

---

[51] Primat, *Chronique*, p. 80.

[52] Primat, *Chronique*, p. 80.

[53] Lèfevre, *La crociata*, no. 391; *Registri della cancelleria angioina*, 10: no. 51. For the funduk, see Lèfevre, *La crociata*, nos. 412–413.

If Charles of Anjou benefited from peace with Tunis, taking advantage of Louis's presence there but not, out of fear of destroying the city, directing the crusade against it, we must examine the possibility that Louis planned the diversion himself. Louis may have believed that a strike against Tunis would aid the Christian settlements of the Holy Land. He was one of many thirteenth-century crusade enthusiasts who believed one could help Latin Syria without crusading there directly. Egypt, for example, had been a popular target from the late twelfth century onward. But whereas Egypt under Sultan Baybars posed the gravest of threats to the crusader states in the late 1260s, Tunis under al-Mustansir did not. His capital city lay 1,400 miles to the west. His contact with Latin Syria, whether friendly or hostile, was minimal. His foreign policy centered on trade and diplomacy and his relations with Christian powers were peaceful.[54] Commercial interests also dictated his domestic agenda. He welcomed Christian merchants and allowed them to live in specially-built funduks, where they were free to trade and practice their own religion.[55] The worst accusations Western sources could muster against al-Mustansir were that he obstructed the sea route from western Europe to Syria and provided arms to Baybars.[56] Neither had much basis in fact and both, in any event, paint him as, at most, a secondary threat to the Holy Land. Given the geographical realities, he could hardly have been more than that.

If Tunis was not an attractive primary target for a campaign in aid of the Holy Land, it may instead have figured in Louis's plans as a useful stopping point along the way. Whether he meant Syria or Egypt to be the final destination of the expedition is impossible to determine. The transportation contracts he made with Genoa through 1268 and 1269 suggest only that he wanted to keep his

---

[54]   Brunschvig, *La Berbérie orientale*, 1, pp. 42–52; Charles-Emmanuel Dufourcq, *L'Espagne catalane et le Maghrib au XIIe et XIVe siècles de la bataille de Las Navas de Tolosa (1212) à l'avènement du sultan mérinide Abou-l-Hasan (1331)* (Paris, 1966), pp. 110–131; Harry W. Hazard, "Moslem North Africa 1049–1394," in *A History of the Crusades*, ed. Kenneth M. Setton, 6 vols. (Madison, 1969–89), 3, 471–473; Olivia Remie Constable, *Trade and Traders in Muslim Spain: The Commercial Realignment of the Iberian Peninsula, 900–1500* (Cambridge, 1994), pp. 5, 34–35, and 241–242; Michael Brett, "The Maghrib," in *The New Cambridge Medieval History V*, ed. David Abulafia(Cambridge, 1999), 632.

[55]   On Tunisian funduks see A.B. Hibbert, "Catalan Consulates in the Thirteenth Century," *Cambridge Historical Journal* 9 (1949), 352–358; Felipe Fernández-Armesto, *Before Columbus: Exploration and Colonisation from the Mediterranean to the Atlantic 1229–1492* (London, 1987), pp. 109–110; and Olivia Remie Constable, *Housing the Stranger in the Mediterranean World: Lodging, Trade, and Travel in Late Antiquity and the Middle Ages* (Cambridge, 2003), pp. 298–301.

[56]   Sternfeld, *Kreuzzug nach Tunis*, p. 378; Geoffrey of Beaulieu, *Vita Ludovici*, p. 22.

options open.[57] Some scholars have argued that Egypt was the ultimate target, claiming that Tunis appeared a more likely stop *en route* to attacking Baybars to the crusaders than it does to us because they believed that it was only a four-day journey by horse from Tunis to Cairo, when in fact the cities lie 1,300 difficult miles apart.[58] The argument for geographical ignorance, however, is difficult to credit in the absence of any contemporary source making this claim. Louis used Genoese ships and crews for the Tunis expedition.[59] Genoa had commercial and diplomatic relations with Tunis and its merchants had a long history of traveling the trade routes between Genoa, Tunis, and Alexandria.[60] It is hard to believe that they did not know the distance between Tunis and Egypt or that they withheld this information from Louis. Nor should the geographical ignorance of Louis and his own advisors be overstated. On his first crusade Louis had sailed from Aigues-Mortes to Cyprus, from Cyprus to Damietta, from Damietta to Acre, and from Acre to Hyères. His brother was just across the Strait of Sicily from Tunis. Envoys from Tunis had visited Louis in Paris on several occasions. There is little reason Louis would have chosen Tunis as a good launching point for an attack on Baybars.

Something other than geographical proximity to more urgent crusading targets must have attracted Louis to Tunis in 1270. The city enjoyed a reputation as a prosperous commercial center. Geoffrey of Beaulieu maintained that Tunis was wealthy and ripe for the taking because it had not been conquered since ancient times (so far as he knew).[61] While money was always useful for a crusade, it was not the main reason Louis chose Tunis, according to Geoffrey. Rather, he claimed, Louis directed his crusade there to facilitate the conversion of al-Mustansir and those of his people who would join him in becoming Christian. On the face of it, this explanation seems little more than the imaginings of a devout confessor: al-Mustansir had, after all, taken the title "Caliph" in 1253. But Geoffrey's closeness to Louis, along with the paucity of alternative explanations,

---

[57]   For the contracts, see Luigi Tommaso Belgrano, *Documenti inediti riguardanti le due crociate di San Ludovico IX, re di Francia* (Genoa, 1858), pp. 215–321.

[58]   Jacques Le Goff, *Saint Louis* (Paris, 1996), p. 459, and 546; Michel Mollat, "Le 'passage' de Saint Louis à Tunis: sa place dans l'histoire des croisades," *Revue d'histoire économique et sociale* 50 (1972), 291–292; Sternfeld, *Kreuzzug nach Tunis*, p. 228.

[59]   Primat, *Chronique*, pp. 41–42, William of Nangis, *Gesta Ludovici*, p. 444.

[60]   For Genoese treaties with Tunis, see Mas Latrie, *Traités*, pp. 118–121, and 122–125. For a statistical overview of Genoese trade with Alexandria and Tunis in the thirteenth century, see Steven Epstein, *Genoa and the Genoese, 958–1528* (Chapel Hill, 1996), pp. 141–143.

[61]   Geoffrey of Beaulieu, *Vita Ludovici*, p. 22.

makes the theory worth examining in the context of Louis's other conversion policies.[62]

A baptismal ceremony of a Jew is, in fact, where Geoffrey places Louis's decision to crusade to Tunis. Louis acted as sponsor to the convert at St. Denis in October 1269:

> In the same year, when the pious king had to cross the sea for the last time, the king of Tunis had sent to him solemn ambassadors, and on the feast of St. Denis, the king had baptized a certain famous Jew. . . . As the king raised him from the sacred font, he wished that the ambassadors might take part in the baptismal ceremony. After they were brought over, the king said with great emotion, "Say on my part to your lord the king, that I so strongly desire the health of his soul, that I would wish to be a captive of the Saracens for all the days of my life, I would wish never to see the light of the sun again, so long as your king and his people from their true hearts became Christians."[63]

The ceremony, as Geoffrey describes it, displays both the king's success at conversion and his enthusiasm for further missionary efforts. The proximity of the ambassadors seems to suggest to Louis an even greater success that he wishes could be his, or gives him the opportunity to state publicly a goal he may have formulated in private. It also, then, provides the occasion for announcing his intention to crusade to Tunis:

> The most Catholic king desired with the greatest devotion that the Christian faith, which in the time of Saint Augustine and other orthodox doctors had flourished in Africa, and most of all at Carthage, might flourish again and be extended in our time to the honor and glory of Jesus Christ. He thought, therefore, that if a large and renowned army suddenly placed itself before Tunis, the king of Tunis could scarcely have such a reasonable occasion to be baptized, because, by this means, he could avoid death at the hands of his men, keep possession of his kingdom, and others who wished could become Christian with him. Furthermore, [Louis] was given to understand, that if the aforesaid king utterly did not wish to become

---

[62]   Geoffrey was the king's confessor for twenty years and administered last rites to him in North Africa. For his biography, see *RHGF*, xxviii; Natalis de Wailly, "Examen critique de la vie de Saint Louis par Geoffroy de Beaulieu," *Mémoires de l'Académie royale des inscriptions et belles-lettres* 15 (1845); Auguste Molinier, *Les sources de l'histoire de France. Des origines aux guerres d'Italie (1494)*, 6 vols. (Paris, 1901–1906), 3, p. 116; Thomas Kaeppeli, *Scriptores Ordinis Praedicatorum medii aevi*, 4 vols. (Rome, 1970–93), 2, p. 15; Le Goff, *Saint Louis*, pp. 333–335.

[63]   Geoffrey of Beaulieu, *Vita Ludovici*, p. 22.

Christian, the city of Tunis could be taken quite easily, and by consequence, the whole country.[64]

As Geoffrey presents it, the emir was on the verge of converting but needed an excuse to do so without reprisals from his people. The presence of an army at his gates would provide him with the cover he sought. Or, if even the threat of attack did not allow him to convert (or lead to his conversion), the army could instead conquer Tunis "quite easily," allowing Louis to use the city and its riches for Christian ends.

The plan Geoffrey outlines has striking parallels to Louis's policies at home, both in his approach to conversion and in his idea of spending the money of non-Christians for Christian purposes. When dealing with Jewish communities in his own lands, Louis created a context that would encourage conversion. He personally sponsored the baptism of converts, who would then receive life pensions from the crown. Child converts also received housing until they reached adulthood. The children were recorded as *Ludovici baptisati* and the adults as *Ludovici conversi* (Louis's converts).[65] While offering real incentives for conversion, Louis also made life more difficult for those who did not convert by suppressing the Talmud, limiting the ability of Jews to lend money at interest, and seizing the profits of money-lending (a practice known as the *captio*, or taking).[66]

The *captio* made life harder for Jews who chose to remain Jewish, but Louis worried that he was profiting from the sins of others by collecting it. When he told Gregory IX of his concerns, the pope solved the problem by suggesting that Louis donate the money in support of a crusade.[67] This suggestion was so palatable to Louis that he used it on a number of occasions, channeling the profits from the *captio* toward his own crusading ventures in 1248 and again in

---

[64]   Geoffrey of Beaulieu, *Vita Ludovici*, p. 22.

[65]   Le Goff, *Saint Louis*, pp. 808–809; Gerard Nahon, "Les ordonnances de Saint Louis sur les juifs," *Les nouveaux cahiers* 6 (1970), 23.

[66]   Isidore Loeb, "La controverse de 1240 sur le Talmud," *Revue des études juives* 1 (1880), 247–61, 2 (1881), 248–270, 3 (1881), 39–57; Hyam Maccoby, *Judaism on Trial: Jewish-Christian Disputations in the Middle Ages* (East Brunswick, N.J., 1982), pp. 19–38; Robert Chazan, *Daggers of Faith: Thirteenth-Century Christian Missionizing and Jewish Response* (Berkeley, 1989), pp. 31–33; Jeremy Cohen, *Living Letters of the Law: Ideas of the Jew in Medieval Christianity* (Berkeley, 1999), pp. 317–325. On the anti-usury campaign, see Robert Chazan, *Medieval Jewry in Northern France. A Political and Social History* (Baltimore, 1973), pp. 103–147; and William Chester Jordan, *The French Monarchy and the Jews: From Philip Augustus to the Last Capetians* (Philadelphia, 1989), pp. 129–146.

[67]   *The Apostolic See and the Jews*, ed. Shlomo Simonsohn, 8 vols. (Toronto, 1988–91), 1: no. 157.

1270.[68] That Louis gained financially from these exactions is clear; but it would be wrong to see the motives behind his anti-usury policy as exclusively financial. In 1253–54, in the wake of his failed Egyptian campaign, Louis expelled all usurious Jews from France, showing an apparent willingness to spurn the profits to be made from Jewish money-lending.[69] The model of using sinful money to finance a holy purpose is one that Louis, by Geoffrey's account, had in mind should Tunis need to be destroyed.

Louis's practice of providing positive and negative incentives for conversion intensified in the year leading up to the Tunis expedition. On 18 June 1269 the king issued an ordinance requiring Jews to distinguish themselves from Christians by the manner of their dress.[70] This legislation, enacted on the advice of the converted Jew Paul Christian, a prominent Dominican missionary, was not original to Louis. The Fourth Lateran council had enacted a similar measure in 1215, but few secular princes besides Louis implemented it.[71] On 18 June 1269, in a separate order, Louis instructed royal officials to compel Jews to attend Paul Christian's sermons, respond to his questions, and surrender their books to him.[72] According to a contemporary Latin chronicle and a recently-discovered Hebrew text, Louis also compelled Jews to listen to Paul's sermons in the Dominican chapter house in Paris and in the royal court itself.[73]

Louis thus placed Jews in situations that encouraged their conversion (such as the enforced sermons), rewarded them if they did convert (through life pensions), and punished them if they did not convert (by levying taxes that could advance Christian goals). These strategies closely match the way Geoffrey of Beaulieu says the king approached Tunis. Here, as in France, wealth would be extracted as punishment and put to pious ends if the expected conversions did not take place:

> That city was full of money and gold and infinite riches, as was possible with a
> city that had never been conquered. Thereupon, it was hoped that if, God willing,
> the said city were captured by the Christian army, that the treasures found there

---

    [68]   Nahon, "Les ordonnances de Saint Louis," p. 19.

    [69]   Jordan, *French Monarchy and the Jews*, p. 148.

    [70]   *Ordonnances des roys de France de la troisième race*, ed. Eusèbe-J. de Laurière et al., 21 vols. (Paris, 1723–1849), 1, p. 294.

    [71]   *Decrees of the Ecumenical Councils*, ed. Norman P. Tanner (Washington, DC, 1990), p. 266.

    [72]   Shatzmiller, *La deuxième controverse de Paris*, appendix 1, p. 35.

    [73]   Léopold Delisle, "Notes sur quelques mss. du Musée britannique," *Mémoires de la Société de l'Histoire de Paris* 4 (1877), 189; the text is published along with a French translation in Shatzmiller, *La deuxième controverse de Paris*, pp. 43–76.

would contribute very effectively to the conquest and the restoration of the Holy Land.[74]

The plan, in other words, was to use Muslim riches to finance the conquest and restoration of the Holy Land, just as Louis had used the money of usurious and unconverted Jews for this purpose. What Geoffrey recounts here is the king exporting his domestic Jewish policy to the Muslim world beyond the royal domains.

The win-win strategy Geoffrey of Beaulieu describes, in which Tunis would become Christian by either conversion or force, also features in a letter of King Philip III of France dated 12 September 1270, less than a month after Louis's death. Addressing the clergy of France from the crusader camp, Philip explained how his father

> came to the port of Tunis, took it with no loss of men, and held this very renowned port lying at the entryway to the land of Africa, which he intended, if God had granted him life, to dedicate to God by the increase of the Christian religion and to expel the barbarian lineage and purify of all their filth the execrable treason of the Saracens.[75]

Six months later Philip repeated this explanation to the abbot of St. Denis. The leaders of the crusade had taken the cross and then "come to Africa to extirpate from the roots the errors of the infidel Saracens there."[76] Philip's language is notable in two ways. In the first place, it uses the standard crusade explanations but applies them to Africa rather than the Holy Land, making it seem as though Louis and the others had taken the cross for Africa, which they had not. In the second place, it adds to this crusading language the language of mission, portraying Louis's desire to spread, strengthen, and increase the faith. Both possibilities, that of crusade and that of mission, co-exist in Philip's account, just as they seem to have co-existed in Louis's actions.

Louis was no stranger to proselytizing while on crusade. During his first crusade he had sponsored missionary initiatives to the Mongols.[77] While

---

[74]   Geoffrey of Beaulieu, *Vita Ludovici*, p. 22.

[75]   Primat, *Chronique*, pp. 62–63.

[76]   *Epistola Philippi regis*, p. 669.

[77]   On Louis's Mongol mission, see Amand Rastoul, "Andrew de Longjumeau," *Dictionnaire d'histoire et de géographie écclésiastique* (Paris, 1912–), 1677–1678; *The Mission of Friar William of Rubruck*, trans. Peter Jackson, introduction, notes, and appendices by Peter Jackson with David O. Morgan (London, 1990), pp. 33–39; Paul Pelliot, *Les Mongols et la papauté*, 3 vols. (Paris, 1923), 3, pp. 160–214.

encamped on Cyprus in 1248 he sent three Dominicans bearing cups, liturgies, and a miniature chapel to investigate rumors that the Mongol Khan Güyük had converted to Christianity. By the time the Dominicans reached the court Güyük was dead and the regent demanded Louis's submission rather than celebrating mass. Undeterred, Louis sent a Franciscan missionary back into central Asia in 1253 with a letter of recommendation. He also encouraged Muslim conversion during his first crusade. According to reports, these efforts met with more success: one chronicler counts 40 Muslim converts, another over 500, while according to Matthew Paris the king almost converted the sultan of Egypt. The king's image among contemporaries as a missionary, if not the actual success of his efforts, shines through these episodes.[78]

But what made Louis think that a prominent Muslim ruler would be receptive to a missionary initiative in 1270? According to Geoffrey of Beaulieu, Louis thought that al-Mustansir was on the verge of conversion on the basis of reports from "trustworthy sources."[79] Some historians have suggested that these "trustworthy sources" were the Tunisian envoys who visited Paris in the fall of 1269.[80] The only positive evidence we have about the purpose of the envoys' visits, however, comes from Ibn Khaldun, who writes that they were negotiating a dispute over the debts of a Tunisian customs official who died under scandalous circumstances while owing money to a number of French merchants.[81] I believe that a more likely, although still circumstantial, source for the suggestion that al-Mustansir might convert is the Dominican community of Tunis.

Tunis was an important center of Dominican missionary activity in the thirteenth century. By the early 1240s the order had established a language school there and in 1250 eight Dominican brothers arrived to reinforce its numbers.[82] Many of the Dominicans with whom Louis had close contacts,

---

[78]   Benjamin Z. Kedar, *Crusade and Mission: European Approaches Toward the Muslims* (Princeton, 1984), pp. 161–165.

[79]   Geoffrey of Beaulieu, *Vita Ludovici*, p. 22.

[80]   Henri-Francois Delaborde, review of Sternfeld *Kreuzzug nach Tunis*, in *Revue de l'Orient latin* 4 (1896), 426.

[81]   Ibn Khaldun, *Histoire des Berbéres et des dynasties musulmanes de l'Afrique septentrionale*, trans. William MacGuckin de Slane, new edition published under the direction of Paul Casanova, 3 vols. (Paris, 1925–1934), 2, pp. 359–362.

[82]   *Scriptores ordinis praedicatorum*, eds. Jacques Quétif and Jacques Echard, 2 vols. (Paris, 1719–21), 2, p. 396. For the Dominican language school in Tunis see André Berthier, "Les écoles de langues orientales fondées au XIIIe siècle par les Dominicains en Espagne et en Afrique," *Revue Africaine* 73 (1932); José M. Coll, "Escuelas de lenguas orientales en los siglos XIII-XIV," *Analecta sacra tarraconensia* 17 (1944); Robert I. Burns, "Christian-Muslim Confrontation in the West: The Thirteenth-Century Dream of Conversion," *The American Historical Review* 76 (1971), reprinted with modifications in his *Muslims, Christians, and Jews in the Crusader Kingdom of*

including Raymond of Peñafort, Francis Cendra, Andrew of Longjumeau, and Raymond Marti, were active in the language school and deeply involved in missionizing.[83] Although it may seem surprising that men with such direct knowledge of Tunisian affairs should have thought al-Mustansir was likely to convert, it seems certain that they did. In a letter R.I. Burns dates to 1256–1258, Raymond of Peñafort wrote of "the fruit which is born through the ministry of the brothers in Africa and Spain." His list included "the Saracens, among whom the powerful, and even Miramolinim himself, the king of Tunis, who bears such grace and favor of God towards them [the brothers]." "And furthermore," Raymond continued, "it seems appropriate to remark that at the moment the door appears open, as if for an inestimable harvest."[84] Raymond's letter is the most explicit statement of the belief that the emir was ready to convert, but it was far from the only contemporary assessment that Tunis was fertile ground for missionary activity.[85]

Whether these Dominicans were deceived by al-Mustansir, mistook the emir's tolerance of their activities as encouragement, or simply held fast to what R.I. Burns has called the "thirteenth-century dream of conversion," they do seem to have thought that Tunis was a promising place for missionizing and its leader a promising candidate for conversion.[86] Louis's close ties to the Dominicans and his own enthusiasm for missionizing made him as likely as anyone to take their assessment seriously. This seems to have been al-Mustansir's conclusion: when the crusade army arrived before Tunis, he immediately had the Dominicans and other religious arrested, threatening the crusaders with their deaths if the army did not desist.[87] That he rounded up the Dominicans (rather than, for example, the merchants), suggests that he saw a connection between Dominican activity in Tunis and the arrival of the crusading army.

Whoever the "trustworthy sources" may have been, a story told by Primat shows Louis and the crusaders' willingness to believe that the people in Tunis

---

Valencia: Societies in Symbiosis (Cambridge, 1984). I follow Burns's dating for the foundation of the school.

[83]   For more on these figures and their links to Tunis and Louis's missionary ventures, see Michael Lower "Conversion and Saint Louis's Last Crusade," *Journal of Ecclesiastical History* 58 (2007), 226–229.

[84]   Coll, "Escuelas de lenguas orientales," Appendix 2: 138. He dates the letter 1246. Burns, "The Thirteenth-Century Dream of Conversion," 85, dates it 1256–1258.

[85]   Humbert of Romans and Pope Alexander IV both declared North Africa a thriving region of missionary activity: Benedictus Maria Reichert, *Litterae encyclicae Magistrorum Generalium*, in *Monumenta ordinum fratrum praedicatorum historica*, 25 vols. to date (Rome, 1896-), 5, p. 40; Coll, "Escuelas de lenguas orientales," appendix 1, pp. 136–138.

[86]   Burns, "The Thirteenth-Century Dream of Conversion."

[87]   William of Nangis, *Gesta Ludovici*, p. 478.

were ready to convert. According to this story, the count of Eu and the lord of Acre were standing guard one day when three Hafsid men-at-arms came up to them, asking to be made Christians. The count led them back to the camp and returned to his post, whereupon 100 more soldiers approached, all asking to be made Christian. While the crusaders were occupied with these 103 potential converts, the Hafsids sprang an attack that succeeded in routing the camp guard. After the attack the count logically accused the original three soldiers of treachery. The three defended themselves with tears and excuses. The count relented, and, with Louis's permission, agreed to let them go if they promised they would return with 2,000 men for the crusaders. The Hafsid soldiers, needless to say, did not return.[88]

Other chroniclers also stress conversion as a primary motive behind the king's expedition to North Africa, ascribing to the crusade a degree of success in this arena that it had not actually achieved. In the treaty concluding the crusade, al-Mustansir restored to the Christians their right to build monasteries and churches in their funduks and to preach and pray in those churches.[89] This was the sixth provision in the treaty negotiated, we should recall, by Charles of Anjou not Louis. Peter of Condé moves it to the second provision, and summarizes it accurately.[90] Primat makes it explicitly the first provision of the treaty:

> And it was arranged in the following fashion between our men and the king of Tunis. And first that in all the cities and noble places of the kingdom of Tunis, and in all the lands subject to the kingdom and those that would be subject to it, from now on, priests and religious would have churches and buildings and cemeteries, and would inhabit these places solemnly and in peace, and would ring their bells and would celebrate the divine service, and would perform in common the office of preaching, and would perform and administer the sacraments of the church to Christians who would live there.[91]

Primat's account is not technically inaccurate, but it is ambiguous in ways that the treaty was not. The provision about Christians in the emir's lands was not first in the treaty, although it may have been first in importance for Primat. The churches and buildings and cemeteries were permitted in the funduks, which Primat's construction of "all the cities and noble places" and "all the lands subject to the kingdom" allows but makes potentially more broad than the reality. The bell ringing, celebration of the service, preaching, and performance

---

88   Primat, *Chronique*, pp. 48–49.
89   Mas Latrie, *Traités*, pp. 93–96.
90   Peter of Condé, *Epistola Petri de Condeto, ad Matthaeum Abbatem*, pp. 667–668.
91   Primat, *Chronique*, p. 81.

and administration of the sacraments were similarly confined to the churches in the funduk, which Primat's language again makes possible, while still retaining a suggestion that these liberties might be more widespread.

Rather than walking such a delicate line, William of Nangis provides two distinct accounts of the treaty. In his *Life of Louis IX* he gives an accurate description of the provision about religious activity in the emir's lands.[92] In his universal history, however, he tells a different story altogether. The Saracens, he explains,

> entered into agreements with the Christians. Among which were said to be these especially, that all captive Christians in that kingdom were to be released, and that in monasteries built in honor of Christ's name in all the cities of that kingdom the faith of Christ was to be freely preached by brothers minor and preacher and by whosoever else wished to do so, and those wishing to be baptized were to be baptized freely.[93]

This version of the treaty, with its allowance of free baptism, not only fictionalizes the success of Louis's expedition, it casts that success in terms of conversion. It proved by far the most popular way of understanding Louis's expedition in the years following his death. William's universal history is one of at least eight surviving chronicles from France, Italy, Germany, and England that repeat this account verbatim, presumably from a common source.[94]

The failure of the diversion has probably made the question of who should take responsibility for it more pressing than success would have. Nineteenth-

---

[92]   William of Nangis, *Gesta Ludovici*, p. 478.

[93]   William of Nangis, *Chronique latine de Guillaume de Nangis*, ed. Hercule Géraud, 2 vols. (Paris, 1843), 1, p. 238.

[94]   *Alberti Milioli notarii Regini Liber de temporibus*, in *[M]onumenta [G]ermaniae [h]istorica, scriptores*, ed. Georg H. Pertz et al, 32 vols. (Hannover and Leipzig: Impensis Bibliopolii Hahniani, 1826–1934), 31, p. 538; Salimbene, *Cronica fratris Salimbene de Adam ordinis minorum*, in *MGH SS*, 32: 483–484; Giovanni Villani, *Cronica*, ed. Francesco Gherardi Dragomanni (Florence, 1844), p. 367; anonymous continuator of Gerard Frachet, *Chronicon Girardi de Fracheto et anonyma eiusdem operis continuatio*, in *RHGF*, 21, pp. 5–6; *Bruchstücke aus der Weltchronik des Minoriten Paulinus von Venedig (I. Recension)*, ed. Walther Holtzmann (Rome, 1927), p. 55; Nicolas Trivet, *Annales sex regum Anglie*, 1136–1307, ed. Thomas Hog (London, 1845; repr. Vaduz, 1964), p. 276; *Vita Clementis Papae IV, ex MSi Bernardi Guidonis*, in *Rerum Italicarum scriptores Nova series*, ed. Gisuè Carducci et al., 34 vols. to date (Bologna: N. Zanichelli, 1900-present), part 3, 1, p. 596; *Martini Oppaviensis chronicon*, in *MGH SS*, 22, p. 474. On these chronicles, see Kedar, *Crusade and Mission*, pp. 168–169.

century historians tended to follow Saba Malaspina in blaming Charles.[95] In the last century some have persisted in this attribution, while others have followed Richard Sternfeld in attributing the diversion to Louis instead.[96] Placing the expedition in the context of Charles's other interests shows how unlikely he was to have to wanted to direct a crusade against his Hafsid neighbor. Doing so would not have advanced his plans for Constantinople; worse still, it would have risked the destruction of a traditional source of tribute, trade, and political support. Charles's last-minute arrival on the scene forestalled this possibility and enabled him to forge the long-term economic and political partnership with the city that he seems to have desired. Placing the expedition in the context of Louis's conversion policies, meanwhile, shows its consistency with his other actions. As he sought to missionize on his first crusade, so he seems to have sought to missionize on his last; as he pressured Jews to convert in Paris, so he seems to have pressured Muslims to convert in Tunis.

---

[95]   Henri Wallon, *Saint Louis et son temps*, 2 vols. (Paris, 1876), 2, pp. 435–436; Karl Hampe, *Geschichte Konradins von Hohenstaufen* (Leipzig, 1940), 305, 311, 312, a reissue of the original text (Innsbruck, 1894) with an afterword by Hellmut Kämpf; Michele Amari, *La guerra del Vespro Siciliano* (n.p., 1947), 41, originally published as *Un periodo delle istorie siciliane del secolo XIII* (Palermo, 1842).

[96]   Sternfeld, *Kreuzzug nach Tunis*, pp. 313–314.

Chapter 12

The Place of the Crusades in the
Sanctification of Saint Louis[1]

M.C. Gaposchkin

Dartmouth College

In the year 1270 Louis IX, King of France since 1226, died on crusade outside
the walls of Tunis as he besieged the Muslim city in an effort to persuade its
emir, al-Mustansir, to convert to Christianity.[2] Twenty-seven years later, in
August of 1297, Pope Boniface VIII solemnly canonized Louis IX as a saint
of the church, praising him in a number of canonization-related documents
for his defense of the faith and his efforts against the Muslim infidel. Louis'
devotion to crusading was a principal feature of the numerous texts written
in these years in support of his canonization and in the testimony offered
during the canonization inquiry that was held in 1282 and 1283 at St. Denis,
and historians of sainthood have routinely said that Louis' sanctity was largely

[1]   For the lives of Louis written by Geoffrey of Beaulieu, William of Chartres, Yves
of Saint Denis (listed as "the Anonymous of Saint Denis"), and William of Nangis, I cite
the editions in vols. 20 and 22 of Martin Bouquet, ed., *Recueil des historiens des Gaules et
de la France*, 24 vols. (Paris: 1738; reprint, Gregg: Farnborough: 1967) – hereafter RHGF.
I cite H.-F. Delaborde's more reliable edition of William of Saint-Pathus' life of Saint Louis
(Guillaume of Saint-Pathus, *Vie de Saint Louis*, ed. H. François Delaborde, *Collection
de textes pour servir à l'étude et à l'enseignement de l'histoire 27* (Paris, 1899)), though this
can also be consulted in *RHGF*, v. 20, 58–121. Boniface's bull of canonization is found in
RHGF, v. 23, 154–160. I quote Joinville from R. Hague's translation: John of Joinville, *The
Life of St. Louis*, trans. René Hague from the text edited by Natalis de Wailly (New York,
1955). I refer to two other texts. The first is the liturgical vita that accompanied celebration
of Louis' feast day. It can be found at *RHGF*, v. 23, 161–167. I also cite an unpublished vita
for Louis, *Gloriosissimi Regis*, that I am currently editing for publication. It is cited here by
chapter number (of which there are twelve in total). I am grateful to Sean Field, Christopher
MacEvitt, and Caroline Smith for reading earlier versions of this piece, to Thomas Madden
for organizing the conference on the Crusades and for the opportunity to participate in it,
and finally to William Chester Jordan for his useful comments at the conference itself.
[2]   Michael Lower, "Conversion and Saint Louis's Last Crusade," *Journal of Ecclesiastical
History* 58 (2007), 211–231.

conceived of in terms of his crusading – that he was a "crusader saint."[3] This view is supported by the text through which we best know Louis – that of Jean of Joinville – which, Joinville tells us, was written specifically to show how Louis was a saint, which is centered on the crusade, and in which Joinville speaks of Louis as a chivalric and glorious crusader.

And yet, if Louis could be praised as a crusader, he could not be praised as a particularly successful crusader. The crusade in 1250 to Egypt had ended with the king and that part of his army that had not died or been killed in the captivity of the Sultan. The crusade of 1270 had, for all intents and purposes, ended when Louis died of disease (dysentery).[4] Louis' crusading came under criticism.[5] Salimbene had in the 1280s written about the "shame which the French had received beyond the sea under St. Louis,"[6] and Joinville spoke of how the crusade of 1270 had achieved little.[7] Moreover, these same years – from 1270 to 1297 – spanned the ever-declining fortune of the crusader kingdoms, marked in 1291 by the fall of Acre, the last stronghold of Christian East. That is, the period in which Louis' sanctity was debated, defined, and confirmed – a sanctity that was heavily animated by his crusades – coincided with the death of the crusader states, though not, of course, the crusader ideal.[8]

---

[3] Michael Goodich, "The Politics of Canonization in the Thirteenth Century: Lay and Mendicant Saints," *Church History* 44 (1975), 306, Christopher Tyerman, *Fighting for Christendom: Holy War and the Crusades* (Oxford, 2004), pp. 84–86, André Vauchez, *Sainthood in the later Middle Ages*, trans. Jean Birrell (Cambridge, 1997), p. 360. Note that of the crusaders Tyerman lists in this discussion, only Louis IX was canonized by the papacy – all others fall into the category of men popularly revered for their sanctity. Jacques LeGoff calls him "un des très rares saints de la croisade." Jacques LeGoff, "La sainteté de Saint Louis: Sa place dans la typologie et l'évolution choronlogique des roi saints," in *Fonctions de saints dans le monde occidental (IIIᵉ-XIIIᵉ siècle): actes du colloques* (Rome, 1991), p. 287.

[4] On Louis' crusades, see in English, William Chester Jordan, *Louis IX and the Challenge of the Crusade: A Study in Rulership* (Princeton, 1979), Jean Richard, *Saint Louis: Crusader King of France*, ed. Simon Llyod, trans. Jean Birrell (Cambridge, 1992), Joseph R. Strayer, "The Crusades of Louis IX," in *A History of the Crusades: vol II: The Later Crusades, 1189–1311*, ed. Kenneth M. Setton (Madison, WI: University of Wisconsin Press, 1969). No assessment of Louis can be made now without consulting Jacques LeGoff, *Saint Louis* (Paris: Fayard, 1996) now available in English, Saint Louis, trans. Gareth Evans Gollrad (Notre-Dame, IND: University of Notre Dame Press, 2009).

[5] Elizabeth Siberry, *Criticism of Crusading: 1095–1274* (Oxford, 1985). Edward Billings Ham, *Rutebeuf and Louis IX* (Chapel Hill, 1962).

[6] Salimbene, *The chronicle of Salimbene de Adam* (Binghamton, 1986), p. 571.

[7] Joinville, §§ 732, 734.

[8] Norman Housley, *The Later Crusades, 1274–1580: From Lyons to Alcazar* (Oxford, 1992), ch. 1.

How, then, were contemporaries to account for this? How were they to make sense of the fact that a man whom everyone agreed was a saint of God had failed in an endeavor that everyone agreed was the work of God, sanctioned by God, and a duty to God? Failures on crusade had come routinely to be blamed on the "sins of the crusaders."[9] But, then, why was Louis – of whom his confessor could say he had not in 20 years committed a mortal sin –not rewarded with victory? What did this failure say, on the one hand, about Louis' sainthood? And further, what did it say about the crusades themselves if someone who was both the most powerful secular leader in Europe and a friend of God had been unsuccessful, not once, but twice?

This paper looks at the sources around Louis' sanctification and canonization, asking how they treated the issue of Louis' crusading. These sources include the traditional vitae – those written by Geoffrey of Beaulieu (1273–1274), William of Chartres (probably before 1282), William of Saint Pathus (written in 1302–03 on the basis of the lost canonization proceedings that had been held in 1282–83), and Joinville (written in stages, but completed by 1308) – as well as other individual sources bearing on the issue, such as letters written in support of Louis' canonization and para-liturgical texts written to celebrate Louis' sanctity on his feast day (August 25). As a solution to Louis' crusading failure developed over time, what we find is not a celebration of crusading per se, but rather the use of the crusades a vehicle to celebrate suffering, passion, and devotion to the Lord. Crusading is sanctified only in so far as it is a mechanism of self-sacrifice.

Crusading was certainly integral to people's conception of why Louis was a saint. All the principal hagiographers devoted large sections of their *vitae* of Louis to his experiences in the east. Many of those who accompanied Louis, either in 1250 or in 1270, testified at the canonization proceedings,[10] and it is clear from the mass of evidence included in William of Saint Pathus' vita that crusading was a focus of testimony. Fragments of the testimony of Charles of Anjou, by then King of Sicily, survive, and these focus almost entirely on the events in Egypt in 1250.[11] Joinville tells us that he himself testified for two days – surely about his time with Louis in the East.[12] A "canonization memorandum" written in 1297 by

9   Siberry, *Criticism of Crusading.*

10   We know of these through Wm. of St. Pathus, (Delaborde ed. 7–11). On these men, Louis Carolus-Barré, *Le procès de canonisation de Saint Louis (1272–1297): Essai de reconstitution,* ed. Henri Platelle, *Collection de l'École Française de Rome 195* (Rome, 1994), pp. 59–138.

11   Paul Edouard Didier Riant, "Déposition de Charles d'Anjou pour la canonisation de saint Louis," in *Notices et documents publiés pour la Société de l'histoire de France à l'occasion du cinquantième anniversaire de sa fondation* (Paris: 1884), pp. 155–176.

12   Joinville, §760.

a papal advisor for Boniface in advance of the canonization treated the crusades as *the* principal aspect of his sanctity.[13] After Louis' canonization, liturgical and homiletic texts routinely recounted anecdotes from his crusades.[14]

That said, there seems to have been some anxiety about the failure of Louis' crusading from the standpoint of its military and strategic objectives. This is first evidenced in the discomfited language employed in the earliest vita, written in 1273–74 by Louis' long-time Dominican confessor, Geoffrey of Beaulieu. In his chapter on the 1250 crusade, Geoffrey found himself insisting that all the events were chosen and directed by God. He began his treatment of the crusade of 1250 by saying "On his first trip, after many efforts, God miraculously gave him Damietta, when afterwards, but only by divine permission, he was made captive of the Saracens ... "[15] and then, later "Indeed, one must but remark that he was captured."[16] Geoffrey even tried to cull a miracle from Louis' ransom, saying that Louis and his men were released "against all hope, for a quite modest sum," in reasonably good shape ("healthy and unharmed"), all of which was accomplished through "a divine miracle and by divine power."[17] One senses Geoffrey grasping here – trying to figure out a language with which to talk about the events of 1250 that did not highlight Louis' failure, trying to incorporate Louis' crusade into a mainstream rhetoric of crusading glory and propaganda. Another (feeble) attempt to discuss his captivity claimed that his release was a miracle, saying that the Muslims knew that Louis could do them more harm than any other prince

---

[13]   Peter Linehan and Francisco J. Hernández, " 'Animadverto': A recently discovered *Consilium* concerning the sanctity of King Louis IX," *Revue Mabillon* 66 (1994), 83–105.

[14]   Guido Maria Dreves and Clemens Blume, eds., *Analecta hymnica medii aevi*, 55 vols. (Leipzig, 1886–1922; reprint, New York, 1961), v. 13, 186, 187, 189–190, 192, 193. Louis' crusades were frequently treated in sermons on Louis. Examples include (but are in no way limited to) BNF Lat 16512, 52r–56v (Anonymous Franciscan sermon, where the information is drawn from *Gloriosissimi Regis*); BNF Lat 3303, 183r–193v (Anonymous Franciscan sermon, where the information is drawn from the liturgical vita discussed elsewhere in this paper); Jacob of Lausanne O.P.'s *Videte Regem*, preserved in a number of sermon collections, for which see Jean-Baptist Schneyer, *Repertorium der lateinischen Sermones des Mittelalters für die Zeit von 1150–1350*, 11 vols., *Beiträge zur Geschichte der Philosophie und Theologie des Mittelalters 43* (Münster, 1969–1973), v. 3, pp. 104–105, no. 609; Vat. Capit san Petri D213, col. 487–492 (James of Viterbo's *Tronus eius*).

[15]   G. Beaulieu, *RHGF*, v. 20, 16, ch. 25: "sibi Dominus miraculosus reddiderit Damietam; quomodo postmodum divina permissione a Sarracenis captus."

[16]   G. Beaulieu, *RHGF*, v. 20, 16, ch. 25: "Denique non silendum est, quod quando Rex ipse captus fuit."

[17]   G. Beaulieu, *RHGF*, v. 20, 16, ch. 25. "non est multum mirandum; sed est divino miraculo et ipsius potentiae, necnon sancti Regis meritis adscribendum, quod ita de facili, et satis pro modico pretio, contra spem fere omnem, ipse et fraters sui, et exercitus christianus, fuerint satis sani et incolumes de ipiorum minibus liberati."

of the world and that they could have obtained up to 100 times the ransom.[18]
This story, ironically, had the effect of praising his Muslim captors for their lack
of greed. Others saw no way out other than to suggest that failure and captivity
was the plan of God, designed to showcase ideal Christian humility. William of
Chartres introduced the crusade by saying that "it was necessary that temptation
should test him, and should clearly show him worthy, just as gold and silver are
proved best when subjected to fire,"[19] and he ascribed the release of prisoners
to "the miracle of divine power and the merits of the king."[20] William of Saint-
Pathus could say of the devastation of the king's army and the captivity of the
king himself only that this was brought about by the "just if hidden judgment
of God," a formulation repeated in later vitae.[21] After Louis' canonization, an
anonymous text explained that Louis was captured not because of his own sins,
but because of those of his people "just as the head is afflicted by the sickness
of its members," and that, through this tribulation, Louis "glowed more and
more red" (that is, became more and more saintly).[22] These explanations – that
the events were directed by God, that the crusades were aided by his miracles,
that failure was a result of sin, that defeat was a test, that crusade was a spiritual
opportunity – all accorded with a traditional theology of crusading failure.[23]

---

[18]   Glor. Reg. ch. 10. "Quis enim non cognoscat miraculum ferocissimam gentem regi
quem posse sibi super ceteros mundi principes nocere sciebant parcere eamdemque gentem
cupidissimam pro redemptione minori in parte centupla quam habere potuissent liberum
dimittere." This sentiment is repeated in the liturgical vita associated with Louis' feast day;
RHGF, v. 23, 162, lection 5, "Qui enim non recognoscat miraculum gentem ferocissimam
tam faciliter parcere tanto regi, et gentem cupidissimam regem ditissimum dimittere liberum
pro multo minori redemption quam habere potuissent." Note that this actually contrasts
with Joinville's telling of the negotiations, where he says the Sultan is impressed with Louis
for not haggling over the requested sum; Joinville, §343.

[19]   Wm Chartres, *RHGF*, v. 20, 30. "necesse erat ut tentatio probaret eum, et probatum
ostenderet manifeste, sicut examinatur argentum et aurum optimum in fornace."

[20]   Wm. Chartres, *RHGF* v. 20, 31. "non absque miraculo virtutis divinae, et meritis
ipsius regis."

[21]   Wm. Saint-Pathus, (Delaborde 23) "par le jugement de Nostre Seigneur droiturier
et secré." The formulation was probably established in the summary vita compiled out of
the canonization proceedings and sent to the curia, and appears also in *Beatus Ludovicus*,
Orleans BM 348, 4v (a unique witness to an early vita), "At non multo post uosto sed occulto
dei"; BLQRF (p. 162) "Justo dei iudicio sed occulto." This was taken up by the author of
Glor. Reg, ch. 10, and the liturgical vita, *RHGF*, v. 23, lection 5, p. 162. The sentiment was
not original. See Matthew Paris, Chronica major (6:195) said "Sed haec secreto Dei iudicio
potius, quam humano sunt commendanda" (as quoted in Cole, p. 179, n. 10).

[22]   *RHGF*, v. 23, 173. "Hec miremur fratres karissimi, si pro delictis populi rex in manus
gentium tradebatur; sic pro membrorum aegritudine caput afflicitur."

[23]   Siberry, *Criticism of Crusading*, p. 69.

But Louis, of course, was special, because he was a saint – his intention was "right" and his aims unperverted. Joinville had blamed the disaster at Mansurah on the sins of the crusaders – plural – not on Louis himself, and he famously singled out Louis' brother, Robert of Artois, for particular blame.[24] William of Saint-Pathus and Boniface VIII both suggested that Louis was allowed to fall into captivity in order to showcase his humility. William said God handed Louis over to the Muslims to show Himself [that is, God] more wondrous in his saint.[25] In 1297 the pope wrote that "The Lord had wanted to reveal, moreover, that [Louis] was the instrument of His choice to make known His words to nations [*gentibus*], to kings and to the sons of Israel. He showed him thus what great suffering he had to endure in His name."[26] Louis was God's instrument not as a function of the crusade, but rather as an exemplum of humility. Here Louis is blameless for the military failure. Rather, he was an instrument of divine providence, delivered into the hands of Muslims by God in order that they witness Christian suffering. In this view, failure was a precondition of God's plan.

The merits of "suffering" and "humility" were thus the keys to sanctifying Louis' crusades, the only way to rescue the ideal of crusade within the context of the claims of Louis' sanctity. Hagiographers thus incorporated the crusades into a discourse of passion, hinting that through his crusading Louis suffered and was martyred.[27] Geoffrey himself, in his introductory chapters, suggested

---

24   Joinville, §§166, 218–219.

25   Wm. Saint-Pathus, Delaborde ed., 23, ch. 3: "Et adonques li Peres de misericorde, qui se volt mostrer en son saint merveilleus, bailla le benoiet roy saint Loys en la main des felons Sarrazins." This formulation was repeated exactly in liturgical-vita, lection 5, *RHGF*, v. 23, lection 5, p. 162, ("Volensque pater misericordiarum Dominus in sancto suo se mirabilem ostendere, pugilem fidei dominum regem tradidit impiorum minibus, ut mirabilio appareret") and in Glor. Reg. 10 (in which the Latin is rendered the same).

26   *RHGF* v. 23, 149. "Voluit insuper Dominus manifestare sibi quod erat vas electionis ad portandum verbum suum coram gentibus, et regibus, et filiis Israel. Et ideo ostendit illi quanta oportebat eum pro nomine suo pati: quia licet tot divitiis, deliciis, et honoribus abudnaret, relinquens omnia, corpus suum et vitam suam exposuit pro Christo, mare transfretando, et contra inimicos crucis Christi et fidei catholicae decertando, usque ad captionem et incarcerationem proprii corporis, uxoris et fratrum suorum."

27   On martyrdom and crusading, H.E.J. Cowdrey, "Martyrdom and the First Crusade," in *Crusade and Settlement: Papers read at the First Conference of the Society for the Study of the Latin East and presented to R. C. Smail*, ed. Peter W. Edbury (Cardiff: 1985), 46–56, Caroline Smith, *Crusading in the Age of Joinville* (Burlington, 2006), pp. 98–108, 139–149, and, for further bibliography, 198, n. 113, Caroline Smith, "Martyrdom and Crusading in the Thirteenth Century: Remembering the Dead of Louis IX's Crusades," *Al-Masaq: Islam and the Medieval Mediterranean* 15 (2003), 189–196.

that on Louis' second crossing to Tunis, "for the zeal and the exaltation of the Christian faith, he merited to be shown as a host [*hostium*] of Christ; and there [in Tunis], like an indefatigable martyr and fighter of the Lord [*martyr et pugil domini*], he finished the end of his life blessedly in the Lord."[28] Geoffrey thus presented the two sides of Louis' crusading status – active, as a fighter of the Lord, and passive, as a martyr.

Martyrdom had been defined by Thomas Aquinas (d. 1274) as the voluntary endurance of persecution to the point of death.[29] By no stretch of the canonical definition of martyrdom could Louis have been understood as a martyr since he died of illness while himself besieging the enemy. Yet, the idea that Louis was somehow martyr-like seems to have been an initial and instinctive interpretation of Louis' death. In 1275, a group high-level prelates – including the Archbishops of Sens and Reims, the bishops in their diocese, and the prior of the Dominican order in the Province of France – wrote to Rome in favor of canonization.[30] The letters use identical language and represented a coordinated argument. These men wrote not of kingship or piety, but of crusading. The critical passage is as follows:

> He manifestly revealed how great an enthusiast he was for the propagation of the faith and the expansion of the Christian name when, abandoning his own inheritance and fatherland through a long and double pilgrimage so that he might extend the name of Christ among infidels and foreigners, he was not afraid to expose his entire family, with his brothers and his sons and his noble magnates, for the work of the cross and of the faith, even to the point of offering himself in sacrifice [*sacrificium*], so that this king could in turn pay back the Highest King, who offered himself to God the Father for our salvation as an acceptable host [*hostiam*] on the altar of the cross. And thus, this glorious athlete of Christ and contestant for the cross of the faithful, gloriously taking up death in the struggle of the work of this persecution, is not believed to have lost the palm of martyrdom, whose cause he did not abandon. This pious hearts feel."[31]

---

[28]   G. Beaulieu, *RHGF* 20, 3–4, ch. 2. "ob zelum et exaltationem fidei Christianae, ibidem hostia Christi effici meruit: et illuc, tanquam martyr et pugil Domini indefessus, finem vitae suae feliciter in domino consummavit!"

[29]   Smith, *Crusading*, p. 99.

[30]   Guillaume Marlot, *Histoire de la Ville, Cité et Université de Reims, Métropolitaine de la Gaule Belgique*, 4 vols. (Reims: L. Jacquet, 1843–1846), v. 4, 816. *Gallia Christiana*, v. 12, "Instrumenta," 78–79. The Dominican version varies slightly; this is found in Marie-Dominique Chapotin, *Histoire des Dominicains de la Province de France. Le siècle des fondations* (Rouen, 1898), pp. 648–649, and n. 641.

[31]   I take the transcription from the letter of the Archbishop of Sens (*Gallia Christiana*, v. 12, Instrumenta 78–79): "Quantus denique zelator propagandae fidei & christiani nominis dilatandi fuerit, evidenter ostendit cum propriam hereditatem derelinquens & patriam longo

"From this," echoed the Dominican letter, "it is easy to believe that, even if the sword of the persecutor did not take his saintly soul, the palm of martyrdom is however not lost."[32] These were extraordinary claims. This was no mere popular (read: uneducated, non-elite) devotion, fueled by appellations of "martyrdom" in the *chansons de geste* written for a lay audience.[33] These were elite churchmen who argued purposefully for an official recognition of Louis as a martyr. They compared Louis, the king, to Christ, the "Highest King," in terms of martyrdom – "offering himself up to God ... as the acceptable victim on the altar of the cross"[34] – and called him deserving of the "palm of martyrdom." They did so even as they recognized that he did not – and according to canonical criteria for martyrdom – die at the hands of persecutors. The fact that crusading drew on the language of the cross smoothed an interpretation of taking up the cross in terms of the salvific and self-sacrificing passion of Christ's own carrying of the cross.[35] Describing Louis as a "glorious athlete of Christ" drew on a trope used repeatedly for early Christian martyrs,[36] but it also keyed into the imagery of battle and struggle that was at the heart of the crusades. Louis offered himself in sacrifice as had Christ, and won the "palm of martyrdom" in so doing. Crusading was in and of itself an offer of self-sacrifice and martyrdom.

This was a powerful argument, and it was one way of dealing with the issue of the failed crusades – to belie the actual military aims of crusading in favor of capitalizing on the notion of Louis' suffering and death. The argument failed. The papacy had never been eager to canonize crusaders, and in the second half of

---

& geminato peregrinationis itinere ut Christi nomen apud infideles & barbaros dilataret, sua omnia cum fratribus & filiis ac proceribus inclytis pro negotio crucis & fidei totaliter exponere non expavit, seipsum etiam tandem in sacrificium offerens, ut rex ipse vicem redderet summo regi, qui pro nostra salute semetipsum hostiam acceptabilem in ara crucis obtulit Deo Patri. Sicque gloriosus hic athleta Christi & crucis agonista fidelis in agone persecutionis dicti negotii mortem suscipiens gloriose, palma martyrii, cujus causa non defuit, sicut pia corda sentiunt, non creditur amisisse."

[32]   Chapotin, *Histoire des Dominicains*, pp. 648–649, and n. 642. "Ex quo facile potest credi quod etsi sanctam ejus animam gladius persecutoris non abstulit, palmam tamen martyrii non amisit."

[33]   Smith, *Crusading*, pp. 99–100.

[34]   C. Maier has discussed the eucharistic/crusading/sacrificial imagery as articulated in the crusading theology of Innocent III, echoed here. Christoph T. Maier, "Mass, the Eucharist and the Cross: Innocent III and the Relocation of the Crusade," in *Pope Innocent III and his World*, ed. John Moore (Brookfield, 1999), pp. 358–259.

[35]   Penny Cole, *The Preaching of the Crusades to the Holy Land, 1095–1270* (Cambridge, 1991), p.172.

[36]   Alison Goddard Elliott, *Roads to Paradise: Reading the Lives of the early Saints* (Hanover, 1987).

the thirteenth-century, it even became reluctant to canonize anyone as a martyr.[37] In any event, as Caroline Smith has recently argued, the issue of attributing martyrdom to those who died on crusade was vexed.[38] When Boniface VIII finally did canonize Louis in 1297, he entered him into the College of Saints as a confessor.[39] A decade later Joinville rebuked the papacy. In his dedication, he wrote:

> I cannot but think that it was an injustice to him not to include him in the roll of the martyrs, when you consider the great hardships he suffered as a pilgrim and crusader during the six years that I served with him; in particular because it was even to the Cross that he followed Our Lord – for God died on the Cross and so did St. Louis; for when he died at Tunis it was the Cross of the Crusade that he bore.[40]

Joinville drew on the same complex of imagery and vocabulary of "the cross" as had the senior French prelates in 1275. But Joinville claimed that Louis was a martyr not because he had *died* on crusade, but that he was a martyr because he had suffered long hardship, twice, while doing the work of the Cross. What underlay Joinville's conception here of the role that the crusades played in Louis' sanctity was the pious integrity of purpose and the suffering in hardship that Louis took upon himself in order to do the work of the cross and of Christ. Joinville's interpretation here may well have been a sort of retro-fitting of the central crusade narrative, written in the 1270s or 80s, to the hagiographic life he wrote for Jeanne de Navarre sometime after 1297.[41] Yet other post-canonization authors agreed that Louis deserved the status of martyr.[42] A hagiographic and para-liturgical text preserved in a *vita sanctorum* at St.-Germain des Près[43] written after Louis' canonization ended with the following invocation:

---

[37]   Vauchez, *Sainthood*, pp. 413–420.

[38]   Smith, *Crusading*, pp. 98–103, Smith, "Martyrdom."

[39]   Can. Bull., *RHGF*, v. 23, 154. This was first called to my attention by LeGoff, "La Sainteté de Saint Louis," p. 287.

[40]   Joinville, §5.

[41]   Smith, *Crusading*, pp. 48–58. This is a different view from the one taken by Jacques Monfrin, "Introduction," in *Vie de Saint Louis* (Paris, 1995). I am persuaded by Smith. On Joinville's intentions in writing the central narrative, see §406.

[42]   William Chester Jordan suggested that an endowment made for an altar dedicated to Saint Louis and Stephen Proto-martyr by a well-to-do burgher and prévôt may have been a subtle argument for Louis' status as also a martyr. William Chester Jordan, "Honoring Saint Louis in a Small Town," *Journal of Medieval History* 30 (2004), 267.

[43]   I must extend my thanks to Elizabeth A.R. Brown, who figured out that this volume belonged to Saint-Germain's holdings (based on comparison with a breviary from the abbey)

> Oh confessor of Christ and martyr by merit, even if [your] soul was not taken by the sword of the persecutor, we do not believe the palm of the martyr to be denied to you. O saintly and venerable king Louis, you marked yourself, not once but twice, with the title of the cross and the privilege of indulgence, by the desire of martyrdom, as much by love [*affectu*] as by action [*effectu*].[44]

The vita borrowed some of its language from the letter that the Dominican prior sent to the curia in 1275, pointing to shared texts and thinking.[45] The author from Saint-Germain wanted very much to accord Louis the status of the martyr and insisted both that he was a "martyr by merit" [*martyr merito*] and through action, but also a martyr through love [*affectu*]. In his canonization testimony, Charles of Anjou had spoken of his (other) brother, Alphonse of Poitiers, as a martyr out of *affectu* and as a *martir voluntate*,[46] and these formulas seemed closely related to another trope, that of a martyr by desire [*martyr desiderio*]. Being "martyr by desire" was a trope of sanctification that had been worked out among Franciscans after Francis' death. It was used in the liturgical office for Francis written in 1232, and it was adapted soon after for the office of the stigmata.[47] Around 1300, the Franciscan office for Saint Louis, which was itself a reworking of the office for Saint Francis, adapted one of its antiphon, saying of Louis the following:

> O martyr by desire [*o martyr desiderio*], how you suffer with the Crucified by the zeal of your pious mind, whose cross you twice took upon your shoulders, the passion weakened you, but the fervor and zeal for Christ has made you a martyr.[48]

---

and shared with me these conclusions.

[44] *RHGF* v. 23, 175–176. "O Christi confessor et martir merito, cujus animam etsi gladius persecutoris non abstulit, palmam tamen martirii non te credimus amisisse. Rex sancte et venerabilis Ludovice, qui martirii desiderio tam affectu quam effectu, crucis titulo et indulgenciae privilegio semel et iterum te signasti."

[45] Chapotin, *Histoire des Dominicains*, pp. 648–649, and n.642. "Ex quo facile potest credi quod etsi sanctam ejus animam gladius persecutoris non abstulit, palmam tamen martyrii non amisit."

[46] Riant, "Déposition," p. 175.

[47] "O martyr desiderio, Francisce, quanto studio compatiens hunc sequeris; quem passum libro reperis, quem in aere." For the Latin text of the Office for Saint Francis, see Dreves and Blume, eds., *Analecta hymnica*, v. 5, no. 61. or Enrico Menestò, Stefano Brufani, ed., *Fontes Franciscani* (Assisi, 1995), pp. 1105–1121. On the office, Tiziana Scandaletti, "Una ricognizione sull'ufficio ritmico per S. Francesco," *Musica et storia* 4 (1996).

[48] Dreves and Blume, eds., *Analecta hymnica*, v. 13, 194. "O martyr desiderio, quam pie mentis studio, crucifixo compateris, cuius crucem in umeris, tuis bis affixisti, passio tibi

The language drew on imagery involving the cross, the crusades, passion and suffering, that associated Louis' crusade with Francis' stigmata, and ultimately Christ's death on the cross. Liturgically, the Magnificat was a celebration of inversion – greatness in humility, eternal life in mortal death, and so forth.[49] Here, the Franciscan Magnificat antiphon for Louis sanctified crusading reversal as passion and thus salvation.

What seems clear is that, in spite of Boniface's canonization, Louis' devotees very much accorded him the status of martyr, which they were somehow sure he deserved. And yet, they did not quite agree on the logic of Louis' martyrdom. Was it because Louis had died on crusade, as the senior prelates had argued in 1275? Because he strove for martyrdom, as the Franciscan and Benedictine texts suggested sometime after 1297? Or because he had suffered a kind of *passio* while on crusade, as Joinville argued around 1305?

The chronology suggests a retreat from the strongest of these claims, that of actual martyrdom made in 1275 by senior churchmen. But notions that Louis desired and strove for martyrdom – that he was a "witness" of Christian humility and devotion (in a greater or lesser sense) – provided the most attractive interpretive context for making sense of Louis' crusades within the discourse of his sanctity. In the pre-canonization texts, the valorization of Louis' suffering was not discussed in the language of a desire for penitential redemption, but rather as an example to others of Christian humility. In the canonization dossier itself, Louis' crusades provided evidence of his devotion to God and his willingness to forego the riches and luxuries of his homeland, his kingship, and his family, to endure suffering. Charles of Anjou recalled that Louis refused to abandon his people and took special care to recite the daily office when in captivity.[50] William of Chartres introduced the events of 1250 by noting that, when in captivity, Louis never ceased in his devotions, asking that his confiscated breviary be brought to him so that he could recite the hours.[51] William went out of his way to excuse Louis for returning Damietta to the Saracens, saying this would have happened even if Louis had not negotiated it.[52] Those men who testified at the canonization proceedings in 1282–83 – many of them members of the nobility who had gone on crusade with Louis in the 1250s – remembered in detail the

---

defecit, sed martyrem te effecit, fervor et zelus christi."

[49]   Elizabeth A. Johnson, *Truly our Sister: a Theology of Mary in the Communion of Saints* (New York, 2003), p. 266ff.

[50]   Riant, "Déposition," pp.170–171, (nos. 1, 2).

[51]   Wm. Chartres, *RHGF* v. 20, 30. On this episode, see Larry S. Crist, "The Breviary of Saint Louis: The Development of a Legendary Miracle," *Journal of the Warburg and Courtauld Institutes* 28 (1965), 319–323.

[52]   Wm. Chartres, *RHGF* v. 20, 30.

manner of his acute physical suffering,[53] his refusal to abandon his people for his own safety,[54] his compassion for others (evidenced by his ransoming of prisoners, his feeding of those in the army, and his burial of Christians), the good works he did when in Acre,[55] and so forth.

But it was above all his captivity – that most extreme failure of the aims of the crusade – along with his staunch faith in the face of his captors, which most came to represent his exalted Christian humility. Of his ordeal in Egypt, William of Chartres exclaimed "All the magnates and even Christians who were present were amazed at how untroubled, how unfearful he was, since they [the Muslim magnates] were in no way frightening to him; indeed, he, as a just man, trusted in God, and he thus had no fear."[56] Someone at the inquest recounted how Louis refused to take an oath to deny Christ if he failed to fill his terms of the treaty, quoting the king as exclaiming in horror "never will these words come out of my mouth."[57] Charles of Anjou remembered Louis saying that, even if doing so would not technically be a sin, he was horrified at the mere thought of saying these words.[58] Another witness remembered that a "pagan admiral" (an emir)[59] said to Louis: "You are our prisoner and our slave in our prison and you speak so haughtily? Either you do what we want of you or else you will be crucified, you

---

[53] Wm Saint-Pathus, chs. 8 and 13 (Delaborde ed. 56, 112–113); Joinville, §310; Riant, "Déposition," p. 170 (no. 171).

[54] Joinville, §5–15, 628–629; Riant, "Déposition," p. 170 (no. 171). See also *RHGF* v. 23, 172.

[55] Wm. Chartres, *RHGF* v. 20, 31–32; Wm. Saint-Pathus ch. 10 (Delaborde, 74–75). The lections for the office of translation (*Exultemus Omnes*) spoke of the many agonies he suffered for Christ and the many virtues deeds he performed overseas. BNF Lat 1024, 417ra; BNF Lat 911, 37r (and others): "In partibus illis vir sanctus pro christo tot et tantos agones habuit tam virtuosos actus exercuit, tanta sancte edificationis exempla prebuit, quod lingua vix sufficeret enarrare." The text (as it appears in the Hours of Jeanne de Navarre, but which replicate the office of translation) can be found in Auguste Longnon, *Documents Parisiens sur l'iconographie de S. Louis* (Paris: H. Champion, 1882), 53–66.

[56] Wm. Chartres, *RHGF* v. 20, 31. "Mirantibus cunctis, qui aderant, magnatibus etiam christianis, qualiter tam securus, tam imperterritus erat, cum ipsi non modicum terrerentur; ipse quidem tanquam vir justus in Domino confidebat, et ideo non timebat."

[57] Wm. Saint-Pathus, ch. 3 (Delaborde ed., 23–24): "Certes ce n'istra ja de ma bouche!" This story was recorded in the liturgical vita, *RHGF*, v. 23, lection 7, p. 163; Can. Bull. *RHGF* v. 23, 156; Yves of St. Denis, *RHGF*, *RHGF* v. 20, 55. It was also incorporated into the Franciscan office for Louis, *Francorum Rex*, Dreves and Blume, eds., *Analecta hymnica*, v. 13, 194.

[58] Riant, "Déposition," 173.

[59] Wm. Saint-Pathus, ch. 3 (Delaborde ed., 24): "un paien qui estoit amiral."

and your men [or family]."⁶⁰ It was then recorded that "the blessed king was by no means unaffected, but he responded that if they killed his body, they would not get his soul."⁶¹ Boniface VIII included both episodes in the Canonization Bull, and interestingly, Yves of St. Denis, who retold the story about the threat of crucifixion around 1317, explained here that Louis was "eager for martyrdom."⁶² This view was shared by Joinville, who, though not writing his central narrative as part of the canonization effort in the 1270s, was writing in the context and with knowledge of the ongoing effort at sanctification. Hearing the stories of Louis' captivity when in Acre, he was impressed with the dignity of Louis' faith. He recounted how Louis was threatened with torture and how he refused to deny the faith during negotiations with the Saracens.⁶³

The canonization and early hagiographical record also stressed the theme of willing self-sacrifice. Joinville, in laying out the reasons for Louis' sanctity in his dedication, explained that Louis was willing to "risk death that he might save his people from harm," and evoked, among other things, potential shipwreck off the coast of Cyprus.⁶⁴ The story was repeated in a number of post-1297 texts.⁶⁵ Others recalled how Louis refused to be liberated before other Christians,⁶⁶ how he refused to get on a ship that would take him up the Nile but expose the rest of his army to the enemy.⁶⁷ Charles of Anjou testified that during the retreat down the Nile back to Damietta Louis flatly refused to abandon his people. Charles rebuked him for thereby endangering the entire army, and then he recalled that Louis, exasperated, retorted "Oh, Count of Anjou, Count of Anjou! If you are burdened by me, then why don't you leave! Because I shall never abandon my

---

⁶⁰ Wm. Saint-Pathus, ch. 3 (Delaborde ed., 24): "Vos estes nostre chetiz et nostre esclave et en nostre charter, si parlez si hardimiement! Ou vos ferez ce que nos vodron, ou vos serez crucefiez vos et les voz." See also account of W. Chartres, *RHGF*, v. 20, 38, who was with Louis.

⁶¹ Wm. Saint-Pathus, Delaborde ed., ch. 3, p. 24: "li benoiez rois ne fu meu; ainç respondi que se il avoient ocis le cors, il n'auroient pas toutevoies l'ame de lui."

⁶² Can. Bull, *RHGF*, v. 23, 156. Yves Saint-Denis, *RHGF*, v. 20, 55. "Rex vero promptus ad martyrum." An account of this episode appears in Wm. St.-Pathus, ch. 3, but does not include the notion of martyrdom. William writes only that "onques pour ce li benoiez rois ne fu meu."

⁶³ Joinville, §§362–363.

⁶⁴ G. Beaulieu, *RHGF*, v. 20, 18. ch. 30; Joinville §6, 39–42; *RHGF*, v. 23 174 (Vita from St.-Germain-des-Près).

⁶⁵ Liturgical vita, *RHGF* v. 23, lection 5, p. 162. Glor. Reg. ch. 10.

⁶⁶ Can. Bull. *RHGF*, v. 23, 156–157; Wm. Saint-Pathus, ch. 10 (Delaborde ed., 76–77); Yves of St. Denis, *RHGF* v. 20, 55.

⁶⁷ Wm. Saint-Pathus, ch. 10 (Delaborde ed. 75); Liturgical vita, lection 5, *RHGF* v. 23, 162; Can. Bull.

people."[68] William of Saint-Pathus recorded that Louis said he would rather die with his men than escape.[69] These stories, though not modeled as martyrdom, were sympathetic with the virtue of martyrdom, reconciled with the expectations of kingship and military leadership. They too were designed to demonstrate constancy of faith in God in the face of disaster.

By and large, then, the image of Louis as a crusader in the canonization documents had very little to do with the objectives of the crusades *per se*, either that he himself had put forth in 1250 or 1270, or as they were being reconsidered at the turn of fourteenth century. Boniface VIII did say that Louis went overseas for the "rescue of the holy land,"[70] and Joinville did say that Louis wanted to secure the safety of the Holy Land,[71] but these as values were minimized in comparison to celebration of a "sainthood of suffering." The formulation of Louis' sainthood instead drew on a vocabulary of suffering and service to the Lord that keyed into developments in the larger arc of thirteenth-century sanctity (not treated here, but represented most clearly by the figure of Saint Francis). It also drew on a spiritualization of crusade *suffering*, in imitation of Christ and his sacrifice, and as part of the process and endeavor of the crusades, which clerics had articulated over the two previous centuries. The theology had been fully worked out by men like Bernard of Clairvaux, Innocent III, and Humbert of Romans: crusading was not about objectives on the ground but the benefit to spirit and soul.[72] Penny Cole has described this approach, as seen in sermons on the crusade, as "the idea of soldiering for Christ [being] tied inextricably to the idea of the crusade as an imitation of Christ" and to "a moral and spiritual renewal" in which the crusader bears "Christ's cross of suffering and physical death in battle."[73] Christoph Maier has more recently called attention to the role of Innocent III (d. 1216) in the formulation of a "more radical interpretation of the crusade as an *imitatio*

---

68   Riant, "Déposition," 171. "Comes Andegavensis, comes Andegavensis! Si vos estis oneratus de me, dimittatis, quia ego populum meum non dimittam."

69   Wm. Saint-Pathus, ch. 10 (Delaborde ed., 75).

70   Can. Bull., *RHGF* v. 23, 158.

71   Joinville, §419.

72   Penny Cole, "Humbert of Romans and the Crusade," in *The Experience of Crusading: Western Approaches*, ed. Marcus Bull and Norman Housley (Cambridge, 2003), Christoph T. Maier, "Crisis, Liturgy and the Crusade in the Twelfth and Thirteenth Centuries," *Journal of Ecclesiastical History* 48, no. 4 (1997), 628–657, Maier, "Mass, the Eucharist and the Cross: Innocent III and the Relocation of the Crusade," pp. 351–360.

73   Giles Constable, "The Historiography of the Crusades," in *The Crusades from the Perspective of Byzantium and the Muslim World*, ed. Angeliki Laiou and Roy Parviz Mottahedeh (Washington D.C., 2001), p. 15. quoting Cole, *The Preaching of the Crusades*, pp. 124–125, and 172–173.

Christi" rooted in sacrifice.[74] This was a discourse well-suited to sanctity, and all that was left was to apply it to Louis. Although texts written in the 1270s and 80s struggled to rationalize or explain away Louis' crusading failures, by 1297 Louis could emerge in a sense as a champion crusader, the perfect embodiment of a memorialization of saintly defeat that at once bypassed and capitalized on the uncomfortable reality of what had happened on the ground. In this view, Louis was not so much of a crusader saint, but just another saint of suffering. The crusades themselves were not exalted or valorized as independent ideals, but they were rehabilitated as vehicles of sanctifying devotion. The question, then, is not so much "what did the idea of saint Louis mean to the crusading ideals around 1300?" but rather – if the crusades were in fact only a mechanism for a passion narrative – why is it that the papacy never thought fit to canonize crusaders as passionate and suffering crusaders?

---

[74]   Maier, "Crisis, Liturgy and the Crusade"; Maier, "Mass, the Eucharist and the Cross: Innocent III and the Relocation of the Crusade." See also Giles Constable, "Nudus Nudum Christum Sequi and Parallel Formulas in the Twelfth Century," in *Continuity and Discontinuity in Church History: Essays Presented to George Hunston Williams* (Leiden: 1979).

Index